★ Jerry Baker Presents... ★

America's Best
PRACTICAL
PROBLEM
SOLVERS

www.jerrybaker.com

Other Jerry Baker Books:

Jerry Baker's Can the Clutter!
Jerry Baker's Cleaning Magic!
Jerry Baker's Homespun Magic
Grandma Putt's Old-Time Vinegar, Garlic, and Baking Soda Solutions
Jerry Baker's Supermarket Super Products!
Jerry Baker's It Pays to be Cheap!

Jerry Baker's Supermarket Super Gardens
Jerry Baker's Dear God . . . Please Help It Grow!
Secrets from the Jerry Baker Test Gardens
Jerry Baker's All-American Lawns
Jerry Baker's Bug Off!
Jerry Baker's Terrific Garden Tonics!
Jerry Baker's Giant Book of Garden Solutions
Jerry Baker's Backyard Problem Solver
Jerry Baker's Green Grass Magic
Jerry Baker's Great Green Book of Garden Secrets
Jerry Baker's Old-Time Gardening Wisdom

Jerry Baker's Backyard Birdscaping Bonanza
Jerry Baker's Backyard Bird Feeding Bonanza
Jerry Baker's Year-Round Bloomers
Jerry Baker's Flower Garden Problem Solver
Jerry Baker's Perfect Perennials!

Grandma Putt's Home Health Remedies
Nature's Best Miracle Medicines
Jerry Baker's Supermarket Super Remedies
Jerry Baker's The New Healing Foods
Jerry Baker's Amazing Antidotes
Jerry Baker's Anti-Pain Plan
Jerry Baker's Oddball Ointments, Powerful Potions, and Fabulous Folk Remedies
Jerry Baker's Giant Book of Kitchen Counter Cures

To order any of the above, or for more information on Jerry Baker's
amazing home, health, and garden tips, tricks, and tonics, please write to:

Jerry Baker, P.O. Box 1001
Wixom, MI 48393

Or, visit Jerry Baker online at:

www.jerrybaker.com

★ Jerry Baker Presents... ★

America's Best

PRACTICAL

PROBLEM

SOLVERS

Featuring:
★ Vinegar ★ Panty Hose ★ Milk Jugs ★
★ Banana Peels ★ Coffee Grounds ★ Pickle Juice ★
★ Much, Much More! ★

Published by American Master Products, Inc.

Executive Editor: Kim Adam Gasior
Managing Editor: Cheryl Winters-Tetreau
Copy Editor: Nanette Bendyna
Production Editor: Debby Duvall
Interior Design and Layout: Sandy Freeman
Indexer: Nan Badgett

Publisher's Cataloging-in-Publication Data
(Provided by Quality Books, Inc.)

Baker, Jerry.
    America's best practical problem solvers / Jerry Baker.
    p. cm. — (Jerry Baker's good home, health & garden series)
    Includes index.
    At head of title: Jerry Baker presents.
    ISBN-13: 978-0-922433-99-5
    ISBN-10: 0-922433-99-2

    1. Home economics. 2. Health. 3. Gardening.
I. Title. II. Title: Jerry Baker presents America's best
practical problem solvers. III. Series: Baker, Jerry.
Good home, health & garden series.

TX158.B35 2010   640
                         QBI10-600116

Printed in the United States of America
2 4 6 8 10 9 7 5 3 hardcover

Contents

Introduction

Dear Jerry: As I was planting my sweet corn, I wondered how to keep raccoons from getting to it before me. I shared this question with the "Wise Old-Timers" at coffee the next day. The first said, "Human scent will keep them away," and suggested I take an old stuffed chair he was throwing out and put it in my cornfield. "No," said the second. "Light will keep them away, so string up some lights." "You're all wet," said the third. "Use newspapers; spread 'em around the field." Not knowing what to do—nor wanting to offend any of them—I used all of their ideas. Boy, was I surprised around harvest time when, upon entering my cornfield, I saw a large raccoon sitting in the chair, under the lights, reading a newspaper and eating my corn. I guess you just never know!

 This chuckle came from a reader in Iowa, just one of thousands of folks who have shared their jokes, tall tales, and terrific tips with me over the years. I've heard about their successes (and failures), and that got me thinking. If so many of you have shared your problem solvers with me, why shouldn't I pass them along to *everyone* else?

And that, my friend, is where the idea for this book came from. I've gathered the best of the best tips, tricks, and tonics from folks all across America to share with you. Perhaps your tip is in here, too!

You'll find everything from household hints to gardening tips to health advice, all courtesy of readers just like you. Want to keep your glass shower doors clean as a whistle? Try a dab of baby oil. Got gardenias that aren't blooming like they should? Perk 'em up with pickle juice. Conquer a head cold with a whiff of horseradish, a sip of hot-pepper water, or a lick of honey and black pepper.

But that's not all! No sirree—to complement these terrific tips, I dug deep into my files and pulled out my own favorite time-tested secrets. Look for these fantastic features scattered throughout the book:

Another Great Idea! offers why-didn't-I-think-of-that ways to solve everyday problems. So if you need to know how to remove stubborn laundry stains, get sticky tar off your car, stop heartburn in its tracks, or keep rabbits out of your vegetable patch, you've come to the right place.

Ask Jerry provides commonsense answers to often-asked questions like:

- How can I get my dishes squeaky clean? (Vinegar does the trick.)

- Got any advice for getting out grass stains? (A simple egg white and glycerin mixture works wonders.)

- What's a safe way to move a mouse out of my house? (Try instant mashed potatoes.)

Grandma Putt's Wisdom reveals time-tested secrets that work just as well today as they did back in Grandma's day. You'll find her favorite old-time ways for extending the growing season, keeping a cut from scarring, and polishing pewter with cabbage leaves.

Jerry's Handy Hints let you in on the stuff I myself use to solve problems that crop up around the house, in the garden, and when I'm feeling under the weather.

Quick Fixes give you the lowdown on fast and easy ways to tackle tough issues like stinky fridge odors, pounding headaches, and frisky, flower-trampling felines.

Super-Duper Solutions explain how to think outside the box in any situation. Can't find a rolling pin? Grab a zucchini. Need to stop ants dead in their tracks? Try ground peppermint. Houseplants looking dull? Polish 'em with a banana!

Take 5 lists uncommon uses for everyday items that you've already got on hand. For instance, you'll discover five unusual wax paper tips, five great eggshell tricks, and five healing vinegar tonics, among other things.

Now that I'm done bragging about what's inside, I have to say a few words about how to use this book.

First, keep in mind that these tips come from readers like you who have used them with some success. But that doesn't mean that they'll work for your particular problem, or work in exactly the same way for you.

Second, *before using any cleaning formula,* be sure to test it in an inconspicuous area. That way you'll know if it's safe to use on your item(s).

Third, the health advice is not meant to substitute for professional medical care. If you try a recommended treatment and your ailment doesn't improve within a few days, or if your symptoms get worse, then see your doctor promptly.

Above all else, enjoy yourself and keep an open mind. You may read a tip and think, "I can't believe that works!" But give it a try—you just may be pleasantly surprised! Even if you're not concerned about removing an ink stain, soothing a sore throat, or foiling cutworms, you'll still learn some neat new ways to keep your home, health, and garden in tip-top shape.

And who knows—as you read through the hundreds of practical problem solvers here, you may be inspired to come up with a few of your own. If you do, drop me a line; I'd love to hear from you!

PART 1

Home

America's Best
Practical Problem Solvers

A Clean Sweep

Kitchen Aids

SPRAY ON STAINLESS SHINE. Try using WD-40® as a polish for your stainless steel appliances. Clean the appliances as you normally would, then add a "finishing touch" by spraying WD-40 on a paper towel and polishing your appliances to a beautiful shine. Buff dry with a soft, clean cloth. Keep in mind that a little goes a long way, so use it sparingly. Don't use this method to polish your stainless steel sink—WD-40 is toxic, so any contact with food can be hazardous to your health. And don't spray WD-40 near the stove—it's a fire hazard! ✉ Edward W., NC

SHINE ON, BABY. I polish my stainless steel appliances with baby oil to take away messy fingerprints. It leaves behind a fantastic shine, and it smells good, too! ✉ Val H., PA

STAINLESS SINK POLISHER. Tired of spending so much time trying to make your stainless steel sink gleam? Then try using mineral oil on a soft cotton cloth to restore the shine. It'll clean up easily, yet look like you scrubbed your sink for hours. ✉ Sandy Y., NC

DUST YOUR SINK. For an extra shine after cleaning your stainless steel sink, use a dusting and cleaning spray like Endust®. You'll be amazed by the luster it leaves behind. Just spray it into a dry sink, then buff the sink with a soft, clean cloth. ✉ Patricia H., FL

RUB IT ON. Wanna polish your stainless steel sink? I wipe mine down with rubbing alcohol on a soft, clean cloth. It works as well as (or even better than) any commercial polish. ✉ Lynda G., MI

THE WHITE WAY. If you have a white kitchen sink, you know how easily it can discolor. To get it super-clean, wet the sink and sprinkle on some cream of tartar. Then cut a lemon in half and use it to scrub the sink. It'll take some elbow grease, but you'll be delighted with the results. ✉ Margo F., ME

EASY OVEN CLEANUP. To clean your oven, mix 1 cup of vinegar in a pan of water and bring it to a boil. Place the pan in your oven, close the door, and let it sit overnight. The next morning, you can simply wipe your oven clean. ✉ Suzanne M., VT

OVEN RACKS TAKE A BATH. Clean your oven racks in a snap—by doing the job in the bathroom. Lay them on a towel in your bathtub, get them good and wet, and then pour powdered

Jerry's Handy Hints

BOMBARD IT WITH BLEACH

➜ To make your sink sparkle, line the inside with paper towels and saturate them with a half-and-half solution of household bleach and water. Leave the wet towels in place for about five minutes, then remove them and rinse the sink out thoroughly.

Grandma Putt's Wisdom

You'll foil oven cleaning forever when you use this nifty trick I learned from my Grandma Putt. The next time your electric oven is clean and cool, cover the bottom with overlapping sheets of heavy-duty aluminum foil, slipping the foil under the heating element, not over it. Then pesky spills will collect on the foil and not on the oven. And when the crud builds up, just replace the foil and you're good to go!

dishwasher detergent over them. Let the racks soak for a few hours, then scrub them off and turn on the shower to rinse 'em clean. ✉ Florence P., PA

SUPER-CLEAN YOUR COFFEE MACHINE. If you're noticing that your morning coffee is taking longer than usual to brew, it's probably time to clean the buildup that's been accumulating inside your coffeemaker. Mix ⅛ scoop of OxiClean® with 2 cups of hot water, allow it to cool, and run the mixture through your coffeemaker on the brewing cycle. Then run the machine through a few more cycles with plain water. The next time you make a pot of joe, your machine will work better, and your coffee will taste great, too! ✉ Raeleen B., OR

QUICK FIX

If a plastic bread bag melts onto your coffeepot or toaster, just rub some petroleum jelly on it. Then reheat the appliance and scrub off the softening plastic with a paper towel.

CUT THE COFFEE CRUD. To remove rings of coffee residue from my coffeepot, I put ¼ cup of powdered dishwasher detergent in the bottom of the pot, then fill my coffeemaker with water and start the brewing

4

process. The machine heats the water, which drips into the pot, mixing with the detergent. After letting this sit overnight, I hand wash and rinse the pot the next morning. ✉ **Marcia Y., NY**

CLEAN COFFEE TO GO. When you check into a hotel room, you really don't know how many times the coffeemaker has been used—or cleaned! So do it yourself before making a pot of coffee by dropping two denture-cleaning tablets into a full tank of water. Run the brewing cycle as usual, then run it two more times with plain water. With this trick, you'll know the coffeemaker is clean, and you'll be able to enjoy a fresh-tasting pot of coffee. ✉ **Lillian W., WY**

RICE TO THE RESCUE. Running uncooked rice through your coffee grinder will sharpen the blades as well as clean them, thanks to the abrasive texture of the grain. Pour in about ¼ cup of uncooked white rice, and let the grinder run until the rice is the size of your usual grind. Unplug the machine, dump out the rice, wipe the funnel, and take a sniff inside. If you still smell coffee, repeat the treatment. ✉ **Linda C., NY**

CROCK CLEANUP. A slow cooker's the berries when it comes to low-maintenance cooking, but cleaning the cooked-on food from the crock is another story. Well, not anymore! Mix ¼ cup of white vinegar and 1 squirt of dishwashing liquid in a 32-ounce

TAKE 5

Five not-so-common uses for wax paper are:

1 Make appliances gleam by rubbing them with a piece of wax paper.

2 Shine floors by buffing 'em with a piece of wax paper placed under a mop head.

3 Seal a jar tighter by laying wax paper over the mouth before closing.

4 Slice cheese easily by folding wax paper over a knife before cutting.

5 Preserve leaves by laying them on a piece of wax paper, then covering them with another piece and ironing to seal the deal.

handheld sprayer bottle (with the balance of the bottle filled with water), and spritz it on the gunk. Let the mixture sit for a few minutes, then wipe the crock clean. ✉ Stacey L., OH

A SMOOTH OPENING. Can opener blades will rust quickly if they're exposed to moisture, and getting that darn rust off is way harder than preventing it in the first place. So try this: After you wipe the blades clean, crumple up a piece of wax paper and slice into it with the opener. The can opener teeth will get coated with a thin layer of wax that stops moisture in its tracks, so that rust can't settle on the metal. ✉ Paul T., PA

Jerry's Handy Hints

CRUD-CUTTING COKE®

→ You can freshen up the inside of your dishwasher by using Coca-Cola® to clean up the gunk. Simply pour a 2-liter bottle of the real thing (use the "classic" version, not diet) into the bottom of your machine, and run it through a full cycle. And if the bottom tray is really grungy, let it soak for a few minutes before you start the cycle.

TANGY DISHWASHER CLEANER. If it's good enough for the astronauts to drink, it's good enough for your . . . *dishwasher*? That's right—just fill both detergent dispensers of your empty dishwasher with orange Tang® drink mix, and run the machine through a normal cycle. Your dishwasher will come out as clean as a whistle. ✉ Erich H., MI

BAKING SODA BOOST. Baking soda can add a nice kick to your dishwasher's cleaning cycle. Just add a scoop in the dispenser along with your normal detergent, and run the machine as usual. ✉ John D., TX

FAST FRIDGE CLEANUP. Nobody likes cleaning the fridge—what a chore! So I line my refrigerator shelves with paper towels, which makes spills very easy to clean up. Then I just replace any dirty paper towels with clean ones when necessary. ✉ Jessica G., TX

PERK UP PAINTED PANS. If your once-lovely painted cast-iron pan is now a chipped mess, don't toss it! Bring new life to an old treasure by soaking it in Lestoil® overnight. The paint will "melt" off without ruining the pan. Come morning, you'll be flippin' flapjacks! ✉ Sandra M., CT

KETCHUP FOR CAST IRON. I'd never throw away an old cast-iron skillet because it's rusty. Just cover the affected area with a mix of equal parts ketchup and vinegar, and let it sit for two or three minutes. Then, using a nylon pad, lightly scrub the rust away. ✉ Janine B., IN

QUICK FIX

To remove odors in your refrigerator, dip a cotton ball in vanilla extract and set it on a small plate. Replace the ball every few days, or as needed.

QUICK COPPER CLEANER. Here's a trick for cleaning a copper-bottomed pot or pan without a lot of elbow grease: Wash the pan, turn it upside down, wipe the bottom with white vinegar, and sprinkle it with table salt. Use a nylon scouring pad to rub the copper, and it will quickly become clean. Next, add a squirt of dishwashing liquid to your scouring pad, and buff the copper lightly to give it a super shine. Rinse the pan under hot water, dry it, and you're done! ✉ Roberta B., TX

ANOTHER GREAT IDEA!

WARM AND DRY

Cast iron can really take the heat, so store your skillet in the oven—and keep it there even when you bake something! The heat only makes the finish harder, plus it stops the growth of any bacteria that might be lurking about. And since the oven is nice and dry, whether it's cooking or not, your pan will stay rust-free.

Grandma Putt's Wisdom

Homemade pickles were such a favorite at my Grandma Putt's house that the slices and spears disappeared from her jars in a jiffy. When that last pickle was gobbled up, Grandma put the leftover juice to work—cleaning her copper pots! She'd wet a rag with the brine and go to town, scrubbing the tarnish off with the sour, salty pickle juice. The same trick works great with store-bought pickles, too. So whenever you empty a jar, bring out the copper, and let the brine bring back the shine!

BANISH COPPER TARNISH. To remove tarnish from a copper pan, coat it with tomato-based pasta sauce and leave it alone for an hour. Wipe the area clean with a wet sponge—you won't need to scrub at all! ✉ Robin W., MI

SPIFFY SKILLET SOAK. Instead of breaking a sweat trying to scrape away food stuck to a skillet, I pour some vinegar into the pan and let it stand for about five minutes. Then I wash the pan, and the gunk comes right off. ✉ Betty S., AL

USE PINE TO SHINE. Cooking outdoors when you're camping is great, but you still have to deal with dirty skillets. Don't bring the baked-on food home with you—find a big, sturdy pinecone, and use it as a natural scrub brush at your campsite. ✉ Linda N., TX

PAN DEGREASER. To remove baked-on grease and grime from a pan, put it in a heavy-duty plastic bag and pour about ¼ cup of ammonia into the pan. Tightly close the bag and allow it to sit overnight in a well-ventilated area. The next day, open the bag in the sink and remove the pan. Use a steel wool pad to easily wipe away the softened grime. ✉ Kristin E., IN

RENEW YOUR COOKWARE. You can bring back that shiny, clean look your pots and pans had when you first brought them home from the store with this simple mix: Combine 2 parts vinegar and 1 part salt. Scrub the mixture onto the dirty pot with a dish brush until the dinginess is gone, and rinse thoroughly under warm water. Your pots and pans will look like new! ✉ Susan W., IN

SUPER-DUPER SOLUTIONS

PUT THAT IN YOUR SKILLET AND FRY IT! ● To remove burnt-on food from a skillet, simply add a drop or two of dishwashing liquid and enough water to cover the bottom of the pan. Bring the mixture to a boil, let it cool down a bit, and the skillet will be a cinch to clean.

NO-SCRUB CLEANUP. You can scrub and scrub, but sometimes caked-on, baked-on food just won't budge from your pots and pans. Here's my solution: Put a fabric-softener sheet in the bottom of the pan and fill it with hot water. Let the pan soak overnight and the next morning, the gunk will wash right off. ✉ Heather L., WV

QUICK FIX

While cooking, be sure to keep a box of salt on hand. If food bubbles over or spills on the stove, simply pour some salt on the spot to prevent it from burning.

BAKING SODA SOAK. To clean a pan that seems ruined by burnt-on food, scrape out what you can, then rinse the pan and sprinkle the inside with baking soda. Cover the baking soda with water, and let the pan sit overnight. In the morning, you'll be able to clean off the remaining crud lickety-split! ✉ Emily H., TX

HIT THE BLACK POT. Blackened pots and pans are downright nasty! To rid your pots of yucky gunk, saturate the burned bottoms with dishwasher detergent, then add a little water. Let the pots soak overnight, and use a little elbow grease to scrub away the mess with a dish brush. Your formerly unsightly pots will be nice and clean. ✉ Nadine M., NY

VINEGAR BEATS THE BURN. If you've burned food in the bottom of a pan, don't waste time trying to scrub it clean. Just pour in 1 cup of white vinegar and heat it for a few minutes. Turn off the heat and let the pan stand on the stove for 10 to 15 minutes, and the burnt-on mess will wash right out. ✉ Selma W., LA

A LITTLE HELP FROM THE LAUNDRY ROOM. Tackle tough, baked-on food in your pots and pans with laundry detergent. Just pour half a cup or so of whatever brand of detergent you have on hand into the pot, add some hot water, and let the mess soak for about an hour. You'll be able to rinse the gunk away with no scrubbing. ✉ Carolyn K., OK

DOUBLE-DUTY DENTURE CLEANER. Don't get steamed about baked-on food in your pots and pans. Just drop a couple of denture-cleaning tablets into each water-filled pot or pan and let it soak overnight. The next morning, wash the cookware thoroughly with warm, soapy water, and the mess will rinse away. ✉ Marlene L., NY

RHUBARB TO THE RESCUE. When my steel pots and pans start looking a little grungy, I reach for rhubarb. I simply toss in a few chopped rhubarb stalks, cover them with water, and boil them in the dirty pan until the stains disappear. ✉ Janice B., MI

Jerry's Handy Hints

FOILED AGAIN!

→ Wad or crush some aluminum foil to make a convenient scouring pad for pots, pans, and metal casserole dishes. Just add a little dishwashing liquid, and you'll be amazed at how well it works.

Ask Jerry

Q: I use "grease-cutting" dishwashing liquid, but sometimes it doesn't do the job. Any suggestions for how I can get my dishes squeaky clean?

A: As a matter of fact, I have two. Before tackling a pile of greasy dishes, add a little vinegar to the rinse water. It'll cut the grease and leave your dishes clean as a whistle. Or, you can add 1 tablespoon of baking soda to the soapy dishwater. It'll soften your hands while it cuts the grease.

Shiny Solutions

STAIN-BUSTING PASTE. Stains from grape juice and red wine are tough to clean off light-colored countertops. Here's how I do it: Mix just enough water with baking soda to make a thick paste, and scour the affected area. The dark stain will come right out. ✉ Susan W., IN

KITCHEN FAUCET CLEANER. Is your kitchen faucet looking like it's seen better days? Then get it back to its old self by soaking a washcloth in vinegar and wrapping it around the faucet. This will get rid of mineral deposits and other residue. Leave the cloth on the faucet for about an hour, then remove it and wipe the area clean. There you go—no more buildup! ✉ Sue R., LA

SOAK YOUR FIXTURES. It can be hard to clean all of the filth-filled nooks and crannies in and around bathroom faucets. This easy trick works like a charm: Saturate the area with white vinegar, then cover it with plastic wrap. After about an hour of soaking, remove the plastic wrap, wipe the vinegar away, and the faucet will be nice and clean. In the shower, take a slightly different approach: Fill a plastic bag with white vinegar and tie it around the shower-head, making sure the head is completely covered by the vinegar. After an hour, take off the bag, and your showerhead will be scum-free. ✉ Penny M., AB

Make your chrome fixtures sparkle by lightly spraying them with seltzer and polishing with a soft, dry cloth. Then stand back and admire the shine!

CHROME CONDITIONER. Whenever I need to shine chrome faucets, handles, or other fixtures, I reach for my tube of Alberto VO5® Conditioning Hairdressing. I squeeze a small dab of the conditioner onto a soft, dry cloth and buff the chrome lightly until it gleams. ✉ Jane C., TX

KILL GERMS AND KEEP THE SHINE. How can you kill germs and shine your bathroom fixtures in one fell swoop? It's simple: Pour rubbing alcohol onto faucets, drains, and the shower door frame, then wipe it off with a soft, clean cloth. To take care of any sticky spots on a mirror, dip a soft, clean cloth in rubbing alcohol, and have at it. ✉ Carlos B., GA

FOG-FREE AND CLEAN. Use a dab of shaving cream to clean your bathroom mirror and to keep it from fogging up the next time you hit the shower. Rub the shaving cream all over the mirror, then wipe it off with a soft, clean cloth. While you're at it, use a little of the foamy cream to clean the faucet and any other bathroom fixtures that could use a shiny boost. ✉ Barbara R., NJ

QUICK MIRROR FIX. You can repair a small scratch in your mirror right at home for just pennies. Rub a little dab of white non-gel toothpaste into the mark, let the paste dry, then buff the area with a soft, clean cloth. The excess paste will wipe away, but the scratch will remain filled. ✉ Sheila B., VA

HANDY HOSIERY HELPER. Next time you get a run in your panty hose, don't pitch 'em. I wash mine as usual, and then when I'm cleaning a mirror, I wipe it dry with the recycled panty hose. I always end up with a spotless mirror, with no fuzzy paper towel lint left behind. ✉ Helene R., IN

COOK UP CLEANER GLASS. Keep your glass shower door clean with cooking spray—no kidding! Lightly and evenly spray the door, then leave it alone for 5 or 10 minutes. Use paper towels or a clean, absorbent cloth to wipe away the residue. Turn the cloth frequently as you wipe until the doors are nice and clear. ✉ Lois B., WA

CITRUS A-PEEL. Wipe orange oil across your glass shower door to clear away built-up soap scum and mineral deposits. It's easy: Just wipe it on, then wipe it off. Your shower door will be clean, and the whole bathroom will smell citrusy fresh. ✉ Kate J., OH

ANOTHER GREAT IDEA!

BABY THE BUILDUP

Keep your glass shower doors as clean as a whistle by applying a thin coat of baby oil to them once a month or so. The oil will keep dirt, soap, and hard water from building up.

WAGE WAR ON WATER SPOTS.

Rubbing alcohol does a great job of getting rid of water spots on mirrors, windows, and other glass surfaces. In a bucket, mix 1 part rubbing alcohol with 4 parts warm water. Dip a lint-free towel or rag into the mix, wipe it on the spots, then dry with a clean towel. All of your glass surfaces will have a streak-free shine. ✉ Christine G., WA

TIDY UP THE TRACK. The next time you need to clean a grungy shower door track, do what I do: Put a small amount of nail polish remover on a clean cloth and rub it on the metal. Rinse well, and the track will shine. ✉ Mary R., TN

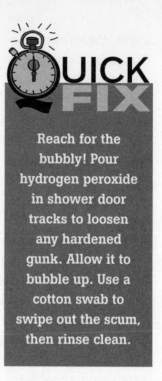

QUICK FIX

Reach for the bubbly! Pour hydrogen peroxide in shower door tracks to loosen any hardened gunk. Allow it to bubble up. Use a cotton swab to swipe out the scum, then rinse clean.

Rub-a-Dub

THE SWEET SMELL OF CLEAN. Mix 1 cup of baking soda with 20 drops of your favorite essential oil to add a pleasant scent to your scrubbin', shinin', and sanitizin'. After adding the oil to the baking soda, let the mixture sit for about 24 hours. Then sprinkle a little of the scented powder mix into the sink, the bathtub, the toilet, or wherever you want to clean. It makes surfaces spic-and-span and smells great, too! ✉ Vicki F., AL

GET RID OF GRIMY GROUT. To make your grungy grout sparkle, scrub it with whitening toothpaste on a clean, moistened tooth-brush, then wipe it with a wet sponge. Not only will your grout be clean, but the whole room will smell minty fresh. ✉ Cat M., OR

GROUT GARGLE. Freshen up your grubby floor grout with Listerine® mouthwash and a good stiff brush. Dip the brush into a container of the mouthwash, and scrub away. Follow with a clean-water mopping and watch that grout glow! ✉ Lisa K., MI

GEL IN THE SHOWER. Because it's so thick, gel-formula toilet bowl cleaner with bleach does a great job of cleaning shower wall grout, even in hard-to-get-at areas. Start at the top of the tile wall and squeeze the gel on the grout lines, letting it slowly run down to the shower floor. The cleaner will do its dirty work in a few minutes, and then you can easily rinse it off. ✉ Cindy M., OH

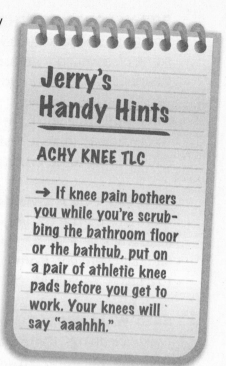

Jerry's Handy Hints

ACHY KNEE TLC

→ If knee pain bothers you while you're scrubbing the bathroom floor or the bathtub, put on a pair of athletic knee pads before you get to work. Your knees will say "aaahhh."

DYE YOUR GROUT. Sometimes plain white grout can be, well, boring. So perk it up with tea! Brew ordinary tea using two bags per cup of water. Let it cool, pour it over the grout, and wipe away the tea once you're satisfied with the color. But what if—yikes!—you change your mind? Any cleaner containing bleach will easily wash the stain away. On the other hand, if you love the new look, preserve it with grout sealer. ✉ Sheri M., GA

ANOTHER GREAT IDEA!

LEMON-AID

Grab a lemon to remove lime and hard-water deposits around drains. Just cut the lemon in half, and rub the deposits with the cut surface. The fruit's acid will work quickly to bring back the shine.

BORAX FOR THE BATHROOM. I use borax to clean my enamel and fiberglass sinks and tubs without scratching them. Simply sprinkle some on a wet sponge, and use it as you would any other powdered cleaner. Just make sure you rinse thoroughly. ✉ Sharon S., AL

SINK PASTE. If you have a tube of toothpaste you don't like, don't throw it away. Instead, use it to clean your bathroom sink. Just squirt it on a scrub brush and have at it. ✉ Melody B., TX

VINEGAR FOR A SHINY SINK. Hard-water buildup in your bathroom sink can be the very dickens to remove, but not if you use a little white vinegar. Just close the drain, pour in some vinegar, and let it sit overnight. Come morning, open the drain and wipe the sink to a shine. ✉ Holly M., CO

EASY WALL WIPE. To keep your shower walls looking good between cleanings, there's no need to buy fancy daily sprays. Just wipe the walls with a towel after each and every shower. (Keep a separate towel handy just for this purpose.) ✉ Meredith D., MO

SUPER-DUPER SOLUTIONS

POLISH THE WALLS ● Even though oily residue can be a slippery subject in the bathtub, on the walls of a *shower*, it's another solution to soap scum. A very light layer of oil will actually slow down the formation of stubborn scum. Try a bit of baby oil for a pleasantly scented preventive—just pour a small amount on a soft, dry cloth, and lightly rub it over the shower walls in circles.

WAX WORKS WONDERS. Prevent those not-so-pretty water spots from showing up on your shower's walls and glass doors by polishing the surfaces twice a year with car wax. Follow the directions on the product's label to polish on and wipe off the wax. And as a bonus, the wax will also make routine cleaning a much easier task. Just make sure you don't use it on the shower floor—it'll make it way too slippery. ✉ Chris N., NY

ONION BAG SCRUBBER. Here's how to make a homemade scrubber that will really help you clean up around the house. Clip the end off an empty onion bag and stuff it with other empty onion bags. Then wad it up and use it to tackle bathtub soap scum, shower walls—even gunky dishes and splattered stovetops. ✉ Rosemary T., PA

SHAMPOO FOR SHINE. Shampoo will do a bang-up job of cleaning grime from your shower walls. The same product that's so good at cutting through the dirt and oils in your hair will do the same on built-up scum on the tiles and glass door, leaving them sparkling clean and shiny. ✉ Eugene W., MD

BRUSH YOUR TILE. To clean tile and grout, I use my electric toothbrush with an old brush head attached. I just apply the cleaner to the surface I'm working on, and brush away! ✉ Jenna P., WA

TILE RUBDOWN. Shine your ceramic tiles and porcelain tub with wintergreen rubbing alcohol on a soft cloth. It cleans to a sparkle, kills germs, and leaves behind a fresh scent. ✉ Eileen I., MD

NO MERCY FOR MILDEW. To eliminate mildew on your shower tiles, spray them with foaming oven cleaner, and let it sit for about 30 minutes. You'll then be able to effortlessly rinse the tiles clean—no need for elbow grease! ✉ Minnie G., TX

QUICK FIX

The next time you clean your old white porcelain or fiberglass tub, follow up the scrubbing with a good, long soak: Fill the tub with hot water, and drop in several denture-cleaning tablets. Let the water sit overnight, rinse the tub out in the morning, and that porcelain will gleam like a Pepsodent® smile!

Ask Jerry

Q: I can't get rid of the mildew in my bathroom. I swab it with a bleach solution, and a week later, it's back again. What else can I do?

A: Keeping your house on the dry side is the only way to win the war against mildew. To dry things out a little, try these battle-tested tips and tricks:

• Use a bathroom ventilation fan or dehumidifier. Turn the fan on before you step into the shower or take a steamy bath, and let it run until the bathroom air loses its extra humidity.

• Set a pan of unscented clay cat litter or silica gel on a bathroom closet shelf. Or, fill one foot of an old pair of panty hose with the litter, knot the panty hose at the ankle, and cut off the extra part above the knot. Then place this nylon sack on a shelf.

• Avoid grouping houseplants together in your bathroom; the water vapor released by their foliage and the soil may encourage mildew on nearby countertops and other surfaces.

• If mildew and mold are common problems throughout your house, install a large-capacity dehumidifier to dry the air out.

GOOP FOR GRIME. Tackle bathtub grime by dipping an old plastic-net bath scrubber into a tub of Goop® Hand Cleaner and rubbing it into the mess. Rinse well, and you'll end up with a shiny, clean tub that's scratch-free. ✉ *Dina S., NJ*

TUB SOAK. Clear out stubborn scum from your bathtub by filling it with hot water, then adding 2 cups of liquid laundry detergent. After letting it soak for an hour, pull the plug, then wash and rinse the tub as usual. ✉ *Timothy R., MO*

RING-AROUND-THE-TUB SCRUB. To remove bathtub rings lickety-split, I make a paste of 3 parts cream of tartar and 1 part hydrogen peroxide. Then I rub it onto the stain and let it dry. When I wipe the paste off with a clean, damp sponge, my bathtub looks as clean as freshly fallen snow. ✉ *Hurdie R., NV*

Down the Drain

CUT THE CLOG. Hydrogen peroxide is a great choice for clearing clogged or sluggish drains. Pour ¼ cup of 3% hydrogen peroxide down the drain. If there's standing water in the sink, carefully use your plunger to clear the gunk away. Otherwise, flush the drain with water, and it'll be flowing freely in no time. ✉ *Katherine O., CA*

CLEAR AS A BELL. Try this for clearing a clogged drain: Mix ½ cup of table salt, ½ cup of baking soda, and 1½ tablespoons of cream of tartar. Slowly pour the powdery mixture down the drain, following it with 2 cups of cold water. Repeat, if necessary. ✉ *Jackie D., KY*

GO WITH THE FLOW. Slow drains can drive you nuts! So make 'em flow by pouring a cup of baking soda into the sink or bathtub drain, followed by a cup of vinegar. Wait five minutes, and flush the drain with 2 quarts of hot water. For extra-stubborn clogs, you may have to repeat this process, but before you know it, your sink will be back to normal. ✉ LaWanda K., OK

A BIT OF FIZZ'LL DO IT. Clear a clogged drain easily with Alka-Seltzer® Original antacid tablets. Just drop two tablets into standing water and let the effervescent fizz do all the work. After about 30 minutes, flush the drain with water. Your drain will be on the go—er, flow—just like that! ✉ Janet E., IA

Grandma Putt's Wisdom

When your drains are so clogged up that water goes down s-l-o-w-l-y, try my Grandma Putt's quick fix, and plunge the problem away. Grab a "plumber's friend" (a hand plunger), hold it over the drain, then give it one or two quick, hard pumps to dislodge the stuff that's causing the backup. Wear long rubber gloves for this job because you'll need to grab the hair ball or other gunk that comes up before it tries to slide back down the drain.

GO-GO DRAIN CLEANER. Get a sluggish drain flowing again by mixing 1 cup of baking soda, 1 cup of salt, and 1/2 cup of white vinegar and pouring it down the drain. Wait 15 minutes, then follow up with about 2 quarts of boiling water. ✉ Don Q., SD

LET IT POUR. Has your showerhead gone from the bathroom version of Niagara Falls to a feeble trickle? Hard-water deposits are probably clogging the holes. To keep your shower flowing freely, fill your sink with hot water and add a couple of denture-cleaning tablets. Then unscrew the showerhead and soak it in the mix for several hours. Rinse it well, screw it back in place, and you'll enjoy a full-force shower again. ✉ Bill W., DE

A Tidy Bowl

MAKE YOUR BOWL SHINE. There are lots of commercial products that get rid of lime buildup and other grime in your toilet. But why buy those pricey (not to mention toxic) potions when all you need are a few denture-cleaning tablets? Drop two in the bowl, let them do their work for about 30 minutes, and then scrub the toilet clean. It works for me! ✉ **Norma N., TN**

C HOW EASY IT IS? Here's my no-sweat approach to toilet cleaning—I simply drop a few vitamin C tablets into my toilet bowl at bedtime. In the morning, I just swish the bowl with a toilet brush and flush. The bowl is clean and smells fresh, without the need for any harmful chemicals. ✉ **Sharon L., CA**

TOOTHPASTE FOR THE TOILET. I know this sounds a bit crazy, but do what I do and squirt some fluoride toothpaste into your toilet bowl. Then use a toilet brush to clean the inside of the bowl. Your toilet will be clean, and your bathroom will be left with a wonderful, minty-fresh scent. ✉ **LaShonna S., IL**

SUPER-DUPER SOLUTIONS

STOP YER FLAPPIN'! ● When hard-water minerals build up in a toilet tank, the deposits keep the flapper valve from closing tight—and that leads to an annoying trickle. If jiggling the handle doesn't make the toilet stop running, shut off the water, flush the toilet to empty the tank, and scrub off the pesky buildup with Zud® scouring powder. You can also use Lime-Away® or CLR® to dissolve the minerals. Just remember to protect your skin and eyes while you work. When you're finished, turn the water back on and flush the toilet a few times to rinse out the residue.

A CLEANER COMMODE. If you're cleaning the bathroom and reach for the toilet bowl cleaner only to discover that the bottle is empty, grab some Listerine® mouthwash instead. Listerine not only smells great (especially the citrus variety), but it'll clean your commode just as well as toilet bowl cleaner does. ✉ **Terri M., UT**

SODA SOLUTION. For a refreshing way to clean in the bathroom, pour a can of Coke® into your toilet and let it sit for about an hour. Then brush the inside of the bowl, and your toilet will be sparkling fresh. ✉ **Marie M., WA**

Fabulous Floors

TEA TIME. Black tea is a terrific shiner-upper for hardwood floors and wood furniture. Put about 20 tea bags in a saucepan with 2 quarts of water. Let the liquid come to a boil, then turn off the heat and let the tea steep until it's cold. Mop the tea onto your floors with a sponge mop—no rinsing required! For furniture, dampen a clean cloth with the tea and polish away. ✉ **Erin T., MN**

THE PERFECT PAD. Nothing's easier to use on a dirty floor than disposable floor-cleaning pads—they're convenient and work well. But when I run out and need my floor cleaned pronto, I reach for a

---

SUPER-DUPER SOLUTIONS

TACKLE THE TOUGH STUFF ● To clean your dirtiest floors, combine ¼ cup of Murphy® Oil Soap and ½ cup of vinegar in 2 gallons of warm water. Mop the mixture on, or use a scrub brush. It'll take the toughest scum off and leave your floor gleaming.

maxi pad instead. It sticks right on to the swivel head of my mop, and I can either dry-dust the floor with it or spritz on an all-purpose cleaner to get things really spotless. ✉ **Sharon S., ON**

MOP TO A SHINE. Clean and shine your hardwood floors with a mix of ½ cup of white vinegar in 1 gallon of warm water. Use a sponge mop to apply; no rinsing required. It's an easy way to keep your floors looking their best. ✉ **Colleen S., MI**

SPRAY AWAY GRIME. Make your own all-purpose spray cleaner by filling a 1-quart handheld sprayer bottle with equal parts dishwashing liquid, bleach, and pine oil. I use this homemade cleaner on vinyl floors, laminate countertops, sinks, and other hard surfaces. ✉ **Jean M., LA**

RUB OUT SCUFFS. Scuff marks on your linoleum or vinyl floor can drive you crazy, so here's a simple way to get rid of them. Squeeze a glob of white non-gel toothpaste onto a clean cloth and rub away. Then all you have to do is rinse, and the offending marks will disappear. ✉ **Ronda C., SC**

DYNAMIC DUO. To remove grease and dirty buildup from a linoleum or vinyl floor, make a paste of equal parts baking soda and hydrogen peroxide. This combination makes a spot-on cleaner, and it helps to preserve the color of the linoleum as well. Scrub the grime away using the paste on a wet sponge, then follow up by mopping with clean water. ✉ **Arlene B., WA**

SALT AWAY STAINS. If you've got a stain on your marble floor, cover it with salt, then brush it away. Reapply and brush off the salt as many times as you need to until the stain has been completely absorbed. ✉ **Wendy L., PA**

QUICK FIX

When a leaky pen makes a mess on your vinyl floor, here's how to clean it up in a flash: Put a dollop of solid shortening on the stain and rub it in with a clean cloth or paper towel. After you smear the grease on, wipe it away, then wash the area with a warm, soapy cloth to remove the oily residue.

ANOTHER GREAT IDEA!

READ ALL ABOUT IT

Got crumbs on the floor, but can't locate your dustpan? Not to worry—use newspaper instead. Just wet the edge so that it sticks to the floor, then sweep the mess away. Now that's what I call news you can use!

ERASE PENCIL MARKS. I use good ol' baking soda to get rid of pencil marks on my vinyl floor. I just sprinkle the marks with the soda and add enough water to make a paste. Then I lightly rub the paste until the marks lift right off. ✉ Meredith S., FL

Off the Wall

GIVE MARKS THE BRUSH-OFF. Did your artistic children or grand-kids leave crayon marks on the walls? Try this neat trick: Squirt a generous amount of white non-gel toothpaste onto the marks, rub the area with a scrub brush, and rinse with a water-soaked sponge. You'll be back to a blank canvas in no time! ✉ Lisa H., IN

A SOFT SOLUTION. I dab a little Avon Skin So Soft Original Bath Oil onto a cotton ball, and use it to remove crayon marks from my walls and furniture. It cleans up the mess and leaves a nice scent behind. ✉ Rosie F., MO

1-2-3 . . . GONE! Removing crayon marks from a wall or other hard surface is as easy as 1-2-3. One, grab a baby wipe; two, rub the marks away; and three, rub it again with a fresh wipe if any stain remains. That's all there is to it! ✉ Denise L., NB

SIMPLE SODA SCRUB. Dip a damp cloth in baking soda to remove pencil or crayon marks from your walls. It'll take any unwanted "artwork" right off, lickety-split! ✉ Jennifer D., KY

NIX NAIL POLISH. When nail polish lands on a painted wall, first blot up as much as you can. Then mix 1 teaspoon of borax in 1 cup of water, dip a sponge into the solution, and scrub away. ✉ Susan N., PA

VINEGAR VICTORY. You can remove dirt and grime from your pine paneling by mixing ¼ cup of white vinegar in a bucket of warm water. Dip a rag in the mixture, wring it out, and then wipe the paneling clean. ✉ Dan M., NJ

Ask Jerry

Q: I quit smoking more than a year ago, but I still can't get the nicotine stains off my walls, no matter how hard I scrub. Is there any hope, or do I need to call in the painters?

A: I have just the cleaning solution you need. Trisodium phosphate (TSP) will get rid of the dirt and discoloration, though you may have to repeat the treatment. Test TSP in an inconspicuous area first to make sure it won't damage the paint. Then mix 1 to 2 tablespoons of TSP powder in 1 gallon of warm water. Use the cleaner to wash the walls from the bottom up, and rinse them thoroughly. Wear protective clothing, and cover all rugs, floors, and furniture to protect them from any wayward drips and splashes.

Grandma Putt's Wisdom

Washing a ceiling can be a real chore, but my Grandma Putt had a couple of neat tricks for cutting the job down to size. First, she used the two-bucket system—the cleaning solution went into one bucket and clean water in the other. That way, she could rinse out her sponge as often as she wanted to without trekking back to the sink or dirtying the cleaning solution—because frequent rinsing means a streak-free job! Plus, she made sure to dip only about one-third of the sponge into the cleaner to prevent drips from running down her arm or streaking the walls. Now that's what I call using the old noggin!

BRANCH OUT YOUR DUSTING. I sweep away cobwebs on basement walls and ceilings with a branch from a pine tree. Just swipe the branch through the web, turning it as you go, then discard the whole mess. *Note:* Don't try this upstairs on your painted walls and ceilings because the branch could leave green or brown marks on the paint. ✉ Carl B., NC

ROLL CEILINGS CLEAN. To remove dust and cobwebs from your ceilings, put a clean paint roller on the end of a roller extension pole. You'll reach the dusty areas easily, and will be able to roll the webs away in a flash. ✉ Darlene B., FL

GROW A LONGER ARM. Clean those hard-to-reach places like ceilings by stretching your reach with a clean old T-shirt attached to a broom to snag the dust. No ladders required! ✉ Mike T., CT

WOOLLY WALLPAPER CLEANER. I use fine steel wool to erase crayon marks on my wallpaper. Just employ a light touch and gently rub the marks with the wool until they disappear. ✉ Greg C., FL

WALLPAPER PASTE. Get a grease spot to release its grip from wallpaper like this: Make a paste of cornstarch and a little water, spread it over the stain, and let it dry. Then brush off the powder and check the spot—if you can still see it, repeat the treatment until it has vanished completely. ✉ Sherry K., PA

REMOVE PAPER GENTLY. Don't let the thought of removing wallpaper overwhelm you. Make it easy on yourself—just fill a handheld sprayer bottle with liquid fabric softener and spray it all over the wall covering. Let the liquid soak into the paper for a few minutes, and then it'll be easy to peel or scrape it off with a putty knife. ✉ Karen T., IL

PAPER BE GONE! To strip off wallpaper—even several layers— quickly and easily, mix 4 cups of boiling water with 1 cup of white vinegar in a paint-roller tray. Dip in a clean paint roller until it's saturated, then apply the mixture to the wall, wetting it thoroughly. Wait about five minutes, and peel the old wallpaper right off. ✉ Vicki B., VT

PACK IT WITH PASTE. Need to fill a nail hole in the wall, but you're fresh out of Spackle™? Just use white non-gel tooth-paste to fill the hole, then smooth out the surface with a putty knife. Let the area dry, and touch up the spot with paint to match. ✉ Shirley A., WA

COLOR YOUR WALL. To quickly and easily patch a nail hole in a wall, push the tip of a matching-color crayon into the hole until the wax fills it up. Then use the crayon to color over the hole in a circular motion, and rub with a tissue to "sand" it smooth. Voilà—no more hole! ✉ Shannon W., NY

Jerry's Handy Hints

GET STEAMED

➔ To remove stubborn pieces of old wallpaper, carefully hold the spout of a steaming kettle near the paper, and after it has darkened with moisture, peel it off. This trick is as easy as pie!

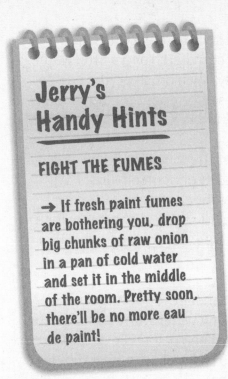

Jerry's Handy Hints

FIGHT THE FUMES

→ If fresh paint fumes are bothering you, drop big chunks of raw onion in a pan of cold water and set it in the middle of the room. Pretty soon, there'll be no more eau de paint!

PLASTER PATCH. Mix a paste of equal parts white glue and baking soda, and use it to patch old plaster walls. The cracks will disappear in just a few minutes, and you can paint right over the patch once it's dry. ✉ Elaine W., PA

PORTABLE PAINT. For small wall touch-ups, you really don't want to haul around a whole can of paint. Just cut a clean, dry 2-liter plastic soda bottle in half and set the bottom aside. Take the top and turn it upside down, making sure the cap is screwed on tight. Holding the "neck" of the bottle as a handle, pour some paint into your new container, grab a paintbrush, and you're good to go! ✉ Marty S., IN

THIS'LL STIR THINGS UP. When I'm ready to paint but find that I'm fresh out of paint stirrers, I use an old plastic hanger without a bottom bar. It works like a charm! ✉ Janice N., OH

ANOTHER GREAT IDEA!

COUNT ON CHALK

When a plaster wall has a hole in it that's too deep to fill with just spackling compound, reach for a stick of chalk. Simply insert the stick into the hole, cut it off even with the wall, then apply Spackle™ over it.

A SMOOTH IDEA. Don't dump an old can of paint that's full of lumps and clumps—it's still okay to use. Just do what I do and strain the paint through a piece of panty hose into a new container. Then get ready to roll. ✉ Neil W., CT

STICK TO IT. If you're getting ready to paint a vinyl, metal, plastic, or laminated surface, wipe it down with vinegar first, and start painting as soon as the vinegar dries. The vinegar makes the paint stick better and helps prevent chipping. ✉ Leroy P., TN

ROOM FRESHENER. I add a teaspoonful of vanilla extract to my water-based paint before painting my walls. It cuts down on the odor of the paint while I'm working, and it keeps the room smelling nice, even after the paint dries. ✉ Shirley T., TN

Ask Jerry

Q: I've got some leftover paint stored in my garage in case I need it for touch-ups. How long can I keep it before it goes bad?

A: It all depends on the conditions in your garage. If the temperature inside goes below freezing in the winter and/or gets blistering hot in the summer, your paint could become unusable in less than a year. On the other hand, if your garage is well insulated, paint can last a long time. I recently touched up some spots in my house using latex paint that I've had for more than 10 years! I just gave it a good, thorough stirring, and it worked just like it did the day I bought it. Oil-based paint will store equally well, as long as you keep the lid on real tight.

Window Dressing

I CAN SEE CLEARLY NOW... When it's time to wash your windows, add a squirt of dishwashing liquid to a bucket of warm water for an extra shine. Wipe your windows clean with the soapy solution, and dry them with a lint-free clean cloth. The glass will end up crystal clear, with no need to rinse. ✉ *Renee Z., TX*

A CORNY IDEA. For the cleanest windows around, I do what folks did in the old days. Just fill a bucket with water and add enough cornstarch to make the water cloudy. Wipe the mixture onto the windows with a clean cloth. Let it dry, and then buff the glass to a shine with an old T-shirt. If the outside temperatures are below freezing, I simply add a splash of rubbing alcohol to keep the solution from icing up. ✉ *Sherry P., IN*

FILTER OUT LINT. Looking for the perfect lint-free cloth to dry your windows and mirrors? Try paper coffee filters. They're inexpensive and won't leave a telltale paper trail behind. ✉ *Judy S., ME*

Grandma Putt's Wisdom

Figuring out which side of the glass a streak is on can be awfully frustrating. You peer, you smear, you walk outside and back in again. To tell the difference at a glance, my Grandma Putt came up with a neat trick: She used vertical strokes on the inside of her windows, and horizontal strokes on the outside. Then if that doggone streak was horizontal, why, she knew it was on the outside looking in!

HANDY CLEANER. If the change of life has left you with a closet full of feminine products, put them to good use! Spray the glass cleaner of your choice onto a maxi pad that you've stuck to the palm of your hand, and use it to clean your windows. You can also use the pads, along with the appropriate cleaners, to spiff up ceiling fans and furniture. ✉ Cheryl L., OH

WINDOW WASH ON THE CHEAP. Here's a do-it-yourself window wash that practically pays for itself. Fill an empty handheld sprayer bottle with club soda and use it to wash your windows, wiping them clean and dry with bunched-up newspaper. You'll appreciate your nice clear glass, and your homemade spray cleaner will cost a whole lot less than those store-bought brands. ✉ Meredith M., IL

LOOSEN UP. Are your windows sticking when you open and close them? Then you need to take action. Here's what I recommend: Spray furniture polish on the gliders. A little squirt and the windows will move much more easily. ✉ Julie R., MA

WAX WORKS WONDERS. When your windows and sliding doors are hard to budge, here's how to make them run more smoothly. After cleaning the tracks, rub a white, unscented candle back and forth along the gliders. Your windows and doors won't stick, and the wax won't attract dirt. ✉ Sandra A., NM

PICTURE-PERFECT FRAMES. Toothpaste is just the ticket for cleaning aluminum window frames. Gently scrub it into the grime with an old toothbrush, making sure to get into those hard-to-reach corners. Then wipe the area clean with a wet cloth. ✉ Sandra H., MI

FAST FILLER FOR HOLES. I fix small holes in my window screens by applying several layers of clear nail polish or model airplane cement over each hole. Once the sealer dries, the holes will barely be noticeable. ✉ Doug C., NJ

PANTY HOSE PATCH. To temporarily mend a torn window screen, I cut a piece of panty hose that's about half an inch larger all around than the tear in my screen. Then I brush rubber cement over the tear and press the patch into place. When it's time to make a more permanent patch, I simply peel off the panty hose and rub the cement away with my finger. ✉ Nicole W., PA

BATH FOR BLINDS. Clean the nasty grime that seems to cling to mini blinds by removing the blinds from your windows and placing them in your bathtub. Saturate them thoroughly with a basin, tub, and tile cleaner, and leave them alone for about 15 minutes. Scrub the extra-stubborn dirt with a soft brush, rinse the blinds off under the shower, and let them air-dry. ✉ Kathy K., MI

SWIPE AND WIPE. Use baby wipes to clean your mini blinds. You can wrap a wipe around your finger to get into even the narrowest spots, especially around the blind pulls. And to get the most out of each sheet, use both sides of the wipe. ✉ Carol G., MA

SOCK IT TO ME. You don't have to spend hours dusting your blinds. Do the job in a flash by putting an old sock on your hand,

---

SUPER-DUPER SOLUTIONS

KNOW YOUR NUMBERS ● When you take the screens out of your windows, you might think you'll remember what screen came from which window, but it's easy to get them mixed up. So use a permanent marker to write a number on each screen frame in an inconspicuous place and mark the corresponding window with the same number. That way, you'll know right away which screen goes where.

Grandma Putt's Wisdom

Finding clever shortcuts was my Grandma Putt's specialty, and she used a neat trick to make sure her drapes and curtains never ended up in her ironing basket—she hung them back up on the rod while they were still a little bit damp. She'd simply retrieve one curtain at a time from the dryer while the cycle was still going and slip that piece onto the rod at the window. Then she'd get the next one, and the next, and so on, so the curtains never had time to stop spinning and end up in a wrinkled heap in the dryer. The weight of the slightly damp cloth helped the curtains dry straight, as did the nice cool breeze that was coming in the open window.

spritzing it with water, and running it along the slats. The sock picks up the dust like magic. ✉ **Patty J., NH**

DRY OFF DUST. Dusty window treatments will spiff up in a flash if you put them in your dryer on the "no heat" setting, and toss in a Swiffer® dry cloth. After about five minutes of tumbling around, your window treatments will be fresh and clean—without a bit of dust on them! ✉ **Phyllis S., IL**

DELICATE LACE WASH. You can gently clean your fragile lace curtains by washing them on your washer's delicate cycle with ¼ cup of Epsom salts added. Remove the curtains immediately after the wash cycle stops, and hang them to air-dry. ✉ **Maribeth H., WA**

CODDLE YOUR CURTAINS. I use a soft-bristled baby brush to clean my delicate curtain and lamp shade fabrics. Just remember to use a light touch as you gently brush the fabric to get rid of the dust and dirt. ✉ **Alyssa L., NY**

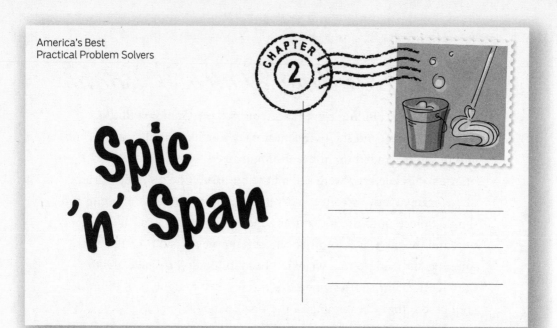

America's Best
Practical Problem Solvers

CHAPTER (2)

Spic 'n' Span

Laundry Lessons

HOMEMADE HELPER. Store-bought multipurpose cleaners cost a pretty penny. So do what I do and make your own with a mixture of Octagon Soap® and powdered Tide® laundry detergent. Dissolve a shredded bar of Octagon in boiling water, then mix in ½ cup of Tide. Pour the hot mixture into a glass jar and let it cool; it will turn into a gel. You can use your homemade cleaner on stained, washable clothing, plus anything that you would normally wash with soap and water. ✉ Halimah S., NC

DIY DETERGENT. I make my own inexpensive, suds-free laundry detergent. Here's how: Grate ⅓ bar of Fels-Naptha® soap and add it to a pan with 6 cups of very hot water. Heat the pan on the stove until the soap is dissolved, then stir in ½ cup of washing soda and

½ cup of borax. Continue to stir until all of the ingredients are dissolved and the mixture has thickened and looks like honey. Remove the pan from the heat, then mix the melted soap blend with 1 quart of hot water in a 6-gallon bucket. Add another 5½ quarts of water, and stir until completely blended. Set the mixture aside for 24 hours, then pour it into clean plastic milk jugs for storage. For a regular load of laundry, add ½ cup of mix per load. ✉ Claudia A., IA

ODOR EATER. Laundry detergents clean your clothes, but they won't always wash away stubborn, lingering odors, like those from cigarette or barbecue smoke. For a deodorizing laundry boost, add ½ cup of white vinegar to your wash cycle, along with your regular detergent. ✉ Pam O., PA

A PINEY FIX. To deodorize extra-smelly laundry, add ½ cup of pine oil to your washing machine when you pour in your detergent. It also works wonders as a stain remover. Just rub some of the cleaner directly on the spot before laundering. ✉ Robin D., MI

ANOTHER GREAT IDEA!

HANDLE WITH CARE

Instead of buying an expensive liquid soap to clean your delicate fabrics, mix up a batch of this remarkable recipe. Simply combine ½ cup of powdered laundry detergent and ½ cup of borax in a saucepan with 2 cups of water. Simmer over low heat for about 10 minutes, stirring constantly (beat with a wire whisk occasionally to break up the lumps). Remove the pan from the stove and let it cool, then pour the mix into a clean plastic bottle. Use it as you would any commercial product for delicate fabrics. This gentle soap keeps practically forever, so it'll be ready whenever you need to treat your hand-washable items with TLC.

NIX THE SOFTENER. If you use rags to clean your windows, don't add fabric softener to the water when you wash them. The same additive that keeps fabric soft will make the rags less absorbent and leave streaks behind when you dry the windows. ✉ **Ellie T., OH**

SOFTENER SUBSTITUTE. Next time you run out of fabric softener, don't buy a new bottle. Make your own by mixing 1 part hair conditioner with 10 parts water. Add the mixture to your washing machine's fabric-softener dispenser, and run your wash cycle. Your laundry will feel soft and smell great! ✉ **Julia B., AZ**

BLOODSTAIN S.O.S. Cut yourself? First, grab the hydrogen peroxide and tend to your injury. When you're done, keep the bottle out and use the hydrogen peroxide to get out any blood that may have gotten on your clothes. Wet the spots with water, then soak those sections of the clothing in a bowl filled with hydrogen peroxide. After about 30 minutes, remove the item and rinse with cold water, then wash it as you normally would. ✉ **Melissa L., IN**

SALTY SOLUTION. Remove a fresh bloodstain by covering it with salt, then dabbing at the spot with a cold, wet cloth. Continue to rub it with cold water until the stain is gone. Then launder the item as usual. ✉ **Angela P., BC**

HAIR SPRAY HELPS. If I'm not able to get to a bloodstain while it's fresh, I spray the spot with hair spray, then rinse it with cold water. The blood clings to the hair spray and washes away. For deep stains, you may have to repeat the steps before you put the treated item in the washing machine. ✉ **Laurie H., IN**

BAKING SODA BRIGHTENER. Get whiter whites and brighter brights in one fell swoop—simply by tossing a scoop of baking soda into each load of

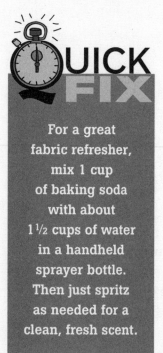

QUICK FIX

For a great fabric refresher, mix 1 cup of baking soda with about 1½ cups of water in a handheld sprayer bottle. Then just spritz as needed for a clean, fresh scent.

laundry. Your clothes will come out cleaner and with a great fresh scent to boot! ✉ Carolyn Y., CO

TAME THAT BLEACH. Bleach in your washing machine gets your whites super bright, but it can be hard on fabric. So try adding 1 cup of white vinegar along with the bleach to help keep the bleach from harming your clothes. ✉ Megan G., FL

CREAM (SODA) FOR YOUR COFFEE. To eliminate a stubborn coffee stain from fabric, apply cream soda directly to the stain. Blot it, rinse it, and let it dry. Then launder as usual. It works like a dream! ✉ Anita G., GA

Jerry's Handy Hints

OUT, DARN SPOT!

→ Get bloodstains out fast by first rinsing the spot with cold water. Then pour a little ammonia onto the stained area and rub well. Ammonia is safe for cotton and most synthetic fabrics, but don't try this trick on silk, batiks, or any tie-dyed items.

STAIN REMOVAL ON THE RUN. If I'm on the go and have a spill, I just reach for the baby wipes. It's so easy to rub one on the stain to help keep it from becoming permanent until I can get back to my laundry room and treat the spot properly. The wipes are gentle enough that the fabric won't be damaged and the color won't fade. ✉ Wendy A., PA

TOOTHPASTE TOUCH-UP. For extra-stubborn food stains, squeeze a dab of white non-gel toothpaste onto the spot. Hold the item under cool water while gently rubbing the toothpaste into the stain with your fingertips or a soft brush. Repeat as necessary, then rinse the toothpaste out and launder the item. ✉ Mary O., KY

POWDER POWER. When you're saddled with tough clothing stains, make a paste of powdered dishwasher detergent and water, and work it into the spots. Let the item sit for a few hours, then launder the clothing. As with all stain removers, this should be tested on an inconspicuous section of the clothing first, to be sure it doesn't damage or fade the fabric. ✉ **Cindy S., CA**

STAIN SOLUTION. You can easily remove grease, grass stains, ring-around-the-collar, and other common laundry stains with a mixture of 1 part Murphy® Oil Soap and 1 part water. Simply combine the liquids in a handheld sprayer bottle and apply liberally to any stain. ✉ **Roseanne O., LA**

SHAMPOO YOUR COLLAR. Since the filthy ring that appears around the inside of your shirt collar comes from your hair products and the natural oils your body produces, try using the same product you wash your hair with to get rid of the dirt. Work a small amount of shampoo—formulas for oily hair work best—into the grime, and follow it with a squirt of laundry-stain spray. After machine washing and drying, the shirt should come out fresh and clean. ✉ **Debbie M., GA**

LATHER UP! I've found that clear shampoo mixed with a dab of honey will get tough stains out of clothing. Just squirt the mixture onto the stain, rub it with a soft brush, and rinse it out

Grandma Putt's Wisdom

My Grandma Putt shaved a piece of Fels-Naptha® soap into every load of her laundry, but when she needed extra power to eliminate stains, she'd rub the bar right on the cloth like a stain stick. Fels-Naptha worked like magic on grass stains, chocolate stains, and all kinds of other spots—we even scrubbed it onto our skin to prevent poison ivy! To put this old-fashioned helper to work on your tough laundry stains, wet the stained fabric and vigorously rub the soap into the spot before you machine wash the garment. Look for Fels-Naptha in the laundry section of your supermarket.

with water. Then you can launder the garment. ✉ Doris S., MN

DON'T WHINE ABOUT IT. It never fails. Every time red wine is spilled, it seems to end up on a light-colored tablecloth or shirt. When this happens to you, blot up as much of the liquid as you can with an absorbent cloth. Then pour a little cold water on the spot. Blot it again, and sprinkle some salt on the remaining stain. Repeat the process until there's no longer any sign of the wine. Launder the item as usual. ✉ Dave C., OH

DISHWASHER WHITES. Liquid dishwasher detergent makes a spot-on treatment for stains on white laundry. Simply squirt the detergent on the stain, then machine wash the item. *Note:* This works like a charm, but the detergent contains bleach, so it's only safe to use on white fabrics. ✉ Sandy H., MI

AN EASY SEPARATION. I keep two laundry baskets for our dirty laundry—a light-colored one and a dark-colored one. My family knows to put their dirty whites in the white basket, and their dirty darks in the dark basket. That way, the laundry is presorted, saving me precious time. ✉ Belinda L., PA

BABY THOSE STAINS. Use a baby wipe to swipe away unsightly deodorant stains. The alcohol in the wipe will dissolve the marks

TAKE 5

Here are five not-so-common uses for chalk:

1 Erase ring-around-the-collar by rubbing white chalk on the spot; then wash the shirt as usual.

2 Lift grease from a washable fabric. Just rub the spots with chalk, wait until the grease is absorbed, then launder.

3 Cover spots on suede by rubbing the marks with chalk of the same color.

4 Prevent dampness by hanging bags of chalk in closets and basements.

5 Clean marble with a soft, damp cloth dipped in powdered chalk. Rinse with water, and dry thoroughly.

QUICK FIX

To eliminate white deodorant stains from dark clothes, just rub a scrunched-up pair of panty hose over the stains, and the gentle abrasive action will make them vanish!

and evaporate, leaving you clean and dry. If you keep wipes in your purse or car, you'll always be ready for emergency touch-ups. ✉ Amanda T., PA

POWER WASH. Mix baking soda, liquid dishwasher detergent, and powdered dishwasher detergent in equal parts to make a solution that will remove just about any stain. Rub the mixture on the spot, wait for it to dry, then wipe it away with a wet cloth before you wash the clothing as usual. This powerful combination of ingredients will tackle even the toughest of stains. *Note:* Because dishwasher detergent contains bleach, use this cleaner on white fabrics only. ✉ Janet B., TX

GO AFTER GRASS STAINS. To mow down grass stains in a snap, mix 1 cup of laundry detergent, 1 cup of ammonia, and 2 cups of water in a handheld sprayer bottle. Apply this solution directly to the stained area before tossing the clothes into the wash. ✉ Arianna K., OK

ANOTHER GREAT IDEA!

LAST-DITCH CLEANER

To remove a really stubborn mystery stain on an old white tablecloth, try my tried-and-true last-ditch effort: Put the cloth into an extra-large cooking pot, pour in 4 tablespoons of dishwasher detergent (liquid or powder), and add enough water to cover the fabric. Heat the mixture to a boil, and let it simmer on low for about 20 minutes, stirring occasionally. Carefully lift the steaming tablecloth out with a pair of tongs, put it in a bucket, and then dump it in your washing machine. Wash it immediately on the usual cycle.

GIVE GRASS STAINS THE HEAVE-HO. A grass stain can be a real bear to get rid of. So make your job easier by mixing a thick paste of baking soda and water. Rub the paste on the stain, then scrub the area with a brush dipped in plain club soda. ✉ Juanita T., MI

Ask Jerry

Q: I've got a pair of jeans with some old grass stains on them. Is there anything I can do to make them come clean?

A: There sure is, and it's easy, too. Just combine egg white and glycerin in equal parts, apply the mixture to the stains to loosen them up, and then treat the area as you would a fresh stain. That should do the trick!

A CORNY APPROACH. I remove ground-in grass stains from my clothing by pouring a little light corn syrup directly on the stains. I gently rub the fabric with a laundry brush, then toss the item into the washing machine with the next load of wash. The grass stains vanish into thin air! ✉ Sandy F., PA

GREASE BUSTER. Yikes! While you were frying chicken, grease spattered all over your favorite blouse. Don't panic—just reach for the Goop®, a mechanic's hand cleaner (available at supermarkets). Apply it directly to the stains and launder your blouse as usual. It'll come out fresh, clean, and grease-free. ✉ Gayle B., FL

A REFRESHING DEGREASER. Here's an easy way to remove grease stains from clothing—add half a can of cola to your washing machine along with your regular detergent, then toss in the stained clothes. For really stubborn stains, rub a little cola right into the spots, let it sit for a few minutes, then wash the item. ✉ Rhonda H., LA

Grandma Putt's Wisdom

Whether she was cleaning a cruddy kitchen floor or scrubbing greasy work clothes, my Grandma Putt relied on the same hardworking helper for all of her toughest jobs—Lestoil®. To take out grease stains, she simply poured some heavy-duty, full-strength Lestoil directly onto the spots and rubbed the fabric vigorously to work it in. And as an extra precaution, she'd rinse the spots under running water and pour on another dose of Lestoil before the stained item went into her washing machine. Give Lestoil a try. You'll find this old-time standby in the floor-cleaning products aisle (not the laundry aisle) of your local supermarket.

FLOUR FOILS GREASE. Get rid of a greasy clothing stain easily by sprinkling the oily area with flour until it's totally covered. Let the item sit for at least an hour, then brush the flour off. All of the excess oil will be absorbed, then you can pretreat the spot with a liquid laundry-stain lifter before you toss the garment into the wash. ✉ Iris S., NJ

MIGHTY GREASE FIGHTER. You can use WD-40® to remove greasy stains from clothing, but beware—it's harsh stuff. Make sure to test it on an inconspicuous spot first, then treat the grease stain by rubbing some WD-40 into it before laundering the item as you normally would. ✉ David B., WI

A STICKY SITUATION. Somehow, you've managed to get gum stuck on your clothes. What a mess! Get rid of it by spreading peanut butter all over the spot and working it in with your fingers. The peanut butter will loosen the stickiness, so you'll be able to scrape the gum off. Then pretreat the area with a liquid stain remover and launder as usual. ✉ Rocky C., IN

GET OUT THE GUNK. Use a dab of WD-40® to remove gum that's gotten stuck to your clothing. Just spray it on, wait a few minutes, and then pull the gunk away. ✉ Crystal G., WV

SPRAY OUT INK STAINS. As anybody who's ever worked in an office knows, ink has a tendency to wind up smack-dab on your clothing. The last time I had a too-close encounter with a pen, I spritzed the area with hair spray before tossing the garment in the wash. The ink was gone in a flash! ✉ Brenda R., VA

QUICK FIX

Apply cornstarch to an oil or grease stain on your clothing. After the cornstarch has soaked up the stain, just brush it away, and launder the item as usual.

GIVE MURPHY A KISS. To remove a lipstick stain, pretreat and scrub the area with Murphy® Oil Soap. It may take a fair amount of scrubbing, but the lipstick will eventually disappear. Then launder the garment as usual. ✉ Diane R., AL

USE YOUR HEAD. Can't get a lipstick stain off a shirt collar? Reach for the hair spray. Saturate the spot with the spray, and scrub the fabric until the stain disappears. Then wash your shirt as you normally would, and the stain should be history. ✉ Stephanie S., IN

SUPER-DUPER SOLUTIONS

DISAPPEARING INK ● To make an ink stain vanish, lay the stained item on top of a clean, old white towel or T-shirt. Dab rubbing alcohol directly onto the stain, folding the cloth underneath to a fresh part as it absorbs the ink. Continue dabbing and refolding until the stain is gone, then rinse and launder the item as usual. Keep in mind that the towel or T-shirt will become stained, so use one that's ready for the ragbag.

CLEAN YOUR SCREEN. A clean lint screen helps your dryer run as efficiently as possible. If yours has seen better days, remove the screen from your dryer's vent and saturate it with dishwashing liquid. Then grab a couple of rags (enough to cover your lint screen in two layers). Saturate the rags with white vinegar, and lay them on the screen in a double layer. Let the screen sit this way overnight. In the morning, rinse the screen, and it will be as good as new! ✉ Constance P., VA

MACHINE MAINTENANCE. Once a month, I put a cup of vinegar in my washing machine and run it through the wash cycle without any clothes. This monthly "flushing" cleans out the hoses and gets rid of any built-up detergent gunk. ✉ Pauline C., AL

Grandma Putt's Wisdom

Although red was my Grandma Putt's favorite color of lipstick, it's one of the hardest shades to get out when it's smeared on a collar or shirt. Why? Because a lipstick stain is part grease and part dye. So Grandma came up with a great three-step trick for handling this tough customer. Here's how to do it:

1. Gently rub a bit of vegetable or mineral oil into the stain, letting it soak in for about 15 minutes. Then blot the spot with paper towels to remove as much oil and lipstick as possible.

2. Sponge the stain with rubbing alcohol to lift the dye and cut the grease.

3. Wait about five minutes for the alcohol to work its magic, and then toss the item into the washing machine, using the cold-water setting. If any stain remains after washing, don't put the garment in the dryer—apply more alcohol, wait about five minutes, and then wash it again.

HOSIERY FOR HOSES. Recycle an old nylon knee-high and use it as a filter to keep lint from clogging the washing machine drain. Secure the nylon to the drainage hose with a rubber band, and replace the knee-high when it's about half full. This is an easy, mess-free solution that'll keep your machine in tip-top shape. ✉ Mary J., IL

SEARCH AND RESCUE. Small items that roll behind or between the washer and dryer always seem to be just out of reach. Here's how I get at them: Cover the end of your vacuum's hose attachment with an old nylon knee-high, then push an empty cardboard paper towel or gift wrap tube onto the hose. Bend or flatten the tube to fit the opening where the item rolled, then turn on the vacuum and have at it. The item will be sucked up and trapped inside the tube, where you can easily retrieve it. ✉ Wendy C., IN

QUICK FIX

One way to get rid of your dryer lint is to use it to start fires. Place it under the kindling to really get your blaze going fast.

Fabric Fixes

THIS HITS THE SPOT. Use a dab of shaving cream to spot-clean stained upholstery and carpets. Just spray a small amount of the foam on the stain, and rub it gently with a damp cloth until the mark is gone. ✉ Lynn M., SC

SUDS UP. If your upholstery can be cleaned with water, try this trick to spot-clean your sofa or chairs: With a hand mixer, whip ¼ cup of dishwashing liquid and 1 cup of warm water until foamy. Then scoop some foam onto a cloth or soft brush and lightly scrub the fabric. Lift the dirty suds off with a spatula, and use a clean, damp cloth to remove any remaining soap. ✉ Rob T., CT

Grandma Putt's Wisdom

My Grandma Putt used cream of tartar for baking—but she also used it as an all-purpose rust remover on her upholstery and carpet. She made a paste by mixing it with a little water, and then she spread the paste on the stained areas. After 15 minutes or so, she washed the residue off, repeating the treatment as necessary. You'll only need a small amount of cream of tartar for most rust stains, so start with 1 tablespoon, and add more if it doesn't make enough paste to cover the stains.

VINEGAR SOAK. You can easily remove sticky decal residue and chewing gum from carpets, upholstery, and other fabrics by saturating the area with warm vinegar. Then work the sticky goop out with your fingers. Follow up by cleaning the fabric as you normally would to remove any lingering vinegar odor. ✉ Lois S., MO

STEAMY STAIN RELIEF. To remove a stain from a rug, gather up a bottle of Windex®, a clean rag, and your steam iron. Spray the Windex onto the spot, then dampen the rag and set your iron on steam. Once the iron is hot, put the rag on the stain and lightly press it with the iron for about 30 seconds. Repeat the steps until the stain has vanished completely. ✉ Mildred L., WA

LET THERE BE LIGHT. Light-colored carpeting can be a real bear to keep clean! For the toughest stains on the lightest carpeting, I use toilet bowl cleaner with bleach. Just work a little bit of the cleaner into the stain, being careful not to overdo it. Once the stain's gone, wipe the area with a wet cloth, repeating as necessary. Then vacuum as usual after the spot has dried. But be careful—toilet bowl cleaner is mighty strong stuff, so first test it in a hidden area of your carpet. ✉ Cathy T., PA

ICE IS NICE. When you find a stain on your carpet, try this icy maneuver. Start by sprinkling baking soda and vinegar on the spot, then placing a clean towel over the area. Cover the towel with ice cubes and wait until all of the ice has melted. Then remove the towel and let the carpet dry. Vacuum up any baking soda residue, and the stain should be gone. ✉ Colleen G., PA

IRON STAINS AWAY. Want to remove Kool-Aid® or another similar stain from your carpet? First, spray the spot liberally with carpet and upholstery cleaner, and let it soak in for 15 to 20 minutes. Then place a clean white cotton T-shirt or hand towel over the stained area and, keeping the cloth on the stain, iron it on a cotton/steam setting. As the cloth becomes saturated, fold it to a clean spot and keep ironing. The stain will come out in no time. ✉ John K., GA

POWER OUT PAINT. If you spill latex paint onto your carpet, don't try rubbing it out. The easiest way to remove it is with a wet/dry vac. For this to work, the paint needs to be wet, so if it's spread over a large area, keep it from drying out before you get to it by covering the paint with a water-soaked towel or plastic sheeting. Then start vacuuming up the wet paint. Keep rewetting the area and vacuuming until a clean towel laid over the entire spill remains paint-free after you stomp on it. ✉ Marion B., NE

Jerry's Handy Hints

DID SOMEONE SAY SPOON?

→ Here's a neat trick I learned way back when: The back of a spoon makes the perfect tool for blotting up ketchup stains on carpet. Just lay a moist cloth over the spot and press the spoon against the cloth to soak up the remains of the stain. Then work in a bit of dishwashing liquid and water, using the same technique. Finally, sponge the soap away with fresh water, and blot it up by pressing the spoon against a clean, dry cloth.

SNACK-STAIN SOLUTION. The next time your late-night snack winds up facedown on the living room carpet, spritz the area with diluted ammonia (1 part ammonia to 1 part water). Then blot the spot with a clean rag, and repeat the process until the stain is gone. This works like a charm for most stains, but whatever you do, don't—and I mean don't—use ammonia, or anything

Ask Jerry

Q: Do you have any advice on how to remove urine stains from a carpet and get rid of the lingering odor, too?

A: I sure do. To remove yellow or brownish urine stains from your carpet or upholstery and neutralize the odor, try this trick. Blot up the urine, then wet the stained area thoroughly with a mixture of 1 cup of white vinegar and 1 cup of water. Blot it with paper towels until it's damp, not wet, and then sprinkle about 1 cup of baking soda liberally over the stained area. Finally, mix 1/4 cup of hydrogen peroxide with 1 teaspoon of dishwashing liquid, and pour the solution over the baking soda. (Be sure to test the potion in an inconspicuous area first to make sure the peroxide doesn't bleach the color out of the carpet or upholstery fabric.) Work it in with a scrub brush until the baking soda is dissolved and the mixture penetrates the fibers. Allow the carpet or fabric to dry, and then vacuum up the residue. If you still see a stain, repeat the treatment.

containing ammonia, on your carpet if you have a dog. It smells like urine to your four-legged pal, and that'll make him think it's A-OK to lift his leg in that area. And that's just about the last thing you want! ✉ **Lisa H., NE**

FIZZ FOILS STAINS. Did someone get too tipsy at last night's party? Just use some seltzer to clean all the stains from your rugs and carpets. Pour a little over the area, and let the fizz do the work. Blot the spots dry, and watch the stains disappear. ✉ **Paul T., PA**

OIL ABSORBER. Oily stains are tricky to completely remove from your carpeting. Try dabbing rubbing alcohol onto the stain with a clean cloth, folding it so you're always working with a clean section, until the spot has vanished. ✉ **Brenda M., IN**

STEAM MACHINE BOOSTER. If you're planning on using a steam cleaner on your carpet and you have a particularly stubborn stain to deal with, do what I do. Presoak the spot with a multipurpose

Grandma Putt's Wisdom

When my Grandma Putt wanted to make her wall-to-wall carpet smell extra good, she borrowed a magic ingredient from her spice rack—and added a pinch of cinnamon to her home-made carpet freshener. To spice things up yourself, mix ⅛ teaspoon of cinnamon with 1 cup of baking soda, sprinkle the powder lightly over your dry carpet, and wait about half an hour so the scent can soak in before you vacuum it up. The fine cinnamon dust can leave a stain if you grind it into the fibers, so don't walk on the mixture, and don't use this trick on white or pale carpets. For those, try light-colored powdered ginger instead of the darker-colored cinnamon.

cleaner to neutralize the odor and give an extra boost to the steam cleaning. ✉ Pamela B., WV

GET THE RED OUT. If you spill red wine on your carpet, pour some white wine immediately over the area. Blot well, and dab with a sponge soaked with warm water. Then pat dry with a clean towel. Repeat if necessary. ✉ Katherine P., PA

FREEZE OFF GUM. Gum is great, but not when it's stuck in your carpeting! So pack a ziplock plastic bag full of ice (don't forget to zip it closed), and lay it on the gum. After 15 minutes or so, the gum will freeze and you'll be able to gently pry it up. Move the ice bag around as you peel up the gunk, so the remaining gum doesn't thaw and become sticky again. ✉ Paul E., MD

BROWN BAG IT. To get candle wax drippings out of my carpet, I start by using a spoon to pick up as much of the drip as I can, or scrape at the hardened wax with my fingernails. Then I place a brown paper bag over the area, set my iron to warm, and iron over the bag. The wax should lift off the carpet and stick to the bag. ✉ Amanda L., NY

ANOTHER BROWN BAG TRICK. When candle wax has dripped onto a tablecloth, cloth napkin or placemat, or even—yikes!—your clothing, don't panic. Once the wax has hardened, freeze it with an ice cube to make it brittle, then chip it away with the edge of a credit card. To remove the wax that has soaked in, put your iron on its hottest setting, place a paper bag beneath the item, and another on top of it, and gently iron the area until the wax has transferred

QUICK FIX

To help soak up and neutralize the sickly smell from vomit on your carpet or rug, blot up as much of the moisture as you can, then sprinkle a layer of baking soda over the area. Let it sit for about an hour, and vacuum up the residue. You can use 1 part borax powder and 2 parts cornstarch in place of the baking soda with the same results.

to the bags. Keep moving the bags to a clean area until the wax is gone. If the wax came from a colored candle, it may leave a stain. So pretreat the area ASAP and launder the item. ✉ Tina Y., NV

CHILL OUT. I've been using this trick for years to keep birthday candles from dripping all over the place. Put the candles on ice for a day before using them on a cake, and they'll burn more slowly and evenly, without all that drippy mess. ✉ Sheryl R., PA

Wonderful Wood

MAYO MAGIC. Oh, no! You forgot to use a coaster under your icy beverage and now your wooden table has a water spot on it. All is not lost—just spread a coating of mayonnaise over the stain and let it sit overnight. In the morning, wipe the surface with a clean, dry cloth and buff the spot with matching furniture polish. There you go—no more water stain! ✉ Michael P., NC

WOOD ON WOOD. When you have a water stain on a wooden table, wood ashes will work wonders to get it off. Simply sprinkle some

ANOTHER GREAT IDEA!

DON'T LET IT BURN YOU UP

If an ember or candle drops on your carpet and singes it a bit, boil up a mixture of 1 cup of white vinegar, ½ cup of talcum powder, and 2 coarsely chopped onions. Let it cool, then spread it over the stain. Once the spot is dry, brush away the residue, and vacuum the area as usual.

ashes on the stain, add a few drops of vegetable oil, and rub the spot away. Then polish the table clean. ✉ Amanda T., PA

RING REMOVER. Get rid of a white water ring from your wooden table by smearing the spot with a squirt of hand lotion, and letting it sit for an hour or so. Then wipe the lotion off with a soft, clean cloth and buff the surface. It might take a few applications, but the white marks will eventually disappear. ✉ Margaret D., ON

MARK OUT BURNS. Got a cigarette burn on your coffee table or hardwood floor where someone missed the ashtray? Apply a paste made of equal parts vinegar and baking soda to the mark, and use a pencil eraser to rub it in. Wipe off the residue with a damp sponge, and let the spot dry thoroughly. Then use a wood-stain marker to color the spot until it blends right in. These pens come in a wide range of colors and shades, so choose the one that matches your furniture or floor best. ✉ Bill T., FL

SKIN-DEEP SOLUTION. To remove a burn mark that has penetrated the finish on my wooden furniture but not the wood

Grandma Putt's Wisdom

Whenever a scratch showed up on my Grandma Putt's favorite wooden sewing table, she mixed up a little "salad dressing" to make it vanish. All it takes is about 1 teaspoon of fresh lemon juice mixed with 1 teaspoon of vegetable oil to get rid of unsightly scratches. Dip a soft cloth into the mixture, rub the scratch, and it'll simply disappear! For deeper scratches, Grandma had another great trick—she rubbed the nut meat of a black walnut or pecan into the scratch and let the "juice" sit for about half an hour to darken the wood. When she polished the table, the scratch was darn near invisible.

itself, I just wrap a small piece of extra-fine steel wool around my finger and use it to carefully sand the stain out. Then I brush the dust away, apply a coat of wax or furniture polish, and it's hardly noticeable. ✉ Julie W., NY

Ask Jerry

Q: There's an ugly white ring on my wooden end table where I had a vase of flowers. What can I do to make it disappear?

A: When water soaks into wood, try one of these quick fixes to get rid of that stain:

• Rub the spot with a bit of white non-gel toothpaste on a damp cloth.

• Dab a moist cloth into a mixture of 1 tablespoon of baking soda and 1 tablespoon of white non-gel toothpaste, and rub the stain in circles for about five minutes.

• Mix a little table salt and olive oil, and rub the area until the stain vanishes.

After any of these treatments, wipe off the residue and polish the table as usual. And next time, don't forget to put a coaster under your vase!

GREASY KID STUFF. Furniture polish sprays are so easy to use and smell so good that it's tempting to use them often. But they'll eventually build up until the wood feels greasy and every fingerprint shows clearly. If your wood furniture has a buildup of polish, clean it up by sprinkling a little cornstarch over the surface and letting it sit for at least an hour. Then wipe it away with a soft, clean cloth and your furniture will glow. ✉ Nicole W., NY

INSTANT WOOD STAIN. Here's my recipe for a homemade finish for unstained wood furniture: Create a mix of 2 parts instant coffee to 1 part black shoe polish and brush it on your pieces. After it dries, seal in the stain with a coat of polyurethane. ✉ Horace R., GA

GET RID OF GREASE STAINS. Wood furniture that's not coated with polyurethane or another tough finish can absorb grease, leaving a nasty stain behind. It's not easy to remove the mark because the oil penetrates the wood fibers. So try this: Place a folded paper towel over the spot and iron it gently to draw out the grease. Then dust the surface with talcum powder or cornstarch, and let it sit overnight to soak up still more. If you can still see a spot, use extra-fine sandpaper (0000 grade) and gently sand the area down to fresh wood. Then rub in some furniture wax or polish to make the area match the rest of the furniture. ✉ Tim G., LA

DO THE SOCK HOP. When you're moving heavy furniture, put socks on the feet of the piece to prevent scratching your floor or the furniture. You can also put socks on the tops of ladder legs to protect your paint and woodwork. ✉ Sean K., PA

SUPER-DUPER SOLUTIONS

HOLD THE OIL ● If you're like me, you probably reach for the oil soap when it's time to clean wood. That's fine, except when it comes to your wood stairs. In that case, save the soap for the banister only. Why? Because any cleaning product that contains oil can make steps a little slippery—and even a little is too much when you need secure footing! So instead of using oil soap on your stairs, use a simple mixture of ¼ cup of white vinegar in a bucket of warm water, and damp mop the treads. There's no need to rinse because the vinegar smell will disappear without a trace, leaving a nice clean, nonslip surface behind.

ANOTHER GREAT IDEA!

ROLLING RIGHT ALONG . . .

If casters drop out of your wooden furniture, fill the holes with melted paraffin, and then put the casters back in. That should do the trick. Or you can wrap a narrow strip of adhesive tape around the stem of the caster until it fills up the hole. Either way, it won't slip out again.

QUICK FIX

If your kitchen cabinets are feeling a bit sticky, get rid of the greasy buildup with a monthly wipe-down. Use a damp sponge with a dab of grease-cutting dishwashing liquid or Murphy® Oil Soap on it. Rinse with a clean, damp sponge, and dry with a lint-free cloth. The finish will look good as new!

CARDBOARD COASTERS. Do you have furniture you need to move? Just place pieces of cardboard under the legs and push. The cardboard will help the furniture slide easily over carpet, and if you have hardwood floors, the cardboard will protect both your furniture *and* the floor. ✉ Sylvia L., OH

END WICKER WILT. If your wicker furniture is sagging, then try this trick: Take the furniture outside and sponge it with hot water. Then let it air-dry. The wood will shrink as it dries and tighten right up. ✉ Viv W., DE

NOT YOUR USUAL GLUE. Next time you've got some wood items that need gluing, try my homemade adhesive: Rinse and strain a quart of cottage cheese until the curds are clean and dry. Then add the juice of one lime and stir well. Let the mixture sit for about an hour, and you've got yourself a strong wood glue! ✉ Stanley S., GA

FRESHEN IT UP. Every now and then you should revive and deodorize your butcher block with fresh lemon juice. First, pretreat any stained areas by sprinkling a little salt over them. Then slice a lemon in half and rub the cut side all over the block, paying special attention to the stains. Let it air-dry for 15 minutes or so, rinse, then dry with a clean cloth. ✉ Fran C., NY

WELCOME TO THE CLUB! Fizzy club soda breaks right through dull, greasy buildup on cabinet surfaces. So whenever I have a little extra left in the bottle, I don't let it go flat in the fridge. Instead, I use it to dampen a cleaning cloth and wipe the grime away. ✉ Sheryl R., PA

CABINETS TAKE A SHINE. Nicks and scratches that mark up your kitchen cabinets and wood furniture can be covered up easily with a matching shade of shoe polish. Simply wipe the polish onto the mark with a soft, clean cloth, then buff it off with a second clean cloth. No more nicks! ✉ Kay M., OH

Grandma Putt's Wisdom

My Grandma Putt used her big ol' butcher block for everything from cutting up chicken to chopping tomatoes. You'd think that block would've been full of stains, but Grandma had a trick up her sleeve that kept it looking like new. Every so often, she'd melt down some beeswax to add to the oil she wiped the block with— and that kept liquids from soaking in before she could wipe them away.

To mind your own beeswax, shave about 1/2 teaspoon of it into 1 cup of mineral oil, and microwave the mix on "high" for about 45 seconds to melt the wax. Stir the mixture, pour some on your butcher block, and rub it in while it's still warm. Now that's what I call bee-ing smart!

SPRUCE UP BASEBOARDS. To clean the wooden baseboards in my home, I use Murphy® Oil Soap, Formula 409®, and ammonia. Mix all three ingredients in equal parts in a handheld sprayer bottle, spritz the liquid on the baseboards, and wipe them clean with a soft, dry cloth. If your baseboards are painted, test the spray in a small, inconspicuous area first to make sure it doesn't discolor the paint. ✉ Anthony L., IL

Precious Metals

BRASS BOOSTER. Polish up your old brass candlesticks with baking soda. Simply dip a damp cloth in the soda and gently rub it into the brass. Wipe the candlesticks with a clean, damp cloth, then polish them to a brassy shine with a soft, dry cloth. That's all there is to it! ✉ Jack D., MI

QUICK FIX

To remove stubborn tarnish from brass, rub it with a paste made of $\frac{1}{2}$ teaspoon of salt mixed into $\frac{1}{2}$ cup of vinegar. Or dip half of a lemon in salt to rub it clean.

ADD A LITTLE LEMON. Make a great brass-cleaning paste with 2 parts baking soda and 1 part lemon juice. Rub the paste into the brass and let it sit for five minutes. Then wipe it off with a clean, damp cloth and buff to a shine. Or, cut a lemon in half, sprinkle it with baking soda, and rub the lemon directly on the brass for an even quicker cleaner. ✉ Elizabeth H., OR

TACKLE TARNISH. You can remove tarnish from brass with ketchup. The acids in the condiment help cut through the nasty stuff with minimal rubbing. Just squeeze some ketchup into a bowl, then use a soft, clean cloth to dab it onto the tarnished areas. Buff it off with another clean cloth for a brilliant shine. ✉ Janet A., IL

Grandma Putt's Wisdom

Old-timers like my Grandma Putt had a terrific trick for polishing their pewter—they used cabbage leaves! Just peel off a few leaves from a head of regular cabbage and use them to rub down the surface of your pewter pieces. The leaves will remove the grime and restore a gentle gleam without scratching the metal.

ASHES TO ASHES. To clean and polish silver and brass, or any metal appliance, I make a paste of wood ashes and water. I rub it onto the item with a soft cloth, then gently buff it clean with a dry cloth. ✉ Milton F., KY

AUTO POLISH FOR SILVER. You treasure your silver pieces, and you want them to really sparkle. So use auto-body scratch remover instead of silver polish to restore the shine. Just put some of the scratch-remover paste on a soft, clean cloth and buff until you're satisfied. Your silver will look better than new! ✉ Ishmael S., OR

SILVER TAKES A POWDER. For a great silver polish, try powdered laundry detergent. Dip a moistened paper towel into the detergent, and lightly rub it onto the tarnished silver. Then use a clean cloth to wipe the silver dry, and buff it with a soft, clean cloth. ✉ Betsey H., IL

SCRUB-FREE SILVER POLISH. Don't spend hours scrubbing the tarnish off your silverware piece by piece. You can polish an entire batch in one easy step. Simply line your kitchen sink or a large glass baking dish with aluminum foil, shiny side up. Then lay your silverware on the foil. Pour hot water into the sink or dish until the silver is covered, and add 1 teaspoon of regular table salt. The tarnish will lift right off after just a few minutes of soaking. When the water cools, rinse the silver and use a soft, clean cloth to dry it. ✉ Detra D., TX

BAKING SODA SPARKLER. You can get your silverware sparkly clean with this simple solution: Line a 9 x 13-inch pan with foil, and fill it with an inch or two of warm water. Then add 1 teaspoon of baking soda and soak the silverware in the pan for about 10 minutes. Rinse your pieces, and dry them with a soft cloth before putting them away. ✉ Alexandra R., VA

All That Glitters . . .

SEALED WITH A KISS. Try using good old-fashioned lipstick (nothing glossy) to polish your gold rings. It'll remove built-up oxidation and make the gold shine. Simply rub it on, then use a soft, clean cloth to buff it off. ✉ Wanda C., OH

SOAK YOUR JEWELS. Hydrogen peroxide does a terrific job of cleaning jewelry. It makes my diamonds sparkle, and cleans gold and silver, too. Just pour some hydrogen peroxide in a bowl, and soak your jewelry in it for a few minutes. Rinse, then dry the pieces with a soft, clean cloth. ✉ Sherry K., MI

ANOTHER GREAT IDEA!

PROTECT YOUR PEARLS

Do you have a strand of pearls that's starting to look a bit dingy? Here's a great way to clean 'em up and protect them at the same time. Start by putting a dab of olive oil on a soft, clean cloth, and smoothing it onto each pearl. Then wipe it off with a second clean cloth. And here's another trick of the (jeweler's) trade: If you wear your pearls frequently, your skin oils will help preserve their luster.

GET GEMS GLEAMING. Don't put the cap back on the toothpaste when you're done brushing—use it to clean your jewelry! Squeeze a small glob of toothpaste on your fingertip and gently rub it onto your jewelry. Then rinse and wipe dry with a soft, clean cloth. It will sparkle like new! *Note:* This technique is not safe on all jewelry; for example, some stones like tanzanite, lapis, and turquoise are too soft for the abrasiveness of toothpaste, and softer metals may scratch. ✉ Tressa N., OH

DAZZLING DIAMONDS. I make my diamonds gleam by soaking them for two minutes or so in a glass of water with one denture-cleaning tablet. Then I rinse my jewels with clear water and polish them dry with a soft cloth. Just don't use this trick with pearls or opals. ✉ Sophie M., CA

PLOP, PLOP, FIZZ, FIZZ. For quick jewelry cleaning, I place my gold or silver item in a cup of water, then add two Alka-Seltzer® Original antacid tablets. After five minutes, I rinse the jewelry and gently dry it with a soft, clean cloth. Oh, what a relief it is! ✉ Lois P., FL

A SILVER LINING. Here's a nifty trick that'll make your treasured silver jewelry sparkle: Place your jewelry on a square of foil in the sink (shiny side up). In a clean pitcher, mix 1 tablespoon of baking soda with enough hot water to make a cloudy solution. Pour the baking soda mixture over the jewelry, covering it completely. Let it soak for about five minutes, then rinse. Buff all the pieces with a soft, dry cloth. ✉ Michelle J., KY

Jerry's Handy Hints

GIVE GOLD A BATH

→ Here's a really simple way to clean precious gold pieces—it takes just a minute to make, and another minute to work its magic. Mix 1 part ammonia with 6 parts warm water in a small bowl that's deep enough to cover the gold. Set the gold in the solution and let it soak for one minute. Then remove the items, rinse them under cold running water, and dry them with a soft, clean cloth.

Grandma Putt's Wisdom

Whenever my Grandma Putt boiled a pot of potatoes, she saved the water—not for soup, but to clean her silver. She simply soaked her silver earrings and other small pieces in the potato water for about 30 minutes and then dipped a soft cloth in the water to rub the tarnish away. It worked like a (sterling silver) charm!

TOOTHPASTE FIGHTS TARNISH. You just inherited your Grandma's lovely sterling silver jewelry (you lucky dog), but it's all terribly tarnished. Don't toss it in the junk drawer! Simply rub it with a dab of toothpaste on a soft, clean cloth to bring out the sparkle it had back in Grandma's day. ✉ Sharon G., OR

CLEVER CLEANER. Make your own jewelry cleaner by mixing ½ cup of warm water with 2 drops of dishwashing liquid and a capful of ammonia. Gently rub your jewelry with an old toothbrush dipped in the homemade solution. *Note:* This cleaner should not be used on soft or porous stones such as lapis, turquoise, opal, or pearls. ✉ Jeanne W., OH

DOUBLE-DUTY DETERGENT. It makes your dishes and flatware shine, so why not use dishwasher detergent to get the same results on your jewelry? I squeeze a dab of liquid gel detergent onto a soft, clean cloth and gently rub it into my jewelry. After rinsing the piece, I buff it with a clean part of the cloth. ✉ Laurie M., FL

SANDY SOLUTION. Don't just sit there and relax the next time you vacation at the shore. Scoop up some wet, salty sand and use it to scrub your gold and silver jewelry pieces—they'll clean up in two shakes of a beach towel. ✉ Robert K., NC

CHAPTER
3

A Place for Everything

Kitchen Confidential

RECIPE ROUNDUP. Do you have a heap of recipes that you need to search through every time you want to cook? If so, then it's time to organize them all in separate color-coded binders. Use one each for appetizers, salads, side dishes, main courses, desserts, and so forth. Fill the three-ring binders with plastic sleeves to hold your recipes, and arrange the recipes in alphabetical order. Then the next time you're looking for that pineapple upside-down cake recipe, you'll find it lickety-split. ✉ Allison B., TX

CLEVER CLIPPING. To keep a recipe card or page close at hand while you're referring to it, use this simple trick: Place a clipboard nearby and clip the recipe to it. You can either hang the clipboard up or lean it against the wall above your countertop. Your recipe will stay out of the way, but still be close enough for you to read as you cook. ✉ Emma G., ME

HANG 'EM HIGH. Here's a clever idea for kitchen storage: Hang a clipboard on the inside of a kitchen cupboard or pantry door, and clip your cloth placemats and napkins to it. That way, they'll stay nice and wrinkle-free. ✉ Cicely B., VA

DON'T WASTE YOUR WINE. If you've ever wondered how best to store leftover wine, here's what I've learned. Recork white and rosé wines (or use a cap made for sealing wine bottles) and store them in the fridge for up to five days. Recork reds and set the bottles in a cool, dark place like a kitchen cabinet for up to three days. If you know you won't have time to drink your wine—red or white—before it goes south, pour it into ice cube trays, and put them in the freezer. Then use the cubes to perk up soups, marinades, and casseroles. ✉ Neil D., MI

A BETTER BREAD IDEA. Whether you keep your bread in a bread box or in a drawer, you know that within a week it dries out. If you're

Grandma Putt's Wisdom

My Grandma Putt knew that the worst place to store dried herbs and spices is on a shelf above or near the stove. That's because heat and light dry up the volatile oils, making the fragrance and flavor go downhill fast. The ideal storage space is in a closed cupboard. But if you're short on cupboard shelves, don't fret. Do what Grandma did and tack a strip of elastic to each interior side of one of your kitchen drawers. Then tuck the herb and spice bottles and tins under the stretchy band. They'll stay upright, organized, and easy to reach—and they'll keep their flavor a whole lot longer!

not going to eat the bread immediately (especially the fresh-baked kind), simply toss the loaf in the freezer. It'll keep for several months, and when you're ready to enjoy it, just thaw it out. The bread will be as fresh and tasty as the day you bought it! ✉ Carol K., GA

KEEP THE HEAT. To keep bread and rolls piping hot at the table, I place a sheet of aluminum foil, shiny side up, in the bottom of my bread basket, under the napkin. It keeps the goodies nice and warm *and* protects the basket from grease stains. ✉ Angela R., KY

SAVE THE SPACE. Unless you have a big family—or you only shop for groceries once a month or so—don't buy giant-size containers of ketchup, mustard, mayo, and salad dressings, no matter how low the price per ounce may be. Instead, choose smaller sizes, and restock your supply as needed. Besides freeing up valuable space in your refrigerator, you'll always know that your condiments will be at their freshest, tastiest best. ✉ John T., NV

TOGETHERNESS IS GOOD. You can save a load of time and money simply by keeping like items together in both your fridge and freezer. For example, put all the salad dressings in one place, the condiments in another place, and so on. In the freezer, keep the vegetables, baked goods, and meats in separate areas. This way,

ANOTHER GREAT IDEA!

SUPER SCRAPER FOR BAKERS

Do you like to bake your own bread, rolls, and pastries? If so, then you know what a sticky mess the dough leaves on your countertop or pastry board. But don't waste your money on a fancy dough scraper from a kitchen-supply store. Instead, clean it all up with an inexpensive plastic ice scraper you can get at any dollar store. It'll remove those gloppy blobs without damaging your countertop.

Ask Jerry

Q: I've heard that a freezer works best when it's filled to capacity. Is this true? And if so, does the same thing apply to the refrigerator as well?

A: First things first: Yes, it is true that a freezer operates most efficiently—and therefore keeps your food fresher, longer—when it's fully loaded. So anytime you find yourself with empty freezer space, fill it immediately. (My favorite filler-uppers are milk cartons or jugs filled with water.)

On the other hand, a refrigerator does its best work when air can circulate freely around the contents. As a general rule, that means you don't want to use up any more than three-quarters of the inside space. And be sure to keep beverages and moist foods tightly covered, so moisture can't escape into the unit. The more humid the air is, the harder the fridge has to work to keep it cool, and the faster the food inside will deteriorate.

you'll know right where to find everything—and you won't end up buying duplicates of food you already have. ✉ Tina G., CA

QUICK ON THE THAW. When you need to heat up a frozen meal in a hurry, do what I do and grab your blow dryer. Set the dryer on hot and blast the meat, vegetables, or frozen dinner. Then immediately cook it and serve. ✉ Teresa R., NM

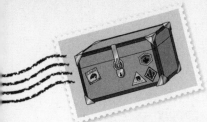

Under the Eaves

LET THERE BE LIGHT. For years I struggled with trying to find stuff in my attic because the lone overhead lightbulb threw shadows in every corner. Then I hit upon this bright idea: Bring in a floor lamp to light the way. If you don't have any electrical outlets in your attic, use an extension cord to plug the lamp into the nearest downstairs receptacle. ✉ *Annemarie E., NH*

HAMMOCK HOUSING. Do you have an old net hammock stashed away somewhere? If so, then don't let it go to waste. Pull it out and hang it from the ceiling in your attic, and use it to store lightweight, nonbreakable stuff like sleeping bags, pillows, and out-of-season clothes. ✉ *Don R., NY*

GIVE YOUR LUGGAGE A JOB. Lots of folks use old suitcases for storage, but don't overlook the ones that are still in service. Put

---

SUPER-DUPER SOLUTIONS

DEODORIZE YOUR BAGS ● If you've got some old suitcases in your attic that you'd like to use for storage, but they smell musty inside, don't send them to the recycling bin. Instead, make 'em smell sweet again by putting half a dozen charcoal briquettes inside each bag. Lay the charcoal on sheets of paper or plastic to keep the black powder from rubbing off onto the lining. Then every few days, take the charcoal out and replace it with a new supply. Repeat the procedure until your vintage holdalls smell as clean and fresh as daisies. The deodorizing process could take anywhere from a couple of days to several weeks. And just remember to use plain, old-fashioned charcoal and not the kind that's been doused with lighter fluid.

---

off-season clothes, linens, or what have you into old pillowcases, and tuck them inside your luggage. Then when it's time to pack the luggage for a trip, pull out the filled pillowcase and set it aside until you return. ✉ Theresa L., AL

BANISH MOTHBALL SMELLS. I've tried all kinds of ways to get rid of mothball odors in trunks and other containers that I wanted to store clothes in. Then I found this solution: I sand the inside of each trunk, and brush on a coat of polyurethane. The trunks smell fresh and clean. Now I protect my clothes with herbal moth repellents, which have a much more pleasant scent than mothballs. I just make sure the polyurethane is completely dry, not tacky, before I put any clothing into the trunk. ✉ Gladys M., MT

EASY LUGGAGE LOCATOR. If you're a frequent flier, you know how frustrating it is to grab the wrong bags off the luggage carousel. After all, they all look alike! I make my bags stand out by sticking bathtub appliqués onto each suitcase. When the carousel comes around, I can spot my bags from a mile away, and the appliqués stay put for years. ✉ Catherine D., IL

QUICK FIX

Here's a super-simple way to easily identify your luggage: Use duct tape. Buy several rolls of brightly colored tape and wrap it around the handles, spell out your initials, and/or make a funky design on the sides of your bags. Now you'll recognize 'em anywhere!

ARTFUL ID. To easily identify my luggage at the airport baggage claim, I painted my monogram in big, bold, colorful letters using fabric paints. If your luggage is made from a material other than fabric, stop by an art-supply store and ask for a recommendation. If you're artistic, you could go beyond simply painting your initials and include a picture or design on your bags, too. Then they'll truly stand out from the crowd! ✉ Colleen M., NY

Cellar Secrets

ON A ROLL. You can keep odds and ends in your basement high and dry by storing your stuff in an old kids' wagon (or two). The rubber wheels won't be harmed by dampness, and you can easily roll it out of hiding to get at what's sitting inside. I use an old red wagon to hold my power tools and extension cords. ✉ Ted K., DE

BINS FOR THE BASEMENT. When I store items in my basement, I use plastic storage containers with snap-on lids. They keep everything dry and free from smelling musty. Plus, if you buy the clear ones, you can see what's inside at a glance. ✉ Leslie G., OK

Ask Jerry

Q: My basement is dry and I haven't seen more than an occasional spider lurking about. So I can store just about anything down there, right?

A: Yep, anything your little heart desires—as long as it isn't hazardous, does not attract pests, and will not be easily damaged by dampness. In particular, the basement is the perfect place to store nonperishable foods and beverages in cans, bottles, or jars (no cardboard boxes!). It's also acceptable for things like sports equipment and outdoor Christmas decorations. In short, anything that's made of plastic, rubber, or rustproof metal will fare just fine down there.

TRUSTY TINS. Over the years, I've gotten my share of large gift tins filled with popcorn and other tasty goodies. I've held on to the empty tins and put them to good use for all kinds of storage in my basement. They come in handy for holding cat litter and dog food and for storing Christmas lights and ornaments. I also keep a large tin just inside the door of my walkout basement. It makes a convenient container for my gardening gloves, trowels, and bug spray. ✉ Stephanie L., PA

Creative Closets

CONQUER CLOSET CLUTTER. Here's an easy way to clean up cluttered closets: Tie the handles of drawstring trash bags to sturdy coat hangers, and hang one bag in each closet. Then every time you come across a piece of clothing that no longer fits, has seen better days, or just isn't your style, drop it into the bag. You can also do this in your kids' rooms for collecting toys they no longer play with and books they've long since lost interest in. When the bags are full, drop them off at your local thrift store. ✉ Shelly R., VA

POCKET POWER. Shoe bags with multiple pockets come in handy all around the house. Hang one in your hall closet and use the pockets to hold gloves, scarves, earmuffs, and other small outdoor gear. Put one in your bedroom closet to store rolled-up socks, panty hose, and underwear. Believe me—they really free up precious drawer space! ✉ Patty L., WI

HANG ON. I've found a simple way to keep lightweight clothes from sliding off wooden hangers: Slip an old cotton T-shirt onto the hanger first. Then hang up your blouse, dress, or other garment right over the shirt. The cotton cover will keep your clothing hanging in place. ✉ Tillie B., TN

GET A GRIP. I keep my shirts from sliding off hangers by wrapping rubber bands around each end of the hanger. The rubber gives the shirt something to grip on to, so it'll stay put. ✉ Bill A., GA

TUBES FOR TROUSERS. I never throw out those cardboard tubes from rolls of aluminum foil, wax paper, or plastic wrap because they're great for hanging pants! Just cut a tube lengthwise, and pop it over the bottom of a wire hanger. Then fold your trousers over the tube. The legs won't get creases in the middle, the way they do on uncovered hangers. ✉ Carl T., MA

Jerry's Handy Hints

THE CHAIN GANG

➜ If you're short on space in your closet, use this neat trick to make room: Start by purchasing a piece of plastic chain from a hardware store. Hang it up by one end from a hanger in your closet, then hang another hanger from each chain link, all the way down the chain. The vertical storage conserves space and keeps your clothes flat and wrinkle-free!

SIMPLE SHOE SHAPERS. Wad up pairs of old panty hose and shove them into the toes of your shoes before you put them away in your closet. The nylons will gently help your shoes keep their shape. ✉ Sarah M., OH

STOP SINGING THE (BLACK AND) BLUES. Do you have a hard time telling apart your navy blue clothes from your black ones in the wee hours of the morning? Try this trick: Use different-colored plastic hangers. For instance, hang your navy clothes on white hangers, and your black clothes on black hangers. That way, you'll never again show up at work wearing a navy blazer with a black skirt! ✉ Cathy P., OH

SMOOTH OPERATOR. Don't spend money on commercial wrinkle-release sprays when it's easy to make your own. Just mix 1 part fabric softener with 15 parts water. Pour the mix into a handheld sprayer bottle and mist your garments lightly. Then give them a gentle tug and smooth those wrinkles away. ✉ Joelle P., AZ

RING MY BELT. Here's an easy way to keep your belts, handbags, and costume jewelry organized and right at hand. Just pop shower curtain rings over the rod in your closet and hang your items from them. Now you won't waste another minute hunting for that certain something! ✉ Denise L., PA

NO MORE JEWELRY JUMBLE. Bracelets and necklaces can turn into a tangled mess when you store them in a drawer. A better way to keep them ready to wear is to hang 'em up. I take an old wooden clothes hanger and screw cup hooks into it at intervals of 1 inch or so. Then I hang it in my closet, and drape my beads, chains, and pendants over the hooks. This is also a great way to organize belts. ✉ Tanya G., NJ

TAKE 5

Five not-so-common uses for empty cardboard tubes around the house include these tips:

1 Preserve your boots by tying three paper towel tubes together and placing a set in each leg.

2 Save old posters inside wrapping paper tubes.

3 Coil electrical cords around the tubes to keep 'em tidy.

4 Make easy gifts by filling toilet paper tubes with candy, wrapping them in tissue paper, and tying the ends with ribbon.

5 Make napkin rings out of 2-inch sections of cardboard tube, and decorate them with paint.

SOAP SCENTS. Keep your closet smelling fresh with soap. Simply place a bar of scented soap in the foot of an old pair of panty hose and tie it shut with a pretty ribbon. Your homemade sachet will add just the right amount of fragrance. ✉ Lorraine N., MI

SPREAD THE NEWS. I've found some neat ways to use newspaper in my closets. I stuff wads of newspaper in my shoes and boots to deodorize them overnight. And I've discovered that moths hate newsprint. So when I store my winter clothes, I pack them away in newspaper. Yesterday's news also can freshen up your luggage. Just crumple up enough sheets to half fill your suitcase, and let them sit in the closed case for a few weeks. After you take them out, your suitcase will smell nice and clean again. ✉ Pete D., NC

WHO PUT THE "UGH" IN THE LUGGAGE? To prevent luggage from acquiring a stale, musty smell, place a bar of unwrapped soap inside the bag when it's not in use. It'll stay fresh as a daisy until your next trip. ✉ Gerald P., FL

IS THAT A PEBBLE IN MY BOOT? When you need to get your sopping wet boots dry quickly, try this trick: Heat a pan of clean, round pebbles in the oven and carefully pour them into your boots. Shake each boot until the stones are cool and your boots are ready to take a hike! ✉ Connie S., WY

ANOTHER GREAT IDEA!

PETRO POLISH

Petroleum jelly does more than soothe chapped skin and lips—it makes a super shoe and boot polish, too! Its oily base makes leather items supple and shiny, so just a dab will do it. Put a bit on a soft, clean cloth and rub it vigorously over your footwear to make the leather shine.

TAKE 5

Here are five reader-tested, tried-and-true shoe shiners. I'll bet a few (or all) of them will surprise you!

1 Shine up your patent leather shoes with a piece of bacon fat. Just rub it on, buff it off, and your shoes'll be shining like they did the day you bought 'em. And the neighborhood dogs'll love you, too! ✉ Gwen H., SC

2 Use furniture polish to spiff up your leather shoes. Just spray it on, and buff it off with a soft, clean cloth. That's all there is to it. ✉ Jerri Lynn S., NJ

3 Simply cut off a piece of banana peel (it's best if it's slightly green), and rub your shoes with the inside of it, using circular motions. As the peel becomes thin, cut off a new piece and continue until you've worked over the entire surface. Then buff your shoes to a shine with a clean, dry cloth or paper towel. ✉ Tom D., OH

4 Mousse adds a terrific shine to your hair, so why not use it to shine your shoes? Pump some of the foam onto a clean cloth, and rub the mousse into your shoes. Buff it off with another clean cloth, and there you are—smart, shiny shoes to go with your smooth, shiny hair! ✉ Cheryl W., IA

5 For an oldfangled way to polish your leather shoes, use cold, leftover biscuits. The oil rises to the surface of the biscuit when it's cold, and that's what gives your shoes a nifty, thrifty shine. ✉ Mary D., TN

Now You're Cooking!

CHAPTER 4

Produce Know-How

NO MORE TEARS. For dry-eyed onion cutting, try this technique: Cut a small slice off the flower end and peel back the skin and first layer of onion. Next, slice a small piece off one side of the onion, allowing it to sit flat on the cutting board. Then slice the onion to within ¼ inch of the root end, and cut the root end off and discard it—that's where the tear-forming enzymes are. ✉ Carole V., NV

YOUR DAILY BREAD. Here's a trick that works for me every time I cut up onions: Chew on a piece of bread. For some reason, it'll keep you from crying. Give it a try! ✉ Lori H., IL

RUB APPEAL. Rub your hands on a stainless steel sink or spoon before you peel onions, and you won't shed a tear when you start chopping. Rub the stainless steel again when you're done handling the onions to take care of any lingering odor. ✉ **Sue E., MI**

NO MORE ONION OUCH. I always pour a little lemon juice on my cutting board before I start chopping onions. That way, I know I won't be in tears while I'm slicing. ✉ **Lillian T., OH**

LONG-LIVED LEFTOVERS. Keep a leftover onion fresh by wrapping the cut portion in a wrapper from a stick of butter and storing it in an airtight container in the fridge. The greasy wax wrapper keeps the onion from spoiling. ✉ **Jennifer L., MN**

GIVE GARLIC A SQUEEZE. To peel garlic quickly and easily, place the bulb on a cutting board and press firmly on all sides with the flat side of a knife. Then cut through the root end and pull the skin away—it should easily come off in one piece. ✉ **Christie V., NV**

GIVE CUKES THE RUB. Before you peel a cucumber, try this trick to remove any bitterness. Slice a half-inch off the vine end of the cucumber, and hold the rest in one hand and the sliced-off piece in the other. Rub the cut ends together, until you see a little foam forming. The bitterness will be gone from the cuke. ✉ **Darby H., OK**

QUICK FIX

After slicing onions or garlic, remove the lingering scent from your cutting board by rubbing it down with the cut side of half a lemon. Then wash the board as usual, and it'll be clean, fresh, and odor-free!

ANOTHER GREAT IDEA!

A PRESSING MATTER

If your garlic press becomes clogged, reach for a toothbrush. Dip the brush in a little soapy water and scrub away. The bristles do a great job of cleaning out the tiny holes.

QUICK CORN. To cook corn on the cob the easy way, I microwave the whole ear of corn (without shucking it first) on "high" for two minutes. Then I carefully remove it from the microwave, and shuck the corn—the silks come right off with the husk, and my corn is cooked to perfection! ✉ Nancy G., TN

SUPER-DUPER SOLUTIONS

ROLLIN' ALONG ● In a pinch for a rolling pin? Grab a zucchini, and roll away! Just be sure to choose one that's nice and firm and not starting to go soft, so you can put some pressure on it without worrying that it might burst.

MILK YOUR ZUCCHINI. It seems like all the zucchini plants in the garden ripen at the same time. But don't give the whole bunch away! Peel several zucchinis, dice them, and put the pieces in a blender with enough water to cover. Puree until a milky liquid forms, adding more water if necessary. Refrigerate or freeze the "milk," then use it in batter for pancakes, biscuits, and muffins; in meat loaf; and in any recipe that could use a little greening up. ✉ Margaret H., WA

POP IN SOME PEPPERS. When frying a large quantity of vegetables, usually the first pieces are a perfect golden color, while pieces fried later become darker as the oil loses its freshness. To keep that from happening, try this trick: Squeeze the liquid out of two or three jarred pickled peppers, and stick them in the oil with the vegetables as you fry them. Believe it or not, the last thing you cook will be just as perfect as the first, and you won't be able to taste the pickled peppers at all. ✉ Lillian S., AL

QUICK FIX

To ripen avocados and bananas, stick them in a brown paper bag with an apple for a couple of days. Then enjoy!

SUPER SPUD SCRUB. When a recipe calls for potatoes or carrots, I wash mine in my sink with a scrubbing pad that's made for stainless steel. It quickly washes away all of the dirt and even scrubs some of the skin away, making my prep job easier. ✉ Valerie N., NY

SASSY SAUCE. Here's a neat way to liven up your spaghetti sauce: Add half a teaspoon of instant coffee crystals to your sauce right when you start cooking it. The result will be a richer-tasting, more delicious topping for your pasta. ✉ Lenora B., CA

CHILI Rx. Who doesn't love a bowl of chili? I know we do, and we eat a lot of it in our house. But sometimes when I taste-test it, I find that it's too tomatoey. If that happens to you, here's a quick and easy way to bring back the zing: Simply add a spoonful or two of powdered, unsweetened baking cocoa to the batch while it's cooking. It'll tame the tomato, and your chili will end up tasting just right to the whole family. ✉ Karen W., OK

SPRAY TO KEEP STAINS AWAY. I spray all my plastic bowls with nonstick cooking spray before putting tomato sauce, chili, and other tomato-based foods in them for storage. That way, the colorful contents won't leave any stains behind. ✉ Kim R., OH

LEMON LIFT. When preparing a fruit salad, keep the bananas and apples from becoming brown by sprinkling a little lemon juice over the slices. The juice won't change the flavor of the fruit, but it'll keep the pieces looking good and tasting fresh. ✉ Linda M., CO

Jerry's Handy Hints

NO-BUD SPUDS

→ To keep potatoes from budding, there are a few steps you need to take. First, don't wash them. Second, keep them in a cool, dark place where light and humidity can't get to them. And third, place an apple in the bag along with the potatoes—it really does help keep them from sprouting.

STICK A FORK IN IT

To get only a few drops of lemon juice from a lemon, prick one end with a fork and squeeze. The juice will come out slowly so you'll get just the amount you need.

FOILED AGAIN. To keep bananas fresh longer, wrap them in aluminum foil, and put 'em in your fridge. The skins will turn black, but don't let that stop you from eating 'em—the bananas themselves will stay fresh and taste delicious. By the way, this also works for celery. Wrap it in foil and it'll keep for weeks! ✉ **Roberta T., IL**

JOLTS FOR MORE JUICE. Before juicing a lemon, put it in a 350°F oven for a few minutes, or zap it for 10 seconds on "high" in the microwave. This simple trick will get you twice as much juice out of it, *guaranteed!* ✉ **Isabel M., TX**

Where's the Beef?

LOVE ME TENDER. I enjoy grilled beef, but I don't like chewy meat. Some time ago, I discovered that bromelain (the enzyme found in pineapples) makes a terrific meat tenderizer. Just look for capsules in your local health-food and vitamin supplement stores. Then right before grilling, open a capsule, smear the contents on the steak, and poke the meat all over with a fork. Throw the steak on the grill and cook it to perfection—it'll melt in your mouth! ✉ **Esther T., SD**

PERFECT POULTRY. Now, I love chicken as much as the next gal, but dry chicken is the pits! So to keep my chicken moist and tender, I spread a layer of Miracle Whip® over it before I pop it in the oven. You won't believe how juicy and tender it is. ✉ **Barbara P., SC**

LET'S GET CORNY. If you want the absolute best corned beef you can wrap your taste buds around, forget that canned stuff. Buy fresh corned beef from your butcher, put it in a slow cooker, and add an extra handful of pickling spices. Cook it all day, and you'll never go back to canned corned beef again. ✉ **Sheila L., OR**

Grandma Putt's Wisdom

My Grandma Putt certainly knew her way around the kitchen. Whether she was filleting a fish or broiling a few T-bone steaks, she always knew the best ways to prepare and serve her meals. One neat trick she taught me years ago is this: If you want thinly sliced meat, slice it when it's still partially frozen, then proceed with your cooking method. Just be sure to keep a close eye on it as it cooks—thinly sliced meats cook much more quickly than their thicker cousins.

BACON ROLL CALL. I keep my bacon handy without letting it spoil in the fridge by freezing each slice individually. Here's how to do it: Remove one slice at a time from the package, and roll it up. When you've done this to all the slices, stack the rolls in a freezer container and store it in your freezer. Then whenever you're in the mood for some bacon, take out however many rolls you need, and put them in a skillet over low heat. They'll unwind and thaw quickly, so you can cook 'em up just the way you like 'em. ✉ **Kendra P., TX**

A BETTER BOARD. Here's a surefire way to keep your cutting boards from becoming contaminated by raw meats: Cut beef, pork, and poultry on a heavy-duty paper plate instead. When you're done slicing, you can just toss the plate into the trash. ✉ **Rita T., IL**

FORGET THE FLOUR. The next time you make gravy, try thickening it with arrowroot instead of flour or cornstarch. It never clumps, and it won't change the taste of your gravy. Substitute 1 teaspoon of arrowroot for 1 tablespoon of flour, or 2 teaspoons of arrowroot for 1 tablespoon of cornstarch. You'll love the results! ✉ Jonelle H., FL

A FLAKY IDEA. You can easily thicken soup or stew by adding a few spoonfuls of instant potato flakes to it. The flakes will make the soup thick and creamy, and oh so delicious. ✉ Penelope C., TX

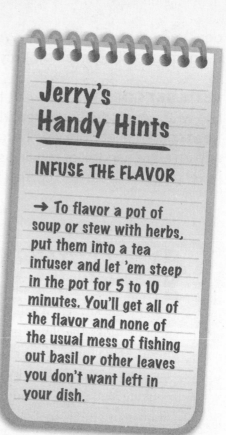

Jerry's Handy Hints

INFUSE THE FLAVOR

→ To flavor a pot of soup or stew with herbs, put them into a tea infuser and let 'em steep in the pot for 5 to 10 minutes. You'll get all of the flavor and none of the usual mess of fishing out basil or other leaves you don't want left in your dish.

Tasty Treats

A DEVIL OF A DISH. For easy, no-mess deviled eggs, seal the cooked egg yolks in a resealable plastic bag, then mash them gently with your fingers. Open up the bag, add the remainder of your ingredients, reseal the bag, and continue mashing. Once the mash is thoroughly mixed, snip off a corner of the bag with scissors, and squeeze the mixture into the waiting egg white halves. This method makes for easy cleanup, too: Just throw the bag away! ✉ Maggie W., IL

SKILLET PIZZA. To reheat pizza, I skip the microwave—I don't like the limp, soggy slices I end up with. Instead, I put the leftovers in a nonstick skillet on top of the stove, with the flame set at medium-low, and heat 'em up until they're warm. This technique keeps the crust nice and crispy. ✉ Miranda P., MI

BOUND BREAD. When a loaf of bagged bread is half gone and the tab is lost or not usable, squish as much air out of the bag as you can, twist it close to the bread, and pull the top of the bag back over the bread like a cuff. This trick keeps the half-eaten loaf from drying out every time. ✉ Kimberly G., UT

BOWL 'EM OVER. If you don't have a crock to keep bread fresh, place a loaf on a wooden breadboard, and cover it with a pottery bowl. Just make sure the bowl completely covers the bread, and your loaf will last longer. ✉ Mike M., NE

WARM YOUR BUNS. To warm biscuits, pancakes, or muffins that were refrigerated, I place them in the microwave along with a cup of water and heat them on "medium" for about 30 seconds. The increased moisture will keep the food from drying out. ✉ Anna L., MI

CIRCLE THIS. Have you ever wondered how to get perfectly round pancakes without using one of those fancy pancake rings? I have

ANOTHER GREAT IDEA!

ZAP AND CRUNCH

If your tortilla chips are past their prime, don't throw them away! Just place a single layer on a paper towel or plate, and microwave them on "high" for about one minute. They'll bounce right back to their original crispness. Then all you've got to do is rustle up some guacamole!

just the solution: Use a meat baster. Fill the baster with your pancake batter, then squeeze the bulb to release the amount you want onto the hot griddle. You'll have perfectly shaped pancakes every time! ✉ Danielle S., MI

Jerry's Handy Hints

FAT'S WHERE IT'S AT

→ To plump up dried fruit for muffins, breads, or pancakes, try soaking the fruit in warm tea instead of water. It'll give the fruit just a bit of something extra and make your baked goods taste dee-lish.

REUSE THOSE WRAPPERS. Save the wrappers from your sticks of butter or margarine in a resealable plastic bag in the fridge. Then, when you need to grease a cake or muffin pan, just pull out a wrapper and you'll find that there's more than enough butter left on it to grease your pan. Give the pan a few swipes with the wrapper, and you're good to go! ✉ Lisa P., CA

STOP STICKING AROUND. When a recipe calls for something sticky, like peanut butter or corn syrup, measuring is easy enough, but scraping it all out of the cup and into your mixing bowl can be a real mess. Here's how I solve this little problem. Before adding the gooey substance to the measuring cup, fill the cup with hot water and pour it out. Then measure your sticky ingredient into the still-wet cup, and watch how easily it flows out. ✉ Wendy R., TN

NO MORE STICKY FINGERS. If you like Rice Krispies Treats®, you know what a mess they make on your hands when you press the mix into the pan. You can avoid it all by running your hands under cold water just before you start pressing. The cold water keeps the gooey marshmallow mix from sticking to your fingers. ✉ Debra S., MI

PERK UP YOUR PIES. Here's how to really brighten up your pies. When you're making piecrust for apple or berry pies, replace the

KEEP YOUR DOUGH TOGETHER ● Before you roll out dough, make sure you spritz your tabletop or work board with a little nonstick cooking spray. Your cookies or piecrust will peel right off, without leaving pieces stuck to the surface. Cleanup is a snap, too!

water in the recipe with an equal amount of freshly squeezed orange juice. It'll give your pie a zesty kick! ✉ Irene M., TX

A LITTLE DASH'LL DO IT. Here's a trick I learned years ago: Throw a dash of baking soda into your rhubarb pie filling to enhance the pie's flavor. I don't know why, but it really does make a delightful difference you can taste. ✉ Pauline S., NY

SLICE NICELY. I use unflavored, unwaxed dental floss to slice my cakes. To do it, start by cutting a piece of floss that is longer than the cake, then wrap an end around each hand. Holding it taut, slice quickly through the cake. This quick and easy trick works for creating individual servings, or for slicing a cake in half horizontally to make more layers. ✉ Katherine K., TX

OUT, OUT, DARN CAKE! Can't get your freshly baked cake out of the pan? Don't poke, prod, and pry at it. Instead, soak a dishcloth with hot tap water and wring out most of the water. Put the cloth on your countertop, and set the pan on top of the warm cloth for about three or four minutes. Then when you turn the pan over, the cake will slide right out. ✉ Samantha T., OR

QUICK FIX

At your next birthday party, use Life Savers® to hold the candles on the birthday cake. They're not only great decorations, but they'll also keep the wax from dribbling all over the frosting. Now, how sweet is that?

STRETCH YOUR FROSTING. You can make store-bought cake frosting go a lot farther if you remove it from its container and whip it with an electric hand mixer until it's fluffy. You'll frost more cake with the same amount of frosting and, as a bonus, you'll be eating less sugar and fewer calories per serving! ✉ Eileen M., IL

LET THE RIBBONS FLOW. Whenever I bake a cake, I like to top it off with beautiful cascading ribbons of chocolate. And I've figured out how to get the job done neatly, with very little cleanup. I just fill a bowl with boiling water, and drop in an unopened 6-ounce bag of chocolate chips. After a few minutes I carefully remove the bag and knead it to blend the chocolate. I usually have to repeat the process a few times until the chips have completely melted. Then I snip off a small corner of the bag and squeeze the melted chocolate onto the cake in fun patterns. When I'm done I just toss the bag in the garbage. It's as easy as that! ✉ Gloria V., FL

WE ALL SCREAM FOR ICE CREAM! Nothing refreshes more than a scoop of ice cream on a hot summer day. But dipping a scoop into the carton and expecting creaminess and instead finding a crunchy layer of ice can really frost a gal! I prevent that icy buildup by pressing a piece of plastic wrap over the top of the ice cream, then replacing the lid every time I scoop some out. ✉ Kathy H., MN

ANOTHER GREAT IDEA!

DON'T BE A DRIP

How many times have you loaded up a sugar cone with your favorite ice cream and been enjoying every lick when the bottom suddenly turned to mush and the tasty treat ended up dripping down your arm? Don't let it happen again! The next time you're ready to fill a cone, stuff a miniature marshmallow into the bottom of it first. The marshmallow will prevent drips and make your ice cream cone good to the last lick!

America's Best
Practical Problem Solvers

CHAPTER
5

The Family Pet

The Well-Groomed Companion

DOGGIE DRY CLEANING. Here's a great way to get a dingy dog looking his best without having to get him wet: Dry-clean your pooch. Just rub some cornstarch into his fur, then brush it out. (It's best to do this outside, since your dog will shake and the cornstarch will go flying.) When you're done, you'll have a nice clean dog with no lingering wet-dog odor. ✉ **Flo S., WA**

SWEET VINEGAR TREAT. After giving my dog a bath, I finish the job by rinsing him off with a half-and-half mix of apple cider vinegar and water. This simple treatment leaves his coat smooth, soft, and shiny, and as a bonus, pesky fleas don't come anywhere near him. ✉ **Eva P., IL**

A REAL CLEAN KITTY. As cat lovers know, most kitties hate to get anywhere near water. So when it's time to give your cat a cleaning, forget about soap and water—use cornmeal instead. Just rub a handful into your cat's fur and brush it out. She'll purr with delight, and you'll have a fresh, clean companion. ✉ Rachel B., ID

HALT HAIR BALLS. I found the perfect recipe for keeping my cat free of hair balls, and it couldn't be any easier. I mix 1 teaspoon of butter with 1 teaspoon of dried catnip, spread it on a plate, and offer it to her once a day. The result? One very happy cat, and no more hair balls! ✉ Susan K., OH

QUICK-DRY YOUR DOGS. When your dog gets caught in the rain, you know how important it is to have a towel ready as soon as he reaches the door. But what if you have to deal with two soaking wet dogs? That was my dilemma until I hit upon this solutuion: I've given up on towels altogether—instead, I use a chamois. It absorbs a lot more water faster than a towel does, plus I can wring it out and use it to dry my second dog in a flash. ✉ Ed L., IN

OIL FOILS 'EM. There's nothing as relaxing as a nice long walk in the woods with your dog. But having to pluck burs and prickers off Fido afterward is no fun, so avoid the problem altogether with this ounce of prevention: Spray cooking oil on your dog's legs, underbelly, ears, and tail before taking him outdoors. It'll keep those nasty stickers out of his fur—even if he's a long-haired breed. ✉ Barb K., IA

Jerry's Handy Hints

CLEAN FIDO'S FEET

→ After a winter walk with your pooch, don't let him bring road salt and other debris inside on his paws. Use a baby wipe to clean his paws thoroughly before he ventures into the house. It'll quickly remove salt and other ice-melting chemicals without hassle or harm to your pet.

CAN YOU 'EAR ME NOW? ● Keep Rover's ears clean and clear with this gentle solution: In a small jar with a tight-fitting lid, mix ¼ cup of rubbing alcohol with 10 drops of glycerin (available at your local pharmacy), and give it a shake. Then dampen a cotton swab with it, and gently wipe out the dirt and wax from Rover's ears. *Note:* If your dog starts shaking his head while you're cleaning his ear, immediately stop and remove the swab to avoid damaging his eardrum.

HOW TO PILL A PUP. Want an easy way to get your dog to take a pill with no muss and no fuss? Then simply wrap the pill in soft cheese before popping it into his mouth. He'll gulp down the medication quick as a wink, without even realizing that the cheesy treat was actually good for him. ✉ Betty B., PA

Cleaning Up the Mess

STOP THE STINK. If your pet isn't housebroken, or doesn't always make it outside in time, you can clean up his stinky accidents with white vinegar. I pour it right from the bottle onto the spot, and then blot the mess up with an old sponge. Vinegar will not stain most fabrics, and the strong smell keeps my pet from doing his business in that area again. ✉ Judy S., WA

RUB OUT ODORS. Can't seem to get rid of the lingering odor of dog urine from your carpet? Then give this method a try: Fill a handheld sprayer bottle with rubbing alcohol, and use it to spritz the smelly area. Let the alcohol soak in, then blot it up with a clean, absorbent cloth. Always test this treatment first in an inconspicuous part of your carpet to be sure the alcohol doesn't damage the fibers. ✉ **Bonnie W., OR**

A SPARKLING SOLUTION. I've found a surefire way to get the stench and stain of pet urine out of carpets. First, I blot up as much of the urine as I can with paper towels or absorbent rags. Then I simply douse the area with sparkling water. After I let it seep into the carpet for 10 minutes or so, I use a clean, absorbent cloth to soak up the liquid. I repeat this step until I don't see any more yellow on the cloth, then I sop up the rest of the fluid with more towels or my wet/dry vac. I finish the job with a blast of odor neutralizer like Febreze®. ✉ **Kathleen F., ND**

Grandma Putt's Wisdom

To neutralize odors and remove yellow or brownish pet urine stains on your carpet, mattress, or upholstery, give this potion a try. It's been working its magic since my Grandma Putt's day. Just be sure to test it first in an inconspicuous spot (like under a seat cushion) to make sure the peroxide doesn't bleach the color out of the fabric.

1. Soak up the urine, then wet the stained area thoroughly with a mixture of 1 cup of white vinegar and 1 cup of water.
2. Blot with paper towels until it's damp, not wet, and then sprinkle about 1 cup of baking soda liberally over the stained area.
3. Mix 1/4 cup of hydrogen peroxide with 1 teaspoon of dishwashing liquid, and pour it over the baking soda. Work it in with a scrub brush until the baking soda is dissolved and the mixture penetrates the fabric or carpet fibers. Allow it to dry, and then vacuum up the residue.

If you still see a stain after the fabric is dry, repeat the treatment.

ANOTHER GREAT IDEA!

A FAREWELL TO FLEAS

Here's a flea repellent that does the trick every time: Mix a drop or two of oil of eucalyptus into your pet's shampoo. Be especially careful not to get it in his eyes while you're washing him. The eucalyptus odor, which smells good to us, keeps those pesky fleas far, far away.

PAPER THE PAN. When paper-training a puppy, instead of laying newspaper down on the floor, I layer it in an oil drip pan (available at auto-supply stores). The pans come in several different sizes, so you can choose the size that works best for your pet. If anything soaks through the newspaper, all you have to do is roll up the paper and toss it in the trash, then wash the pan, not your floor. It makes cleanup a snap! ✉ Pattie F., WA

SUDS UP FIDO'S FLEAS. If your dog has a flea problem, then the next time you give him a bath, replace his normal shampoo with Dawn® dishwashing liquid. Lather it in well, and leave it on for as long as Fido can stand it before you rinse it out with warm water. This is a safe, gentle, and effective treatment for your pet's flea infestation. ✉ Danielle S., OK

KEEP FLEAS AWAY. I add 1 teaspoon of white vinegar to every quart of water in my dog's bowl to keep him free of fleas and ticks. Since the vinegar is so diluted, my dog doesn't seem to notice the addition at all. ✉ Cuba M., MI

BRANCH OUT. If your dog's fleas have made themselves at home in your abode, try this easy trick: Stash fresh eucalyptus branches and leaves behind and around your furniture. Their fragrance will keep fleas from hiding out in your carpeting and buggin' you and your pets. ✉ Peggy D., CA

SCENTED SEND-OFF. Here's a simple way of dealing with fleas and other creepy crawlers in your vacuum cleaner bag: Before vacuuming, put a few mothballs on the floor and step on them to crush them, or scatter a handful of moth crystals on the floor. As you vacuum, the mothballs will get sucked up into the vacuum cleaner bag, killing any bugs that are in there. And don't worry—the mothball smell will vanish after about 20 minutes or so. ✉ **Jan A., NM**

Ask Jerry

Q: It seems like every time I turn around, my dear dog is crawling with fleas. I don't want to use potentially poisonous stuff to get rid of these pests. Do you have any suggestions for a kinder, gentler solution to my pet's flea problem?

A: I sure do. Start by sprinkling some powdered brewer's yeast on Fido's food (about ½ teaspoon for a small dog; up to 2 tablespoons a day for a large dog). The yeast seems to make your pet less attractive to fleas. You can also rub some right into his coat.

Another natural flea repellent you may want to try is this herbal concoction: Make a mix of equal parts eucalyptus powder, fennel powder, yellow dock powder, and pennyroyal powder. Brush Fido's fur backward with one hand, and shake the powder onto his skin at the roots of the fur. Use this powder daily for four days, and repeat as needed. That should send those fleas packing!

WATER TREATMENT. My simple method of keeping fleas off dogs might seem a little weird, but it works for me. I put a small amethyst rock in my dog's water bowl, and leave it there. That's all there is to it. ✉ Lawrence D., PA

FLEE, FLEAS! Don't put up with fleas living in your carpet; get rid of them now! Sprinkle your carpet with borax, and use a good stiff broom to work it into the fibers. Let the powder stay in the carpet for 24 hours, then vacuum it—and the fleas—up. *Note:* Don't use borax for flea control in your yard or around children, and keep your pets out of the room until all of the borax has been vacuumed up. ✉ Laura W., MI

PUT 'EM IN THE DEEP FREEZE. After vacuuming flea-infested carpets or pet beds, I remove the bag from my vacuum cleaner and stick it in the freezer overnight. This kills the bugs that are trapped inside, and allows me to continue using the bag until it's full. ✉ Celia B., GA

STOP SKUNK SCENTS. When a skunk leaves its mark on your pet, give Fido a bath using a bar-type laundry soap like Fels-Naptha®. I've found that it tackles the stink better than tomato juice—and doesn't leave your pooch with an orange "afterglow"! ✉ Karen G., UT

SCOPE OUT A SOLUTION. The eighth time my dog got skunked, I finally found a deodorizing solution that works. Scope® peppermint mouthwash not only breaks through the foul-smelling oil; it also leaves behind a minty fresh aroma. ✉ Barbara Ann D., NY

Jerry's Handy Hints

A RIP-ROARING IDEA

→ Pet hair, loose string, and straggly fibers can work themselves into a real snarl around your vacuum cleaner's beater brush. It's difficult to work a scissors blade under the tightly stretched stuff, so try a better tool: the seam ripper from your sewing kit. Use it to slice through the tangled mess in a few spots, then use an old kitchen fork to remove the clumps.

DE-SKUNKING SHAMPOO. This homemade concoction will neutralize the stinky skunk smell your pooch managed to bring home: Combine 1 quart of hydrogen peroxide, ¼ cup of baking soda, and 1 teaspoon of grease-cutting dishwashing liquid in a small bucket. Wet your pet's fur, then douse your dog with the shampoo, rub it in, and thoroughly rinse the smell away. ✉ Pat B., NJ

EASY SKUNK CLEANUP. I've found that ordinary white vinegar eliminates the smell of skunks. So if your dog gets skunked, bathe him in undiluted vinegar and rinse him well. Then put a cup of vinegar in the laundry along with your regular detergent when you wash your clothes and the towels you used to clean and dry your pup. It'll take care of that nasty odor, pronto! ✉ Kari B., ON

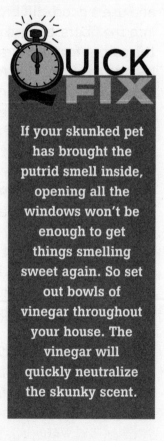

QUICK FIX

If your skunked pet has brought the putrid smell inside, opening all the windows won't be enough to get things smelling sweet again. So set out bowls of vinegar throughout your house. The vinegar will quickly neutralize the skunky scent.

TIDY TANKS. Before cleaning your fish tank, scoop the fish out with an old pair of panty hose. Then float the panty hose and the fish in a water-filled bowl or large jar while you work on the tank. When the tank's clean, use the panty hose to transport your fish back to their home, safe and sound. ✉ Delaine L., MO

SPICE THINGS UP. Here's a fish tank maintenance trick that works for me: Add 1 teaspoon of table salt to your 15-gallon tank each month. It keeps the water clean for a longer time, and your fish will love you for it. ✉ Machell W., OH

DRAWER DUTY. Don't waste your hard-earned money on a fancy aquarium stand. Instead, put your fish tank on top of an old dresser. The drawers underneath are the perfect place to keep all your fish supplies. ✉ Jane E., MA

Pet Pointers

CUT OUT THE CLIMBING. Cats love to climb, yet year after year you probably put a Christmas tree right in the middle of the family room for her to scramble up! Avoid that cat-astrophe and save your beautiful tree and treasured ornaments by stringing cotton balls soaked in ammonia around the trunk of the tree. All it takes is one soaked cotton ball per foot of string, and your cat will be offended enough that she'll stay far away from the tree—and you won't have to deal with broken ornaments. Just replace the cotton balls when the odor disappears. ✉ Joyce B., MI

SHOW HER HOW. If your cat claws your favorite chair to shreds, but refuses to use her scratching post, here's a trick I used to get mine to switch: I showed her how to use the post! I know it sounds funny, but get down on your hands and knees (with kitty watching, of course) and imitate scratching the post with your hands and feet—it really works! ✉ Linda B., MI

THE SWEET SOUND OF SILENCE. Does your dog bark so much that it's driving you bananas? Save your sanity by mixing equal parts of apple cider vinegar and water in a handheld sprayer bottle and giving Fido a good spritz with it every time he barks. Your dog will hate the vinegar taste. After a few days of this treatment, he'll associate it with his own barking and keep his yap shut! ✉ Larry W., CO

Jerry's Handy Hints

PAWS, THEN PAUSE

→ If you find muddy paw prints on your carpet, don't panic— leave 'em alone. Once they're good and dry, you can clean up the mess by simply sweeping the mud off with a good stiff brush. There you have it—no muss, no fuss.

HOUSEPLANT PATROL. If you can't keep your kitty from munching on or digging in your potted houseplants, try this trick: Add a crushed, dried chili pepper, seeds and all, to a gallon of water. Let it soak overnight, strain out the pods and seeds, and pour the remaining liquid into a handheld sprayer bottle. Spritz your houseplants and their surrounding soil with the pepper-water, and your cat will steer clear. ✉ Jennifer M., NM

DON'T SWEAT IT. Moving to a new home can be very stressful for pets. When I moved, I kept my dog's confusion and panic in check by putting him in a securely closed room while I was moving in. I made the transition even smoother by leaving him an unlaundered sweatshirt of mine to snuggle up to. The familiar scent helped ease his fears. ✉ Donna P., MI

ANOTHER GREAT IDEA!

MAKE A FRUGAL FILTER

If your fish tank filter uses an activated charcoal and polyester cartridge, you may be able to save some money by making your own filter. Here's how:

1. Fill a clean, old nylon stocking—or one leg from a pair of panty hose—with about 3 tablespoons of activated charcoal (available at pet-supply stores). Knot the stocking and run it under cool water until the dust is removed.

2. Place the charcoal sack in the cartridge compartment of your filter, along with two or three good-size pinches of polyester pillow stuffing (available at craft stores).

3. Change the poly stuffing whenever it gets soiled—usually after a couple of weeks. At that time, run the charcoal stocking under cool water to rinse it. Replace the charcoal once a month and replace the stocking when it starts to wear out.

America's Best
Practical Problem Solvers

CHAPTER 6

Pest Patrol

Ant Antidotes

CHILI CHASER. Are you tired of seeing ants trooping through your house? Then sprinkle some chili powder around door frames, on windowsills, and anywhere else ants can gain access to your home. They hate the stuff, so they'll stay out. ✉ **Willi B., KS**

ADIOS, ANTS! I say "so long" to ants by mixing 3 tablespoons of borax, 4 cups of water, and 1 cup of sugar in a large saucepan. Once I bring the mixture to a boil, I remove it from the stove and let it cool. Then I pour the cooled mixture into several small plastic containers and set them out wherever I've been seeing lots of ants. The pests are attracted to the sugary mix, and when they eat it, they die. *Note:* Make sure you place this ant killer in spots where children and pets can't get to it. ✉ **Betsy K., CA**

TAKE 5

Five not-so-common uses for vinegar around the house and garden include the following:

1 Send ants packin' by spraying them with vinegar in a handheld sprayer bottle.

2 Fight fleas by adding 1 teaspoon of vinegar per quart of water (ratio based on a 40-pound dog) to Fido's dish.

3 Clean flower vases in a hurry by rubbing them with a vinegar-soaked paper towel.

4 Whack weeds by pouring vinegar over the eyesores, and get rid of 'em just like that!

5 Dazzle azaleas by adding 2 teaspoons of vinegar to 1 quart of water and giving your beauties a refreshing spray.

TELL 'EM TO DROP DEAD. Get rid of ants once and for all by mixing 1 tablespoon of borax, 1 tablespoon of corn syrup, and 3 tablespoons of boiling water in an old tuna fish can until the borax has dissolved. Then, using an eyedropper, place small drops of the mix wherever the ants travel. In 10 days, the ants will be gone. Reapply the drops every three weeks to keep your house ant-free. ✉ Diana K., NY

IN FOR THE KILL. You can kill ants instantly by spraying them with an orange-scented household cleaner. Then prevent their relatives from staging a comeback by spraying a line of the same household cleaner across any entry point to your house. That'll do the trick. ✉ Cynthia A., KY

QUICK ON THE DRAW. I found a quick and easy way to keep ants from invading my kitchen: I hit 'em with a spray of Windex® or Lysol®. Believe me, they can't stand the stuff! ✉ Richard L., CA

SAY "BYE-BYE" WITH BAY. Here's a simple way I keep ants and other pests out of my kitchen: I place loose bay leaves in my cabinets to fend off those pesky ants as well as pantry grain moths and boll weevils. ✉ Sherry M., WV

CUKE YOUR CABINETS. Got ants in your pantry? No problem—just cut a cucumber into ¼- or ½-inch slices, and place the slices inside your cabinets, on pantry shelves, or wherever you have an ant problem. Don't ask me why, but it really works. ✉ **Elaine W., MI**

AN EXPLOSIVE SOLUTION. Don't resort to chemicals to rid your house of ants. Instead, try this trick: Put out small bowls of cornstarch, or sprinkle it along your baseboards and anywhere else the little buggers have made an appearance. Ants and other insects will eat the cornstarch, which dries up their innards as it expands, and . . . POOF! No more ants! ✉ **Markie R., UT**

MAKE MINE MEAL. I place small piles of corn-meal wherever I see ants. The bothersome pests eat it and then take it "home" with them. Since ants can't digest cornmeal, it kills them. And here's more good news—I don't have to worry about pets or tots being harmed in the process. If they happen to sample some corn-meal, they won't suffer any ill consequences. ✉ **Lela W., OK**

TRUE GRITS. You can get rid of ants by pouring boiling water directly onto their anthills, then stirring the wet hills with a stick. Repeat, then wait until the next day to pour uncooked instant grits into the holes. The ants will eat the grits and die when the grains expand inside them. ✉ **Alexa J., FL**

QUICK FIX

When ants invade your kitchen cabinets, reach for some aromatic herbs. Hang sprigs of dried penny-royal, tansy, or rue inside them to repel the rascals without resorting to chemicals.

```
· · · · · · · · · · · · · · · · · · · · · · · · · · · · · · · · · · · · · ·
  SUPER-DUPER SOLUTIONS

  Mmmm . . . Mint ● Here's a surefire way to stop ants dead in
  their tracks: Simply sprinkle ground peppermint around your
  doorstep. It'll have those little buggers heading for the hills in
  no time flat, guaranteed!
· · · · · · · · · · · · · · · · · · · · · · · · · · · · · · · · · · · · · ·
```

Grandma Putt's Wisdom

My Grandma Putt was a live-and-let-live kind of person, even when it came to bugs. But when ants started invading her house, she fought back with this slick solution: Mix 2 tablespoons of sugar and 1 tablespoon of baker's yeast in 1 pint of warm water. Then spread the mixture on pieces of cardboard and set them out in the problem areas. The ants' antics will end in a flash!

RUB 'EM THE WRONG WAY. I've discovered that ants hate Vicks® VapoRub®. So do what I do and dab some on any surfaces where you see ants in your house. That should clear up the problem quick as a wink. ✉ Tamara J., PA

PROTECT YOUR POOCH. To keep ants from eating out of your dog's bowl, draw a line along the bowl's rim with a piece of chalk. Ants will not cross the line, so your dog won't have to fight 'em off for his supper. ✉ Patricia F., OH

Fight Insect Inroads

BAIT FOR BAD BUGS. Sick of pesky cockroaches and water bugs? Then ambush 'em with a homemade trap. Simply apply a liberal glob of petroleum jelly all around the inside of a glass jar, then partially fill the jar with some kind of bait, like beer-soaked bread, bacon drippings, or pieces of fruit. Wrap the outside of the jar with a paper towel, and set it where you've seen the bugs. They'll crawl up the paper towel to get to the bait, fall into the jar, and then won't be able to get back out. ✉ Regina R., CA

ROACHES ON A ROLL. I get rid of cockroaches lickety-split with this concoction: Mix 16 ounces of boric acid, 1 cup of flour, 1 small chopped onion, and ¼ cup of shortening with enough water to form a stiff dough. Shape the mixture into marble-sized balls, and roll them into all the dark, damp areas where roaches hide. The pests will eat the marbles, drink water, and die. ✉ Luana E., CA

KICK 'EM OUT WITH CLOVES. Do you have a problem with roaches and other nasties in your kitchen? Don't fret; simply sprinkle whole cloves in any areas where you have pest problems. It's a safe and effective repellent that'll keep roaches away. Just replace the cloves every few weeks. ✉ Samantha D., FL

LURE THEM IN. Here's a sure cure that I use to keep pesky gnats and fruit flies from hovering around my potted plants and fruit bowls: Mix 5 drops of dishwashing liquid, 2 teaspoons of hot water, and 2 tablespoons of wine in a small glass bowl, and set it out where the gnats congregate. Every gnat in the room will be drawn to it and take the deadly plunge. ✉ Maxine E., OR

ANOTHER GREAT IDEA!

CLOBBER COCKROACHES

No matter where in your house cockroaches are roaming, it's a snap to get rid of them without resorting to dangerous chemicals. All you need to do is make a half-and-half mixture of sugar and baking powder and sprinkle it over the infested territory. The roaches will scurry to gobble up the sugar, and the baking powder will kill them. Replace the supply as needed to prevent further invasions.

TAKE 5

Five not-so-common uses for hair spray around your home include:

1 Get rid of winged household pests with a touch of hair spray that'll stiffen their wings and immobilize 'em for good.

2 Prolong the life of your Christmas tree with a spritz of hair spray to help it hold its needles.

3 Make great wrapping paper out of the Sunday comics. Hair spray will keep the ink from smudging and give the paper a nice shiny gloss.

4 Seal decorative ribbons with a light coating of super-hold hair spray to keep them clean and wilt-free.

5 Preserve dried floral arrangements by lightly spraying all around the arrangement to keep it looking "fresh."

DROWN AND OUT. To get rid of irritating fruit flies, fill a small glass halfway with apple cider vinegar and 2 drops of dishwashing liquid. Mix the solution well, then set the glass away from areas where people gather. The annoying flies will be drawn to the glass, fall in, and then drown. ✉ Barbara K., NC

GROUND FLYING PESTS. When I'm trying to take down flying insects, I don't even think about using toxic bug sprays. Instead, I mix a squirt of dishwashing liquid and 1/4 cup of white vinegar in a 32-ounce handheld sprayer bottle and fill the balance of the bottle with water. Then I spray 'em dead in their tracks. ✉ Ronda C., SC

STEAM OUT MOTHS. Clothes moths don't confine their egg laying to just clothing. If you've got natural-fiber rugs or carpeting, larvae could be lurking in the fibers. To kill them off, saturate a large bath towel with water, wring it out, and spread it over the rug. Then grab your iron, set it on high, and carefully press the towel until it's dry. You don't need to push down very hard—it's the steamy heat that kills the pesky little pests. ✉ Angela B., CA

GET SCRAPPY. I never throw away fabric scraps from my sewing projects. Instead, I use them to make small

HERBAL MOTH CHASERS ● When it comes time to store your winter clothes and blankets for the summer, don't use smelly mothballs. Instead, fasten pouches of dried herbs to the hangers and tuck them onto shelves and into blanket chests. Try some of these moth-chasing herbs: lavender, santolina, southernwood, tansy, thyme, and wormwood. You can use them individually or in a mix, depending on what you have on hand.

sachet pouches. I fill the pouches with dried lavender and place them in all my clothing drawers and closets. They smell great and repel destructive moths. ✉ Martie K., AZ

SOCK IT TO 'EM. Here's a great use for old socks (but only those without holes). Fill 'em with cedar shavings and tie the tops shut. Then tuck 'em among your clothes and linens to fend off moths and silverfish. ✉ Dan D., MI

A SPIDER SOLUTION. If spiders are buggin' you, try this pleasantly scented solution: Place cedar chips in the toes of old panty hose, and hang them in areas where you want to discourage web spinning. The fragrant cedar will keep spiders away. ✉ Barbara R., IN

WAGE WAR ON WEBS. To prevent spiders from webbing up my windows, I spray rubbing alcohol on the sills. If you don't want to run the risk of the alcohol ruining your windowsills' finish, you can scatter a handful of perfumed soap chips on the sills instead. Either method will deter spiders from spinning their webs. ✉ Chip D., MI

AN APPLE A DAY . . . Keeps the spiders away! I put a halt to spider invasions by repelling the creepy crawlers with green hedge apples. They are the fruit of the Osage orange tree and aren't actually apples. They have leathery green skin and can be found in grocery stores and at farmers' markets in early fall. Buy two or three hedge apples for each room you want to treat, then place them around your home. As they age, the "apples" give off an aroma that keeps spiders and other pests away without harming you, your children, or your pets. ✉ **Lamont S., MO**

SHOW FLEAS THE DOOR. Do you have fleas in your basement? Then do what I do to get rid of the little buggers: Cut a few branches from a black walnut tree and place them along the basement walls. The fleas will flee, just like that. ✉ **Rodney P., MO**

IT'S A WRAP! Here's a trick that worked for me: To get rid of a house full of fleas, moisten some wrapping paper with cedar oil, then place the pieces all around the house, under beds and dressers, and beneath every rug. Your home will quickly become flea-free. ✉ **Joanne K., OH**

PUT THE KIBOSH ON CRICKETS. To get rid of crickets in your home, take two plastic lids (like those from coffee cans) and set

Ask Jerry

Q: I'd like to keep plenty of pasta, rice, beans, and other dried foods on hand, but I'm concerned about insects getting into them. How can I keep the invaders out?

A: The answer to this dilemma couldn't be simpler: Just scatter some bay leaves across the shelves where you store these foods. Wily weevils, beastly beetles, and other pesky pests will keep their distance, and at the same time, the herb is safe to use around children and pets.

Grandma Putt's Wisdom

My Grandma knew that cockroaches could invade even the cleanest of houses. So whenever she spotted those nasty creatures inside her home, she mixed up this formula: 4 tablespoons of borax, 2 tablespoons of flour, and 1 tablespoon of cocoa powder. Divvy up the mixture into several jar lids and set them in your cupboards, behind the refrigerator, and anyplace else the roaches are roaming. The roaches will be attracted to the yummy powder, ingest it, and die. Just be sure to place the lids out of reach of children and pets.

them on the floor side by side in the room where you've seen—or heard—these chriping pests. Put some cornmeal in one lid, and pour a little water in the other. The crickets will eat the cornmeal, then drink the water, which will make the cornmeal expand inside of them. Problem solved—no more crickets! ✉ Christine A., IA

Head Off Big Trouble

MAKE MICE RUN. Is there a mouse in your house? Well, here's a safe and easy rodent repellent you can make at the kitchen sink: Start with a small jar with a tight-fitting lid. Remove the lid and make a hole in the middle large enough to pull a piece of cloth through. Then fill the jar with ammonia and add a strip of cloth to the jar (I use a piece from an old T-shirt). Pull up on a corner of the cloth, and thread it through the hole in the lid until the cloth sticks out about an inch. Then bring down the lid and screw it on tightly. Place the jar where you have the rodent problem. The cloth will act as a wick and slowly release the ammonia scent, which repels mice and rats. ✉ Dolores H., WA

MINT FOR MICE. I've discovered that mice won't come anywhere near peppermint. So to take care of any problem areas in and around my house, I saturate cotton balls with peppermint oil and leave them in places that mice are attracted to. As long as I replace the balls when they lose their scent, the mice stay far away. ✉ Betty R., WA

BYE-BYE, BIRDIES. It's nearly impossible to keep birds from nesting in your attic if you can't block all of the tiny entrances they can get through. So if you've got fine-feathered friends trying to take up residence, toss a few mothballs into the spots where they could make their nests. The birds will pack their bags and move on out. ✉ Patti G., MI

Ask Jerry

Q: Help! Mice have invaded my basement, but I have two young children and a very curious dog—so I definitely don't want to use poisons or traps. How can I get rid of the destructive little rodents?

A: I have a simple solution: Just set out shallow containers of instant mashed potato flakes with a dish of water close at hand. The mice will eat the taters, drink the water, swell up, and die. But if your youngsters or dog should manage to get into the basement and take a taste, it won't harm them one little bit. Be sure to check frequently for dead mice, and dispose of them immediately.

PART 2

Health and Beauty

America's Best
Practical Problem Solvers

CHAPTER 7

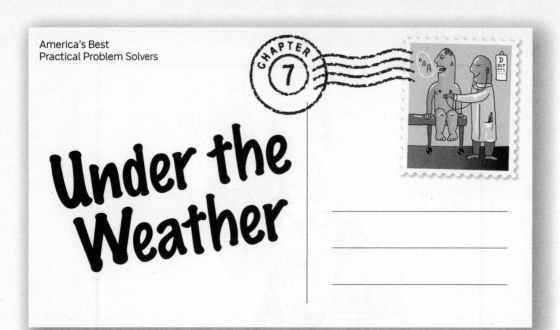

Under the Weather

Aches and Pains

CIDER SOAK. If a hard day at work has left you feeling sore and achy, I've got the perfect cure—a nice long soak in apple cider vinegar. Simply add a few cups of the vinegar to your warm bathwater and slip right in. It'll ease away all your aches and pains, and leave you feeling relaxed and refreshed. ✉ Valerie T., SC

SIP SOME GINGER. When you're aching and creaking with arthritis pain, reach for ginger. It's a powerful anti-inflammatory herb that can take the edge off the discomfort. Here's a recipe I use for a healing ginger tea whenever I'm feeling stiff and sore: Grate about an inch of fresh ginger and steep it in hot water for 10 minutes, then strain. Drink it once or twice a day, hot or cold, to soothe arthritis pain. ✉ Jodi G., NH

UNDO THE TWIST. I twisted my ankle and boy, did it hurt! But I kept the swelling and bruising to a minimum with a mixture of 15 drops of celery seed essential oil and 4 teaspoons of sweet almond oil. I gently rubbed it on my stiff, achy ankle a few times a day for a couple of days. It relieved the soreness and kept the joint from becoming very swollen. *Note:* Don't follow this course of treatment if you are pregnant. ✉ **Kam P., KS**

BANISH BRUISES. If you have a nasty bruise that just won't go away, try this trick: Soak a cotton ball in vinegar, and hold it on the sore spot for an hour with a Band-Aid®. The black and blue will fade, and you'll heal a whole lot faster. ✉ **Yvonne D., IA**

GO BANANAS. You'll always be prepared for sudden bruises, sore joints, and bee stings with this surefire painkiller. Fill a jar with cut-up banana peels, then cover them with rubbing alcohol and put a lid on the jar. Let the mixture sit for two weeks, and store it in your

Ask Jerry

Q: Jerry, it seems that I'm always aching lately. How can I lessen my arthritis pain without taking handfuls of pills every day?

A: It's easy—just add a little spice to your diet! Toss some cayenne pepper into salad dressings, soups, and pasta dishes. The capsaicin that gives the pepper its spicy kick will also help your body block pain impulses. Can't handle the heat? Toss crushed garlic into sauces and stews, and add onion slices to sandwiches and burgers. You'll enjoy terrific, zesty flavor while taming arthritis pain.

medicine cabinet. Then when you're injured, dip a cotton ball into the solution and dab it wherever you're sore, swollen, or stung. It works wonders for me! ✉ **Louise H., OK**

COOL IT. Whether you're bumped, bruised, sprained, or strained, nothing reduces aches and swelling quite as well as a cold compress. But don't wrap ice in a bulky, insulating washcloth. Instead, pack the cubes into the foot of an old, clean pair of panty hose, and hold the compress gently on the injured area. The icy cold will hit the spot quickly and ease the pain. ✉ **Karla C., NJ**

TIME FOR TEA. If you're a nursing mother, you know how difficult it can be to soothe achy nipples between feedings. Here's my

Grandma Putt's Wisdom

My Grandma Putt's homemade poultices and compresses worked wonders on my childhood infections, bruises, insect bites, and sore muscles. As a matter of fact, I still make 'em just the way Grandma did. To whip up one of her special poultices, Grandma would steep a mixture of 1 part herbs and 4 parts oatmeal in water for a short time, then spread it out on a piece of cloth. She'd apply the poultice to an inflamed or infected area for between one and eight hours, replacing it when it cooled.

And her compresses are even easier to make! Just make a strong herbal tea, soak a cloth in it, and apply it while it's still hot (but not so hot that you burn yourself) to a bruise, insect bite, or swollen area.

You can use any herbs you like in your poultices and compresses. Grandma's favorites were burdock, coriander, flaxseed, and slippery elm. But she never used anything spicy, like cayenne, that could burn the skin or cause irritation.

Ask Jerry

Q: I have restless legs syndrome, and I'm having a tough time getting enough sleep because of the constant urge to move my legs and the creepy-crawly tingling. Is there anything I can do to make myself settle down?

A: There are some lifestyle changes that you can make now that'll help control your symptoms in the long run. Start by eliminating caffeine from your diet and cutting back on sugar. Increase the amount of protein you eat every day, and be sure to exercise regularly. Try relaxation therapies like yoga or meditation, and take a hot bath before bed. Sleeping on your side with a pillow between your legs might also help.

remedy: I make a cup of tea with two bags, then I remove the bags without squeezing them and let them cool to lukewarm. I apply the wet bags directly to my sore nipples, leaving them on until the bags are completely cooled. ✉ **Judy C., NV**

PASS THE PEAS. Keep a bag of peas or corn in your freezer and pull it out whenever you need to ice up sore muscles. The bag will mold nicely to the contours of your arm, leg, neck, shoulder, or whatever's bothering you. You can help it stay in place by wrapping an elastic bandage around it. And you can refreeze the bag and use it over and over again. Just be sure to label the bag so it doesn't get opened later and eaten—all of that thawing and refreezing will degrade the quality and flavor of the vegetables, and you don't want them to end up being served for dinner! ✉ **Melody A., TX**

SOAP FOR LEG CRAMPS. If painful leg cramps keep you up at night, place a bar of unwrapped soap underneath the bottom sheet of your bed near your legs. This is one of those "you have to try it to believe it" cures—and believe me, I tried it and it really works! ✉ Deanna W., PA

Jerry's Handy Hints

CRUNCH OUT BACK PAIN

→ Many lower-back injuries and chronic aches can be avoided simply by strengthening your supporting abdominal muscles. It doesn't take a lot of time to do a routine of sit-ups every day. Start out by lying on your back with your arms crossed on your chest and your knees bent (have someone hold your feet on the floor, or hook them in place under a couch). Slowly sit up on your exhale, then lower yourself back to the floor as you inhale. Start with 25 crunches per day, and increase the number by five every week, building to 100 or more.

A BANG-UP BEVERAGE. The next time you bang your shin against a coffee table or smack your elbow on a door frame, resist the urge to cuss and instead, down a glass of pineapple juice. Pineapple contains bromelain—an enzyme that has anti-inflammatory properties—so it'll tame the swelling and keep bruising to a minimum. ✉ Tina R., PA

WALKING DOES WONDERS. Whenever my back is cranky, stiff, and sore, I take a walk. A nice stroll encourages the blood to flow to my fatigued back muscles and really helps relieve the pain in my aching back. ✉ Anna K., NJ

SOCK IT TO ME! For quick back pain relief, put two tennis balls in a sock, and knot the open end. Then lean against a wall, trapping the sock behind your back. With your knees bent, move your back up and down, applying pressure with the balls wherever it hurts the most. ✉ Rob Q., OR

Bronchitis

BREATHE EASY. If you have bronchitis and need to clear your lungs, make your own anti-inflammatory drink. Put a teaspoon of oregano leaves into a mug of water, and heat it in the microwave. This drink tastes just like a nice hot cup of tea, and you'll be breathing easier in no time at all. ✉ Joyce B., MI

GO FOR THE GREEN. Tackle a bad case of bronchitis by eating plenty of magnesium-rich green vegetables like spinach, kale, lima beans, and soybeans. The veggies help relax the smooth muscles of your bronchial tubes and make breathing effortless and a whole lot more comfortable. ✉ Nancy R., AL

Grandma Putt's Wisdom

Before the days of antibiotics and other miracle drugs, folks treated bronchitis, chest colds, and the flu with this remedy. Start by having the patient put on a thick cotton T-shirt and lie down. Then mix 1/4 cup of dry mustard, 1/4 cup of flour, and 3 tablespoons of molasses in a medium bowl. Add enough thick cream or softened lard to get an ointment consistency. Dip a piece of cotton flannel in warm water, wring it out, and lay it on the patient's throat and upper chest, on top of the T-shirt. Apply the mustard mixture in a thick layer onto the damp flannel, and leave it on for 15 minutes, or until the skin starts to turn red. *Caution:* This stuff can burn, so wear rubber gloves as you work with it, and make sure it doesn't come in direct contact with the patient's bare skin.

A PUNGENT CURE. Chicken soup is a great cure for whatever ails you, so when I'm battling bronchitis, I have at least one steaming bowl each day. To boost the soup's potency, I toss several minced garlic cloves into the broth. Garlic is an age-old, reliable respiratory infection fighter, and it tastes great, too! ✉ Debbie D., CA

FULL STEAM AHEAD! When you're suffering with bronchitis, inhaling the steam from a bowl of hot chicken soup will help open up your nasal and bronchial passages. Of course, eating the soup while it's still nice and hot also helps. ✉ Sheri P., IL

MAKE MINE ONION. Onions have been used as a cure for bronchitis for generations and for good reason—the pungent bulbs contain quercetin, a chemical that helps relieve congestion caused by bronchitis and chest colds. So the next time you're stuffed up, do yourself a favor and make a pot of onion soup, or eat the onions raw. You'll feel the warmth spreading through your chest and lungs as your clogged airways open up. ✉ Janice F., KS

Coughs and Colds

THERE'S THE RUB. When I need to get rid of a cough that just won't quit, I generously smear the bottoms of both my feet with Vicks® VapoRub®, then I pull on a pair of socks and climb into bed. The soothing sensations of the VapoRub let me sleep like a baby all night long. ✉ Francis B., TX

AN OILY REMEDY. The next time you get a cough that's a real humdinger, rub the outside of your throat with a little eucalyptus oil. Not only will it get rid of mucus, but it'll also help you relax enough to get some much-needed rest. ✉ Anita C., OH

A HONEY OF A CURE. When you can't stop coughing, don't worry if you don't have a bottle of cough syrup on hand. As long as you have a few staples in your cupboard, you can mix up a batch of homemade syrup right in your own kitchen. Simply mix a cup of honey with a tablespoon of apple cider vinegar and the juice of half a lemon. Swallow 1 to 2 teaspoons per dose, and refrigerate any leftovers. ✉ Angie N., TX

PEPPER, PLEASE. To calm a cough and loosen congestion, try this spicy fix: Swallow a teaspoon of honey that's got a little black pepper mixed in. It's a tried-and-true, time-tested way to solve an age-old problem! ✉ Don D., ME

A SALTY SOOTHER. One of my all-time favorite remedies for a cough is to gargle with warm, salty water several times a day. I simply add 1 teaspoon of salt to a glass of warm water, and gargle as often as necessary to quiet my cough and soothe my sore throat. ✉ Craig B., NY

C IS FOR RELIEF. You can banish your cold symptoms and sore throat pain with a little citrus. Just squeeze the juice out of one lime and drink it in the morning before breakfast (stir in a drop of honey if you can't swallow the sour juice). It'll give you a megadose of vitamin C—just what your body needs to fight off that cold. ✉ Jed Y., TX

MINTY TEA. I say good-bye to nasty cold symptoms by drinking this sooth-ing tea: Put ¼ teaspoon of peppermint extract in 2 teaspoons of sugar, then add ½ cup or so of hot water. Mix

Jerry's Handy Hints

FIGHT COLD WITH COLD

→ Researchers over in Germany have discov-ered that one way to fight the common cold is with . . . cold! That's right—turn the faucet to "cold" for the last two minutes of your shower. It'll improve your body's circulation and increase the flow of white blood cells. And what do white blood cells do? They fight infection!

QUICK FIX

well, and drink it to calm a cough, loosen congestion, or relieve a headache. ✉ Shawn K., MI

SINUS WASH. One way to short-circuit cold symptoms is by cleaning out your nostrils and sinuses. And the best part is that it's not hard to do. Start by mixing ¼ teaspoon of table salt in 1 cup of lukewarm water. Then use whichever method you prefer to get the salted water in one nostril at a time and let it drain out. I like to use a neti pot specifically made for this purpose (available at drugstores and online), but you can also use a spoon to snort the water up your nostrils, or an eyedropper to drop it in. Whichever method you choose, be sure to tilt your head to the side and pour the salted water in the top nostril, allowing it to flow out the bottom one. Then tilt your head to the other side and repeat the process. That's all it takes to breathe freely. ✉ Kris S., NY

SHOWER CLEANSE. Here's how to use your shower to prevent sinus infections. Mix ¼ teaspoon of baking soda with ¼ teaspoon of salt in 1 cup of warm water, and bring that and a bulb syringe

ANOTHER GREAT IDEA!

HERBAL SNIFF

Has your latest cold interfered with your senses of smell and taste? Sprinkle a few drops of eucalyptus essential oil onto a cotton ball, and store it in an old pill bottle. Then when you're congested, take a few quick whiffs. Your passages will open up just like that, and you'll come to your senses.

TAKE 5

Here are five not-so-common ways to use garlic for great health:

1 Clear up nasal and sinus congestion in a hurry by tossing some chopped raw, fresh garlic into a bowl of hot soup, and sipping it slowly to promote drainage.

2 Treat a throbbing earache with a little concentrated garlic oil made from one sliced garlic clove in 2 teaspoons of olive oil, heated for two minutes. Strain the mixture through cheesecloth, and let it cool to lukewarm before dropping it into your achin' ear.

3 Keep biting, stinging insects away by eating lots of garlic throughout the summer.

4 Stop athlete's foot in its tracks by soaking your feet in garlic water. Crush several garlic cloves and drop them into a tub of warm water with a splash of rubbing alcohol added to it, then gently place both feet in the tub for about 10 minutes a day.

5 Strengthen your nails with garlic oil. Prick the end of a garlic oil gel capsule with a pin, and gently squeeze a drop on each fingernail, rubbing it into the entire nail bed. Let it sit for five minutes, then wash your hands with warm water and gentle soap.

with you at shower time. Step into the hot, steamy shower and breathe deeply. Fill the bulb syringe with the salt solution, tilt your head to one side, and squeeze the fluid into one nostril, allowing it to flow out the other nostril. Then tilt your head to the other side and repeat the steps. ✉ Allison G., UT

TAKE THE CHILI CHALLENGE. If you like spicy food, chilies can help cure your congestion. Hot chili peppers work to thin mucus and reduce inflammation in your bronchial passages. So what are you waiting for? Pop a few pepper slices into your mouth throughout the day, and your congestion will soon be nothing more than a distant memory. ✉ **Brenda L., CA**

NO HORSING AROUND. Whenever I have a stuffy nose, I reach in the fridge for horseradish. I just open up the jar and take a good, deep sniff, then screw the lid back on and put the jar back where it belongs. I inhale the horseradish vapors a couple of times a day until I breathe easier. ✉ **Ralph E., UT**

HEAT FOR COLDS. Here's a really simple way to clobber cold symptoms: Grab a bottle of hot-pepper sauce and shake it well. Then put 10 to 20 drops into a glass of water and drink up. Do this three times a day until you're feeling better. ✉ **Carla L., MO**

Ear Issues

A DROP'LL DO IT. I keep my ears clean and healthy by using an eyedropper to dribble a little apple cider vinegar into each ear while I'm showering. I do this a few times a month and I've never had any ear problems. ✉ **Alice D., MI**

HIGH AND DRY. A drop of rubbing alcohol will dry the water in your ears after a shower or a swim. Just drip it in with a bulb syringe, and the alcohol and water will both quickly evaporate, leaving your ears high and dry. ✉ **Sandra M., GA**

KEEP 'EM CLEAN. Clean your ears once a week with 3% hydrogen peroxide squeezed into an ear syringe. With your head tilted to one side, squirt a few drops into the ear and let the peroxide fizz, then tilt your head the other way and let the liquid drip out into a tissue. Repeat this process in the other ear, and you'll never have to deal with waxy buildup. ✉ **Colleen M., NE**

MOVE ON. As we get older, earwax tends to build up, become hardened, and even block the ear canal. Then you need a trip to the doctor to clear everything out. But there's a simple way to keep earwax soft and moving right along: A couple of times a week, put a drop or two of warm vegetable oil into each ear. That'll do the trick! ✉ **Ben P., NM**

DULL THE ACHE. Sometimes an aching ear just won't wait for the morning when you can get to the doctor. When this happens to you, here's a quick fix: Drip a few drops of hydrogen peroxide right into your ear with an eyedropper. It'll help ease the pain until you can get it properly checked out. ✉ **Estelle T., ON**

THE ONION OPTION. When my ears are achy and throbbing, I cut an onion in half and heat one half in the oven until it's warm (not hot). Then I wrap the warm onion in cheesecloth and hold it against my sore ear. The chemicals in the onion help increase blood circulation and flush away the infection and the pain. ✉ **Doug Z., OR**

Grandma Putt's Wisdom

I still remember the very first earache I ever had. I was in third grade, and the pain was so deep in my ear that I couldn't even reach to massage it. To this day, I still do what my Grandma Putt did for me back then: I wrap a cold pack with a towel and hold it against my achin' ear. Nowadays I know that folks usually rely on heat to help stop earache pain, but give this cold cure a try. It'll restrict the blood flow to the area and ease the pain.

HEAT RELIEF. Nothing soothes an aching ear like good ol' heat. But what do you do when an earache strikes and you haven't got a heating pad on hand? Simple—just put a heat-proof plate in the oven until it's toasty warm. Then wrap a towel around the plate, lie down, and rest your achy ear on top of the warm wrapping. Repeat as necessary. ✉ *Bev W., FL*

Headaches

THE CAFFEINE CURE. Brew a cuppa joe the next time a whopper of a headache hits you. And make sure the coffee's caffeinated. Caffeine, you see, constricts blood vessels, and that'll help reduce your head pain and even lessen the length and severity of a migraine. ✉ *Carrie S., WA*

MIND MASSAGE. For quick relief from a nasty headache, massage some Vicks® VapoRub® directly on your forehead and temples, keeping it away from your eyes. The soothing vapors really help ease the pain fast. ✉ *Susan C., GA*

DRINK UP! I know this sounds a bit odd, but it works for me. Keep your favorite flavor of Gatorade® handy, and when a headache strikes, drink two glasses in a row. You'll put your electrolytes back in balance and stop the throbbing pain in its tracks. Aaahhh, relief is so refreshing! ✉ *Emilie S., NY*

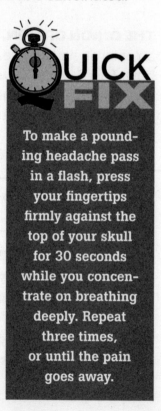

QUICK FIX

To make a pounding headache pass in a flash, press your fingertips firmly against the top of your skull for 30 seconds while you concentrate on breathing deeply. Repeat three times, or until the pain goes away.

PANTRY Rx ● There's more than one way to stop a migraine in its tracks—and even help prevent one from coming on in the first place. And they all start with a trip to your pantry. Check out these easy kitchen counter cures:

• **Ginger.** As soon as you feel the first hint of a migraine attack, mix about ¼ teaspoon of ground ginger in a glass of water, and drink up.

• **Honey.** To stop a migraine before it starts, take 1 teaspoon of honey the minute you feel the early warning signs coming on.

• **Cayenne pepper.** Sprinkle this hot stuff on your lunch or dinner as often as you can. Cayenne pepper is a source of magnesium, a mineral that helps to ward off migraines.

CITRUS RUB. Do you want a natural and easy home remedy for your headache? Then simply cut a fresh lime in half and rub the cut side directly on the area where it hurts. It might sound a little silly, but it really does the trick! ✉ **Larry K., OK**

SOME LIKE IT HOT. If you suffer from migraines, here's a hot tip for you. As soon as you feel one of those monster headaches coming on, take a pinch of cayenne pepper—a natural pain reliever—and sniff it into each nostril. The heat will beat the pain, not to mention what it'll do to your nose. ✉ **Sheila R., CT**

I LOVE LAVENDER. Whenever I have a headache, I reach for some lavender essential oil. Just a drop or two massaged into my temples brings quick relief. If you have sensitive skin, rub a thin layer of your usual moisturizing face lotion into your temples before applying the lavender oil. ✉ **Janice W., OR**

GET IN THE SWING. Here's a neat trick that really helps stifle a pounding headache: Stand up straight with your arms hanging loosely at your sides. Then just swing your arms back and forth in unison (not staggered like when you're walking). Swinging relaxes your mind and directs blood flow away from your head to your hands, thus easing headache pain. ✉ **Lori K., NY**

Stress

BREW UP A BATH. After a long, hard, tension-filled day, grab a few beers and head for the tub. No, you're not going to drink while you bathe—you're going to relax in a beer bath that will help you de-stress and soften your skin at the same time. Just pour three bottles of brew into a tub of warm water, settle in, and think lovely thoughts! ✉ **Mary R., WI**

BOGGLE THE MIND. If you need an offbeat stress buster, take this challenge: Build a tower using only a roll of clear tape and a packet of straws. It's silly, creative, and fun. And it'll get your mind off whatever's buggin' you. ✉ **Charlie L., MI**

Ask Jerry

Q: I've been so stressed out lately that I just can't seem to relax. What do you do when you need to chill out?

A: I always make sure I get plenty of carbs in my diet. Foods that are high in carbohydrates, like pasta, crackers, and bread, actually stimulate the release of chemicals that promote relaxation.

ANOTHER GREAT IDEA!

UNPEEL AND UNWIND

If you're feeling stressed out, try eating two bananas every day. The serotonin and norepinephrine in the fruit can lift your mood and prevent you from falling into a deeper depression.

SPRITZ AND BE CALM. Whenever I'm feeling stressed, I give myself a fragrant lift with a little flower water. Mix 10 drops each of lavender, clary sage, and chamomile oils with 1 teaspoon of rubbing alcohol, then add that to 3½ ounces of distilled water. Store the mixture in a glass spray bottle, and liberally spritz it on your skin whenever you're feeling a bit tense. The essential oils will help ease your stress, so keep the bottle close at hand. ✉ Lisa L., IL

STRESS SOOTHER. When you're tired and cranky, try this simple remedy. In a blender, mix 2 cups of nonfat powdered milk, 1 cup of cornstarch, and (if you like) your favorite scented oil. Add ½ cup of the mixture to your bathwater, sink into the tub, and relax. Store the remaining mixture in an airtight container at room temperature for future use. ✉ Stephanie P., PA

TRANQUILIZING SOAK. For a soothing, great-smelling bath, mix 1 cup of powdered milk, 1 cup of baking soda, 1 cup of salt, and 10 drops of vanilla or lemon extract in an empty milk carton. Add about ¼ cup of the mixture to your bathwater, and soak away your stress-filled day. You'll come out of the tub relaxed and refreshed, and your skin will feel really soft and smooth. ✉ Phyllis W., TX

OPEN WIDE. The next time you're feeling stressed, take note of what your jaw is doing. Chances are, you're clenching down. So force a few big, wide yawns, then try to keep your jaw slack. It really does relieve the tension. ✉ Charlotte W., CO

Toothaches

VINEGAR TO THE RESCUE. For temporary toothache relief, try this old-fashioned remedy: Rub vinegar directly on the sore tooth and the surrounding gum area. It'll help dull the pain until you can get to the dentist. ✉ Alice W., TX

SWISH THE PAIN AWAY. I swish hydrogen peroxide around in my mouth to take the edge off a toothache. I tilt my head to the side where the aching tooth is so that the throbbing area will get the most of this magical mouthwash. Just make sure you spit the hydrogen peroxide out when you're done—don't swallow it! ✉ Susan R., OH

AAAHHH, ANISE. When an aching tooth has you ready to bang your head against the wall, dab a little anise oil on and around it. It'll give you instant relief, and it doesn't taste bad, either! ✉ Phyllis R., IL

TEA FOR TEETH. To stop a toothache from throbbing—and dull the pain until I can get to my dentist—I reach for tea. I simply run a tea bag under warm water to moisten it, then lay it directly on the tooth that's causing my discomfort. It brings quick relief. ✉ Sandy R., TX

ICE IS NICE. Believe it or not, placing a cold pack on the outside of your mouth really does help ease toothache pain. Wrap a washcloth around some ice cubes

QUICK FIX

Your tooth is throbbing, but what if you can't get to the dentist right away? The acupressure point for your teeth is the palm of your hand. So press an ice cube or cold compress on the fleshy area between your thumb and index finger for five minutes at a time throughout the day. It's worth a try, and it certainly won't make your tooth hurt more!

and hold it against the tender area for 15 to 20 minutes every few hours until you can see your dentist. ✉ **Mark L., IA**

SALTY SOOTHER. Here's an easy way to soothe an achy tooth: Swish salt water around your mouth. Mix about ½ teaspoon of salt in 1 cup of warm water until the salt is completely dissolved. Then gargle with the salty mixture for a minute or so, making sure you swoosh the liquid over the throbbing spot as you go. The pain relief doesn't last very long, but you can repeat the procedure as often as necessary until you can make an appointment for your dentist to check out the problem. ✉ **Pat N., MT**

Tummy Troubles

IN A PICKLE. When I want to settle a bout of heartburn fast, I eat a dill pickle. Not in the mood to munch? You can opt for the pickle juice instead—just swallow about a tablespoon of the liquid. Either way, your heartburn will be gone in a flash. ✉ **Annettie R., AL**

ANOTHER GREAT IDEA!

TUMMY TUCK

Don't let heartburn get the best of you. Try this knee-squeeze yoga pose instead: Lie on your back on a firm surface with your arms at your sides and your toes pointed. Inhale while you slowly raise your right knee toward your chin, and hold it for a few seconds. Then release your knee, exhale, and straighten your leg. Repeat with your left knee, and finish by holding both knees to your chest at the same time.

Grandma Putt's Wisdom

If this year's holiday feast leaves your stomach a little, well, irritable, mellow it out with one of my Grandma Putt's tried-and-true tummy tamers:

Mellow meadowsweet tea. Meadowsweet is a digestive herb that protects and soothes the stomach, while reducing excess acidity. To prepare a cup of meadowsweet tea, steep 1 teaspoon of the herb in 1 cup of hot water for 15 minutes, strain out the herb, and sip slowly.

Heavenly angelica tea. Say a quick prayer of thanks for the lovely herb angelica, which has the power to cool just about any heartburn. To make a tea (which tastes a bit like celery), put 1 teaspoon of the dried herb—or 3 teaspoons of crushed fresh leaves—in 1 cup of boiling water. Steep for about 10 minutes, strain out the herb, and enjoy a cup after meals.

CIDER RULES. To calm indigestion, I add 1 tablespoon of apple cider vinegar to an 8-ounce glass of water. I sip it slowly, and my symptoms soon fade away. ✉ George K., CA

GINGER TO THE RESCUE. You can stop indigestion in its tracks with a soothing ginger tea. Steep a piece of ginger in boiling water for five minutes. Remove the ginger and add 1 teaspoon of honey. Then relax while sipping the brew slowly. It'll tame your tumbling tummy before you know it. ✉ Chris H., NJ

I CAN'T BELIEVE I ATE ... The whole thing! Next time you over-stuff yourself at dinner, here's how to put an end to the misery. Just lie down on your left side for a few minutes. Resting in this position helps increase blood flow to your stomach and move the digestion process along. ✉ Tom L., MI

A SOOTHING BREW. Here's a tummy-soothing recipe I've used for years: Steep avocado leaves in a cup of boiling water for 10 to 15 minutes, then strain out the leaves and add a little drizzle of honey. Sip it slowly to settle your upset stomach. ✉ Lillian B., MO

PAUSE WITH PARSLEY. Nothing puts a damper on a good meal like a bout of indigestion. But you can nip your discomfort in the bud by simply eating a few sprigs of fresh parsley. If you don't have any of the fresh herb on hand, stir ¼ teaspoon of dried parsley into a glass of warm water and drink up. Your tummy will feel better in no time at all. ✉ Kelly R., TN

SLEEP EASY. Heartburn used to keep me up at night, until I discovered that I was more comfortable in a semi-seated position. But I didn't want to spend the night sleeping in a chair, so I raised the head of my bed with a few bricks so it's several inches off the floor. Aaahhh! Sweet sleep relief. ✉ Margaret K., PA

MUNCH THE ACHE AWAY. Don't put up with a nagging stomachache. Just reach for a non-diet pop, or munch on a handful of soda crackers—a carbohydrate-packed snack will help settle your stomach in a snap. ✉ Mike M., NJ

END THE MISERY. Dealing with diarrhea? Then buy empty gelatin capsules at your local health-food store and fill them with ground nutmeg. Take two filled capsules at the first sign of trouble to put an end to your runs. ✉ Rebecca M., CO

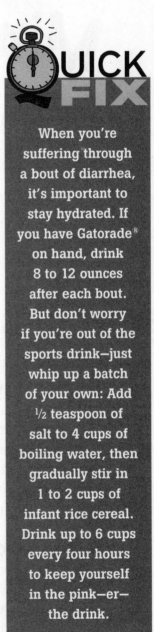

QUICK FIX

When you're suffering through a bout of diarrhea, it's important to stay hydrated. If you have Gatorade® on hand, drink 8 to 12 ounces after each bout. But don't worry if you're out of the sports drink—just whip up a batch of your own: Add ½ teaspoon of salt to 4 cups of boiling water, then gradually stir in 1 to 2 cups of infant rice cereal. Drink up to 6 cups every four hours to keep yourself in the pink—er—the drink.

CHAPTER
8

Minor Complaints

Bad Breath

OUST ONION BREATH. Do you love onions, but hate the pungent breath they leave behind? Here's my simple solution: Chew a teaspoon of ground coffee straight from the can after indulging. Don't worry—you don't have to swallow the grounds. After chewing for a few minutes, spit the coffee out and swish your mouth out with a cold-water rinse. This quick trick will give the boot to onion breath in no time flat. ✉ Sheila T., MS

CLOVES CONQUER ALL. Banish bad breath by chewing on a whole clove (no, not of garlic—the spice!). Crush it with your teeth a little, and roll it around your tongue, then spit it out. Cloves are aromatic and halt halitosis, and they're also good little bacteria fighters. Not a bad combo! ✉ Michele L., LA

LEMON-AID. When my breath smells so bad that even my dog can't stand to be near me, I squeeze the juice of half a lemon into ½ cup of water, swish, and spit. Lemons boost the flow of saliva, which helps flush out whatever's causing the foul odor in the first place. ✉ Jan R., IA

CRUNCH AND FLUSH. Every time you bite into celery, you get a little burst of water that helps flush food particles and odor-causing bacteria from your mouth. So reach for a stalk after eating oniony, garlicky, or spicy meals, and you won't have to worry about bad breath! ✉ Josh C., NE

RAKE YOUR TONGUE. Most bad breath comes from the area in the back of your mouth, where bacteria breed plaque on your tongue. So whenever I brush, I reach as far back as I can with my toothbrush and brush the back of my tongue. When you try this, start slowly so you don't gag. You can buy plastic tongue scrapers at the drugstore, but why waste the money? ✉ Amanda L., RI

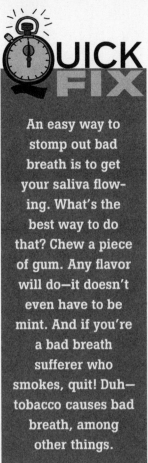

QUICK FIX

An easy way to stomp out bad breath is to get your saliva flowing. What's the best way to do that? Chew a piece of gum. Any flavor will do—it doesn't even have to be mint. And if you're a bad breath sufferer who smokes, quit! Duh—tobacco causes bad breath, among other things.

Blisters

STOP BLISTER PAIN. To relieve the pressure of a blister or boil that needed to be drained, my mom would grate 2 tablespoons of Fels-Naptha® soap and mix it with 1 tablespoon of white sugar to form a paste. Then she'd put it on a large adhesive bandage and place it over the blister. As I recall, the pain and pressure would lessen in just a few minutes. ✉ Vicki B., OH

TAKE 5

Here are five not-so-common healthful uses for petroleum jelly:

1. Ease pierced earrings into your lobes by putting a little petroleum jelly on the posts before you insert them.

2. Shape and tame wayward eyebrows by smoothing the hairs with a dab of petroleum jelly.

3. Soothe red, chapped, or windburned skin by liberally spreading petroleum jelly over the affected areas every hour or so until the burn subsides.

4. Keep suds from running into your baby's eyes at bath time by rubbing a layer of petroleum jelly across the infant's eyebrows.

5. Calm psoriasis with layer after layer of petroleum jelly rubbed into the dry, scaly areas of your skin.

FIGHT THE FRICTION. Keep your feet from blistering by smoothing a thin film of petroleum jelly over them before you put on your socks and shoes. Then be sure to lace up your shoes nice and tight so your feet are held firmly in place. Otherwise, they'll rub around and against the insides of your shoes, creating blisters. ✉ Terri M., PA

KEEP 'EM DRY. My feet get sweaty, so I used to get a lot of blisters. Now I deal with moist feet by dusting some cornstarch between my toes, and sprinkling a bit of cornstarch into my socks before pulling them on. ✉ Sara G., KY

HERBAL HELPERS. When you're worried that a blister may get infected, reach for rosemary and thyme. These powerful bacteria fighters can help prevent infection. Simply add a tablespoon of each herb to a cup of hot water and steep for about 10 minutes. Let the liquid cool to room temperature, pour some on a cloth, and hold it against your blister for about 20 minutes. Repeat the treatment once or twice a day until the blister is gone. ✉ Betsy R., TX

Q: I know you're not supposed to pop blisters, but what should I do if it pops on its own?

A: Wash the area with soapy water, then spread some antibiotic ointment on a piece of clean gauze. Cover the blister with the gauze, and hold it in place with first-aid tape. And you're right: It's never a good idea to pop blisters, no matter how tempting it may be.

Body and Foot Odor

NO SWEAT. Skip the fancy store-bought deodorant; just dab a little petroleum jelly on your armpits. I know it sounds odd, but I've been doing this for years and it works as well as the fancy brands do for me. It makes a great antiperspirant, and my clothes remain sweat-free and smell fresh all day long. Just be sure to use only a small amount of the jelly and rub it into your skin thoroughly so it doesn't stain your clothes. ✉ **Rick V., WV**

SAGE ADVICE. If you have a tendency to sweat a great deal, put a damper on perspiration by drinking tea made from dried sage. Simmer 4 tablespoons of the herb in 1 quart of water for 15 minutes, strain out the solids, let the liquid cool, and then sip away. The effects won't kick in for a few hours, but then you'll be less sweaty for a good two or three days afterward. *Note:* Stay away from sage if you are pregnant or nursing. ✉ **Chris F., IL**

STOP THE STINK. When you sweat, are you noticeably more, er, fragrant? If you're concerned that your sweat comes with a serious stink, then munch on some sprigs of fresh parsley. It's a natural odor eater! ✉ **Sonya C., OH**

HELPING HANDS. Whenever I have to go to an event where I'll be shaking a lot of hands, I never worry that I'll have sweaty palms. That's because before I leave the house, I coat my palms with geranium oil. It closes up my pores and stops the sweat. ✉ **Joel M., KY**

JIGGLE AWAY ODOR. Want to go barefoot, but you're afraid your feet are too stinky? I've got the perfect solution: Soak them in lemon or lime JELL-O®. Mix a box of JELL-O with 2 cups of hot water,

Grandma Putt's Wisdom

We've all had occasions when, no matter how frequently or ferociously we've scrubbed, we still smelled a little sour, and that odor has turned our favorite sweaters into instant rags. The culprits are bacteria that thrive on skin. When they devour the fatty sweat produced by the apocrine glands in your underarms, scalp, and genitals, the result is a very pungent smell.

Nobody in Grandma's house had a body odor problem, but maybe it's because we drank so much vegetable juice. Juices from chlorophyll-rich foods like kale, chard, and other dark green vegetables can restore the pH balance of blood that's too acidic—and therefore too friendly to bad bacteria—as a result of a diet heavy on proteins.

Grandma also knew that the box of baking soda she used to keep her fridge moisture-free and sweet-smelling can do the same for feet and underarms. To freshen things up, simply pat some baking soda under your arms and on the soles of your feet at least twice daily.

SINK THE STINK ● Got stinky feet? Then give this treatment a try: Spray apple cider vinegar on your hardworking dogs to help stop the stench. And if you store the vinegar in the fridge between sprays, it'll make this smell-no-more treatment even more refreshing.

stirring until the gelatin dissolves. Add enough cold water to make a comfortably warm footbath, then soak your feet in the mixture until the JELL-O begins to set. Wash your feet with warm, soapy water, rinse, and dry thoroughly. You'll be good to go! ✉ Sonia K., IN

SPRINKLE THE STARCH. Cornstarch does a fantastic job of absorbing extra moisture from your feet and shoes. And since athlete's foot thrives in places that are moist, cornstarch can help prevent it, too. Just sprinkle some into your shoes and over your clean feet before you put your socks on. *Note:* If you already have athlete's foot, don't use cornstarch to cure it—it can actually set you up for a worse infection. ✉ Stacy R., PA

COCONUT SOAK. At the end of a long day, my feet yearn for a treat, so I soak my tired tootsies in a footbath made with a can of coconut milk, lemon slices, and warm water. Try it—your feet will thank you! ✉ Gwyn P., NC

TEA FOR TOES. I tame my foot odor by soaking my stinkers in a mixture of 1 cup of green tea, 1/2 cup of vinegar, and 2 cups of warm water. It works wonders for me! ✉ Elizabeth G., AL

TEA FOR TOES, TAKE 2. Brew a few quarts of extra-strong black tea to combat foot odor. Let it cool a bit, then soak your feet in the brew for about 10 minutes. The tannins in the tea will dry out your feet and keep 'em dry long after you finish your soak—and dry feet are much less likely to stink. ✉ Dianne R., MI

Burns

COOL YOUR TIPS. Here's a way to quickly cool down a fingertip burn. Immediately touch the finger to the back of your earlobe, and hold it there for four or five minutes. I know it sounds crazy, but you'll be a believer once the burn is quickly extinguished. ✉ Danielle F., NJ

ONION, ANYONE? If you've ever accidentally brushed up against a piping hot grill and singed your finger, you know how painful that little burn can be. Here's my favorite fix: Mash up a raw onion, and apply it directly to the burn. It'll not only cool the area, but also act as an antiseptic and help ease the pain. ✉ Kathy J., MI

BE A SEED EATER. Pumpkin seeds are loaded with the healing power of zinc, so they make a great snack to munch on while you're recovering from a minor burn. I always keep a bag on hand just because the seeds are yummy, and I can reach for them if I need to jump-start the burn-recovery process. ✉ Stephanie B., MA

QUICK FIX

Raw potatoes can offer quick relief for minor burns. Slice 'em thin and lay them directly on the hot spot. Your skin will say "aaahhh."

SWEET RELIEF. Burn your tongue? Then put sugar on it! It'll relieve the pain of the burn and help your taste buds bounce back quickly, too. Simply put a spoonful of sugar on the burnt spot, close your mouth, and let the sugar dissolve. *Note:* Do **not** use sugar on a skin burn; this treatment is reserved for your tongue only. ✉ Mary B., WI

MAKE MINE MILK. The next time you have a minor burn, reach for whole or 2 percent milk. Cold milk cools the burn better than cold water because the fat in the milk coats the area, then sticks around to soothe the pain. ✉ Ralph K., OR

Cold and Canker Sores

LEARN TO LIKE LICORICE. When you have a cold sore, chew on a black licorice whip. Just be sure it's made from real licorice—look for "licorice mass" as the main ingredient, not anise. As an alternative, you can buy some licorice powder and sprinkle it on the sore, or mix up a cream with a pinch of licorice power and a dab of vegetable shortening, then apply it to the sore. Licorice does the trick because it contains glycyrrhetinic acid, which has been shown to kill the cold sore virus. ✉ Maddy A., DE

STOP THE SUN. I have a tendency to get cold sores after being out in the sun, but I find that I can avoid them altogether by using sunscreen. I apply sunscreen with an SPF of 15 or higher that has been made especially for the lips. And, ladies, my wife tells me that you can also find lipsticks that contain sunscreen. ✉ Ryan P., OH

KEEP IT COVERED. You can speed the healing process and help prevent a cold sore from becoming infected by covering it with petroleum jelly. Also try a local anesthetic ointment that contains benzocaine to help numb the pain. ✉ Andrew Q., NJ

CHUCK THE BRUSH. Believe it or not, your toothbrush can harbor the virus that causes cold sores. So whenever I get a blister, I throw away my toothbrush and get a new one, and after the attack has cleared up, I replace the brush again. Now I don't get as many cold sores. ✉ Monica V., WA

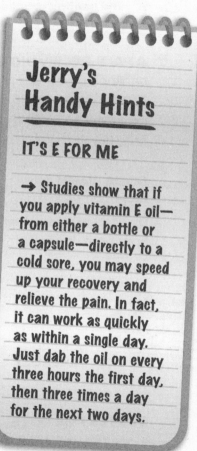

Jerry's Handy Hints

IT'S E FOR ME

→ Studies show that if you apply vitamin E oil—from either a bottle or a capsule—directly to a cold sore, you may speed up your recovery and relieve the pain. In fact, it can work as quickly as within a single day. Just dab the oil on every three hours the first day, then three times a day for the next two days.

ANOTHER GREAT IDEA!

PASS THE PEROXIDE

Hydrogen peroxide is an effective treatment for canker sores. The treatment is simple: Mix 1 part hydrogen peroxide with 1 part water, then use a cotton swab to dab the solution directly onto the canker sores. *Do not swallow the solution.* **Hydrogen peroxide is an antiseptic that will help reduce the amount of bacteria in your mouth and speed up the healing process.**

A PAIN-RELIEVING BREW. When you're suffering from a painful canker sore, brew a mug of your favorite tea, then let it cool down. Remove the tea bag, squeeze it, and tuck it into your mouth to cover the sore. Let it sit in there for five minutes or so and it will help numb the pain. ✉ Eric G., WA

SODA WASH. Here's what I do to keep canker sores at bay, or to help heal an existing one: I add 1 to 2 teaspoons of baking soda to a quart of warm water, swish the mixture around in my mouth, and spit it out. It works for me! ✉ Jack R., OH

Cuts

CLOVES FOR CUTS. To heal your cuts faster and suffer less pain along the way, try the clove treatment. Just crush whole cloves into a powder, then sprinkle the particles directly onto your wound and cover the whole thing with a bandage. Because cloves are a cleansing agent and a painkiller, they fight infection and help your skin heal more quickly. ✉ Elizabeth K., OH

REACH FOR ROSEMARY. You can help prevent cuts from getting infected by washing them with rosemary tea. It's a mild antiseptic that makes wounds dry out quickly, plus it helps hasten the healing process. ✉ Madeleine B., PA

HEAL WITH HONEY. I use raw honey to heal cuts. Raw honey isn't heated to kill the yeast and natural enzymes, and it contains natural antibiotics. You can't buy it in a traditional grocery store, but you may find it in a health-food store, or else contact a local beekeeper

TAKE 5

Here are five not-so-common healthful uses for honey:

1 Halt a hangover by eating a teaspoon or so of honey on a cracker or piece of toast before or after imbibing.

2 Ease allergy symptoms by eating crackers with locally made honey before allergy season hits; you'll ingest small parts of the plants, grasses, and trees that may trigger symptoms, and that'll help you build up resistance and lessen the severity of your allergies when the season arrives.

3 Smooth your skin by applying a thin layer of honey to your face and leaving it in place for 20 minutes. Rinse it off first with cold water, then warm.

4 Calm a cough by drinking tea or juice with a teaspoon or two of honey stirred into it; it'll work like cough syrup to soothe a sore throat or mild laryngitis.

5 Clear up blackheads with a paste made of egg white, dry oatmeal, and honey. Apply it to your skin and wait 10 minutes, then rinse it away with warm water and pat dry.

to get it fresh from the source. To use it, simply clean the cut, apply a thin layer of raw honey, and cover the wound with a sterile gauze pad. Change the pad and clean the area every day or two until the cut has healed. ✉ Fred G., IL

PROTECT PAPER CUTS. If you've got a paper cut, apply instant-bond glue to help the healing. It'll seal the wound and prevent bacteria from getting to the cut. Just be careful not to touch anything until the glue dries! ✉ Barbara S., GA

BALM BASICS. I keep a tube of unscented ChapStick® in my desk drawer so I can reach for it whenever I get a paper cut. I just smear the lip balm right on the cut—it eases the pain and helps my finger heal fast. ✉ Chelsea R., OH

Diaper Rash and Prickly Heat

END THE RASH. To treat persistent diaper rash, reach for the aloe vera. You don't need to go buy the juice or gel if, like many folks, you're already growing an aloe vera plant at home. Just break off a leaf or two and apply the syrupy juice directly to the inflamed area. It'll provide soothing relief in no time at all. If you don't have an aloe vera plant and are using a store-bought preparation, be sure it lists aloe vera as its main ingredient. ✉ Liz P., KY

FORM A BARRIER. One way I help my baby's diaper rash heal quickly is by creating a barrier to the moisture that causes the rash in the first place. After gently cleansing the area, I smear a light coating of petroleum jelly or vegetable shortening on the affected skin, which helps keep the moisture at bay. It protects her skin and speeds up the healing process. ✉ Rachel B., CT

SUPER-DUPER SOLUTIONS

RASH RELIEF ● You can beat diaper rash, prickly heat, and other rashes with this simple kitchen remedy: Add 1 teaspoon of apple cider vinegar to 1 cup of water, then sponge the mixture onto any itchy, rashy skin areas. By balancing the pH of your skin, the vinegar soothes the rash, so it will quickly fade away.

DON'T COUNT ON CORNSTARCH. Here's one important lesson I've learned about treating diaper rash: Never use cornstarch. The rash may be the result of a yeast infection, and if that's the case, cornstarch will only make it worse. Instead, gently wipe your baby's bottom with a solution of 4 tablespoons baking soda per quart of warm water. ✉ Nancy K., MI

AAAHHH, OATS. An almost-instant way to treat a dry, itchy rash like prickly heat is to take an oatmeal bath. You can buy colloidal oatmeal at any drugstore and follow the package directions. Or fill an old stocking or sock with plain dry oatmeal, fasten the open end to your faucet with a rubber band, and let the water flow through the oatmeal as it fills the tub. Either way, you'll get fast relief from the itch. ✉ Marie S., TX

Hemorrhoids

POTATO PATTIES. Here's how I treat hemorrhoids: I grate a medium potato and mix it well with 2 to 3 teaspoons of slippery elm powder (available at most health-food stores). Then I form the mixture into a small patty and place it on the hemorrhoids for 10 to 15 minutes, up to three times a day. It really works! ✉ Darcy J., BC

A DAILY DRINK. To help prevent hemorrhoids, stir ¼ teaspoon of ground nutmeg into a glass of warm water and add a squeeze of fresh lemon juice to it. Drink this mixture twice a day to stay regular and keep hemorrhoids at bay. ✉ Jerry B., FL

SIP TO SOOTHE. I drink a cocktail that's made with equal amounts of cranberry juice and pomegranate juice between meals. It seems to help stop the bleeding that's so often a side effect of my hemorrhoids. ✉ Julie C., IL

Ask Jerry

Q: I get bouts of hemorrhoids so often that I feel like I always have them. Have you got any advice?

A: You bet I do! Keep hemorrhoids away by drinking eight glasses of water a day (herbal tea is okay, too) and cutting back on binding foods like dairy products and meat. To help with the itch, soak a gauze bandage in apple cider vinegar, and place it on the site overnight. Wearing tight underwear or a sanitary pad will keep the gauze in place.

THE FIBER FIX. If you suffer from hemorrhoids regularly, consider changing your diet. Eating more fiber-filled foods like whole grains, crunchy veggies, and oranges will help soften your stools and reduce straining, which in turn can end the recurrence of painful hemorrhoids. ✉ Sylvia B., MD

ANOTHER GREAT IDEA!

THEY'RE BERRY GOOD

Blueberries, blackberries, and cherries are all rich in compounds that strengthen the walls of veins, including those in the anal area. So if you're prone to hemorrhoids, gobble up as many of these tiny, terrific fruits as you can every day.

COOL THE BURN. Aloe is quick to cool the burning irritation of inflamed hemorrhoids, so I just snip a leaf off my plant, slit it open, and apply the gel directly to the area. Commercial aloe gel that says "100% aloe gel" on the label will do the trick, too. ✉ Tim L., TN

Hiccups

THE SWEET SOUND OF SILENCE. There's nothing more annoying than an endless case of the hic—!—hiccups! For a quick, homespun remedy, mix a tablespoon of butter or margarine with a tablespoon of sugar. Put a spoonful of the mixture in your mouth, and let the sweet concoction slowly melt down your throat. ✉ Karen S., OH

FIND A FRIEND. Here's a hiccup remedy to try if you have a friend nearby to help. Stand against a wall with your arms stretched out to the sides. Then have your friend hold a glass of water up to your mouth while you drink quickly. When you're finished, you may be a little wet, but the hiccups will be gone! ✉ **Sam S., MI**

SOUR POWER. When hiccups are driving me crazy, I rely on this remarkable remedy: I cut a small slice of lemon and put it under my tongue. I suck it once and hold the juice in my mouth for 10 seconds. Then, when I swallow the lemon juice, my hiccups are history. ✉ **Shirley R., MI**

SLOW, BUT SURE. I always stop a case of the hiccups right in its tracks with this trick: I mix 1 teaspoon of apple cider vinegar in a glass of warm water. Then I sip it *very* slowly. Voilà! No more hiccups! ✉ **Blair S., NM**

TAKE 5

Five sure cures for a case of the hiccups are:

1 Slowly chew a piece of dry or charred toast.

2 Bite into a lemon wedge that's been generously sprinkled with bitters.

3 Swallow a teaspoon of granulated sugar.

4 Rub an ice cube on the side of your neck.

5 Inhale some black pepper up your nose to make yourself sneeze.

Insect Bites and Stings

BE A SWEETIE. Here's a sweet way to keep biting bugs at bay: Using a cotton ball, dab some vanilla extract behind your ears, on your pulse points, and around your hairline. It'll repel most biting insects, and you'll smell sweet as can be! ✉ **Wynn W., CO**

KEEP MOSQUITOES MOVIN' ALONG. I've found a sure cure to keep mosquitoes from biting. If you drink pickle juice as I do, the mosquitoes will go elsewhere for a snack! ✉ Marie D., VA

SUDS UP. Before heading off into the great outdoors, I take a few minutes to suds myself up with some good old-fashioned Fels-Naptha® soap, and I leave it on my skin. The mosquitoes steer clear of me all day long. ✉ Darlene A., IL

SOAP FOR BITES. You can stop the itch of mosquito bites fast with soap. Just rub a wet bar of soap right on the bite, and the itch will ease up—and so will the swelling. ✉ William V., IL

DITCH THE ITCH. When you've been bitten by a mosquito, pour some vinegar onto a cotton ball and apply it directly to the bite. It'll put a stop to the itch and reduce the swelling, pronto. ✉ Sandi G., WA

DON'T SWEAT IT. I use deodorant to tame itchy bug bites. I just dab a little antiperspirant right on the bites and I get relief, lickety-split. ✉ Eronda H., AL

I'LL DRINK TO THAT! Mosquito bites will disappear in no time if you rub the spot with a few drops of beer. Treat the bite as soon as the pesky little so-and-so flies away, and your bites will disappear as though they never even happened. ✉ Lisa M., TX

Jerry's Handy Hints

DON'T GET THE BLUES

→ Who knows why, but mosquitoes seem to love the color blue. So do yourself a favor if you're headed for an evening outdoors, and wear anything but blue!

RUB IT ON. If mosquitoes always seem to find you attractive, here's one thing you should never be without—lip balm. I keep a tube of it handy so I can rub it on any fresh mosquito bites. The balm quickly stops the itch. ✉ Brenda V., IN

Grandma Putt's Wisdom

My Grandma Putt knew that one sure way to soothe a bite or sting was to make a poultice of sage and vinegar. She'd run a rolling pin over a handful of freshly picked sage leaves to bruise them. Then she'd put the leaves in a pan, cover them with apple cider vinegar, and simmer the mixture on low until they were softened up. After removing the leaves, she'd wrap them in a washcloth and place them on stings and bumps. It worked like a charm!

PUT OUT THE FIRE. To quell the pain, itching, and swelling from fire ant bites, remove a peel from a banana and lay it, inner side down, directly on your affected skin for 20 minutes or so. Wash the area and apply a new peel if the symptoms persist. ✉ Ron M., AZ

WIN THE BATTLE WITH BLEACH. I use ordinary household bleach to destroy fire ant hills without killing my grass (just carefully pour the bleach directly onto and into each hill). And if the little devils happen to bite you while you're doing the deed, you can keep the fiery sting cooled by swabbing your bitten skin with the same bleach soaked into a cotton ball. ✉ Chief S., GA

ANOTHER GREAT IDEA!

FIZZ PAIN AWAY

Stung by a bee? Grab an Alka-Seltzer® tablet, moisten it, and apply it to the site of the sting. The fizz will deliver soothing baking soda right to the heart of the pain. Oh, what a relief it is!

TENDER TREATMENT. To knock out the sting from fire ants, bees, wasps, and other biting and stinging insects, dampen the bite with water, then sprinkle a little meat tenderizer on it—just enough to make a paste. In the time it takes the paste to dry, the sting will be gone! ✉ Ernestine J., AL

A LITTLE DAB'LL DO IT. The next time you're stung by a bee, put a little household ammonia on a cotton ball, and dab it directly on the stung area. Aaahhh—instant relief! ✉ Jessie S., WV

SODA SOOTHER. A quick way to stop the zing of bee stings is to apply a paste made of baking soda and water directly to the achin' area. It'll soothe the painful sting in a snap. ✉ Kimberly C., WI

NO SMOKING ALLOWED. Years ago, folks would put wet tobacco leaves on the site of a bee sting as a spot-on soother. To try this updated cure, dampen the end of a cigarette and gently rub its tobacco on the stung area. ✉ Mary D., TN

ONIONS ARE OKAY. Anytime I get a wasp or hornet sting, I put a cut onion directly on the site. Believe me, it takes the edge off the sting and keeps the swelling to a minimum. ✉ Pete B., ID

QUICK FIX

Freeze a painful insect bite or sting right in its tracks. Just wrap some ice cubes in a washcloth or small towel to make a cold pack, then hold it against the affected area for about 20 minutes. Remove the pack, wait another 20 minutes, then reapply, alternating 20 minutes on and 20 minutes off, until the pain is gone.

SCRAPE A STING. If a bee has left its stinger in you, don't pull it out—you'll squeeze the tiny bulb that contains the venom, and send even more irritating poison into your skin. Instead, scrape the stinger out using the edge of a credit card or your clean fingernail, then wash the area gently with soap and water. ✉ Thomas P., VT

REAL RELIEF. Hemorrhoid cream is good for more than just shrinking hemorrhoids. I use it to soothe the itch, ouch, and swelling from bee stings and chigger bites. Just apply a dab of the cream right to the sore spot and you'll feel soothing relief. ✉ Steven K., FL

QUICK BALM. The itching and swelling from a chigger bite seems to take weeks to go away. But you can end the agony sooner by smoothing Bag Balm® onto the bite site. Trust me, you'll feel better almost instantly! ✉ Donna F., NE

Jerry's Handy Hints

KEEP YOUR SHOES ON

→ Bees often hover just above the ground, gathering pollen from clover and ground flowers. So if you don't want to get stung, don't go barefoot across your lawn.

TA-TA, TICK. To remove a tick that's just bitten you, put a blob of petroleum jelly on it and leave it alone. After about 30 minutes, the tick will loosen its grip, and you'll be able to wipe the little bugger right off or grab it cleanly with a pair of tweezers. ✉ Alice D., FL

UNSTICK THE TICK. If you've discovered a tick embedded in your skin, and it's been there for less than 24 hours, cover it with two drops of clear nail polish. The tick will release its grip and back out so that you can easily wipe it off your skin. ✉ Sarah M., WA

Poison Ivy

THE RIGHT RUB. If you know you've been exposed to poison ivy, rub the affected areas with deodorant, even before a rash breaks out. The swipes will short-circuit the itch right away. Needless to say (but I'll say it anyway), don't use this particular stick of deodorant on your underarms after using it on your poison ivy–covered skin! ✉ Stan M., TX

AN A-PEELING SOLUTION. I lay strips of fresh banana peel, inner side down, across any rash that's been caused by poison ivy. The chemicals in the peel stop the itching, and the rash starts to dry and heal right away. ✉ Patricia W., MO

THE ANSWER IS ACIDIC. What's the best way to soothe poison ivy itch? V-I-N-E-G-A-R! Gently wipe a soft cloth you've soaked in apple cider vinegar across the rash. It'll cool the irritation and dull the itch. ✉ Mary S., OR

TAKE 5

Here are five more not-so-common healthful uses for vinegar:

1 Soothe a sore throat with a gargle made from 2 tablespoons of apple cider vinegar in a glass of warm water.

2 Soak away stinky feet in a solution of 1 part warm water and 1 part vinegar for 10 minutes twice a day for at least three weeks.

3 Baby a bruise by soaking a cotton ball in vinegar and applying it directly to the bruise for one hour to reduce discoloration and speed up healing.

4 Prevent indigestion by drinking a glass of warm water mixed with 2 teaspoons of vinegar before each meal.

5 Stop hiccups by placing a vinegar-saturated lump of sugar in your mouth.

Sunburn

TURN DOWN THE HEAT. You spent an hour—or two—too long in the sun, and now you're paying for it with a throbbing sunburn. What to do? Soothe it with vinegar! If you've only burned a small area, like your face or neck, soak a washcloth in white vinegar, and lay the cloth across the burn. Leave it alone for 10 minutes, then remove it and let your skin air-dry. For larger burns, fill a handheld sprayer bottle with white vinegar and spray the affected areas. ✉ Gina F., LA

COOL WITH CREAM. Stop your sunburn pain in a snap with shaving cream. Foam a glob into the palm of your hand, and apply it thickly wherever you are burned. Leave it on until it dries, and then rinse off the residue with cool water. ✉ Teri C., NC

I'LL TAKE TEA. I don't know why this works, but when I need to soothe sunburn pain, I soak in a bath filled with warm water and the contents of a large container of iced tea mix. After my soak, I rinse off under the shower with lukewarm water so there's no sticky stuff left on my skin. ✉ Monica O., WI

Jerry's Handy Hints

BACK TO THE BEACH

→ Worried about who's got your back when you're at the beach solo? Don't let yourself suffer with a nasty sunburn—rig up your very own sunscreen applicator instead. Just wrap a soft cotton rag or T-shirt around the end of a back scratcher or ruler and secure it with a rubber band. Then squeeze a generous dollop of SPF 15 or higher sunscreen on the rag, and rub the lotion onto all of your hard-to-reach spots. Relax, and enjoy your time in the sun!

MILK SMOOTHIE. If your sunburn is starting to blister, cool the pain with a compress that's made with a soft cloth dipped in buttermilk. Apply the compress to the blistered area for 20 minutes, repeating every three hours as needed. Oh, and next time? Don't forget your sunscreen! ✉ Cheryl C., IA

Toenail Fungus

A SLOW AND STEADY CURE. If your toenails are thick, lifted, or yellowed, dampen a cotton ball with antiseptic mouthwash (like Listerine®), and wipe it over the nails twice a day. Toenails take a long time to grow, so be patient. Just keep using the mouthwash treatment and eventually, the ugly, fungus-y spots on your nails will grow out. ✉ Norma Jean R., MO

RUB OUT FUNGUS. Rub your toenails with a dollop of Vicks® VapoRub® if you suspect they're infected by fungus. Keep applying the rub until your nails become clear and healthy. ✉ Eileen M., IL

TREAT TOES WITH E. Here's how I deal with toenail fungus: I swab some vitamin E oil under and around each and every one of my toenails to knock out the funk. I use a cotton swab to make sure the oil gets to the hard-to-reach spots, repeating the treatment daily until my nails heal. ✉ Helen C., ON

TRY TEA TREE OIL. If you paint your toenails three times a day with tea tree oil, your toenail fungus will clear up in no time at all. Keep the nails short and unpolished and go barefoot as often as you can to increase their exposure to air. Before you know it, the fungus won't be among us anymore! ✉ Betsy D., WI

GO FOR A SOAK. I treat my feet to a weekly soak to soothe them and keep toenail fungus at bay. I fill a small footbath with 1 inch of cornmeal and 1 inch of warm water and let it stand for 30 minutes. Then I soak my feet in the bath for an hour. It's relaxing and keeps my feet nice and soft and fungus-free. ✉ John B., MO

Warts

BELIEVE IN BASIL. Basil contains several antiviral compounds that can help make warts vanish. Just crush a few basil leaves, place them right on the wart, and cover the area with a bandage. Change the dressing every day, and the wart should be history within a week. ✉ Wendy P., IN

YES, WE HAVE BANANAS. You can remove painful plantar warts with banana peels. At bedtime, tape a piece of banana peel, inner side down, over the wart. Cover the peel with a bandage or a tight sock and leave it on overnight. Repeat the process each night until the wart is gone; it usually doesn't take me any more than two or three treatments. ✉ Peter L., OH

WATCH WARTS DISAPPEAR. You can help eliminate warts by rubbing them with half an onion that's been dipped in salt. Use this treatment twice a day until the warts are all gone. ✉ **Christina A., GA**

OIL 'EM AWAY. Use castor oil to get rid of unsightly and bothersome warts on your hands. Simply rub it on once a day, just as you would hand cream. Your warts will vanish in no time. ✉ **Gina D., CA**

TAKE 5

Here are five more not-so-common healthful uses for castor oil:

1 Move things along when you're constipated by soaking a small towel in castor oil, draping it over your abdomen, then covering the towel with plastic wrap and a heating pad set on low for about 20 minutes.

2 Fade liver spots by dabbing castor oil directly on the spots twice a day for several weeks.

3 Treat burns, sunburns, rashes, corns, and calluses by rubbing castor oil on the area twice a day for several days.

4 Soothe and smooth dry hands by mixing 1 teaspoon of castor oil with 1 drop of lemon or peppermint oil, massaging it into your skin before bed, and then wearing cotton gloves while you sleep.

5 Ease bursitis pain by smearing castor oil over the sore area, putting plastic wrap on top of the oil, and covering the whole thing with a heating pad set on low.

America's Best
Practical Problem Solvers

CHAPTER **9**

Lookin' Good

The Eyes Have It

SOOTHE SWOLLEN EYES. Are your eyes swollen, tired, or irritated? If so, then give this soothing cure a try: Soak two cotton pads in ice-cold whole milk, and lie down in a comfortable place. Put one pad over each eye, and relax for 10 minutes or so. Remove the pads and rinse your eyes first with warm water, then with cool water. The fat content of the milk will soothe and moisturize the delicate skin around your eyes, and you'll look and feel refreshed. It always works for me! ✉ *Trish C., CT*

A NICE EYE-DEA. A quick way to ease eyestrain is with a mini massage. I find that I can do it anytime, anywhere—I simply look down, close my eyes, and gently massage the tops of my eyeballs through the lids in tiny circles. Aaahhh, relief! ✉ *Shelly R., PA*

SPUDS STOP CIRCLES. To fade dark circles and reduce bags under my eyes, I grate a raw potato and wrap the shavings in two pieces of cheesecloth (or you can use pieces cut from panty hose). Then I lie down, put one sack over each eye, and relax for about 15 minutes. I do this daily until the circles fade away. ✉ Ellie M., CA

COOL AS A CUCUMBER. Here's a simple way to lighten dark circles under your eyes—and soothe eyestrain at the same time: Just cut two slices from a cold cucumber, lie down in a comfortable place, and put one slice over each eye. Relax for 10 or 15 minutes, and you'll be bright-eyed and bushy-tailed when you get up. ✉ Esther L., TN

DRY NO MORE. An unfortunate side effect of dry-eye syndrome is waking up to crusty eyelids every morning. I clear away the gunky buildup by dampening a cotton ball with apple cider vinegar and gently wiping away the crust from my eyes. It works every time! ✉ Elizabeth H., OR

DON'T WIPE. Stop using your shirttail to clean your eyeglasses! A better method is to squirt a small amount of dishwashing liquid onto your fingers, and rub it onto the lenses under slowly running warm water. And instead of wiping (and streaking, or possibly scratching) the lenses, hold the glasses under the warm water so that it can flow over both sides of the lenses at the same time. The

Jerry's Handy Hints

EGGS-ZACTLY WHAT YOU NEED

→ No matter what's caused those baggy pouches under your eyes, I'll tell you eggs-zactly how to get rid of them—with egg whites! Simply separate two eggs and apply the whites to your under-eye area with a soft, clean brush (a new makeup, watercolor, or basting brush will do just fine). Let the egg whites dry while you relax in an easy chair, then rinse them off with cool water. Your skin will be smooth, tight, and bag-free!

soap will rinse off without leaving any residue behind, and your glasses will be clean. Then all you need to do is give them a gentle shake and let them air-dry—there's no need to wipe. ✉ Jay D., NH

FIGHT FOGGING. To keep your glasses or goggles from fogging up, smear a little toothpaste (one that doesn't contain baking soda) across the lenses, then wipe it off with a soft cloth. That's all there is to it! ✉ Tamara O., IN

NO-SLIP ZONE. You know how annoying it is to do battle with slipping, sliding glasses as your nose gets sweaty on a hot summer's day? Well, I have the perfect cure: Dab a bit of deodorant onto the bridge of your nose before you go outside in hot, humid weather, and your eyeglasses and sunglasses will stay in place no matter how steamy you get. ✉ Frances G., BC

EXERCISE YOUR EYES. Most of us don't go around staring wide-eyed all day long. Our eyes blink automatically; we don't even have to think about it. But what about those days when you're doing lots of reading or computer work, and you really start feeling the strain? The solution is to exercise those lids! Just blink quickly six times or so, then close your eyes for a few seconds. This little trick will keep your eyes lubricated and may even boost your vision. Repeat the blinking drill every 20 seconds for a minute or two, then read on! ✉ Tammi C., NY

ANOTHER GREAT IDEA!

CHEERS!

You don't need fancy lens cleaners to keep your eyeglasses clear. Just dampen a lint-free cloth with a little vodka or white vinegar, and use it to wipe your glasses clean just like that!

Touchable Tresses

SPICE AND SHINE. Here's a great way to strengthen your hair and add shine: Massage a few drops of mustard oil into clean, dry hair. Let it sit for 30 minutes, then shampoo and condition as usual. You'll feel and see an amazing difference! ✉ Azeema R., TX

SMOOTH WHIP. If you want shiny, smooth hair—and who doesn't?—deep-condition it once a week with ½ cup of Cool Whip®. Just work the whipped topping through your hair, and leave it on for 30 minutes. Then rinse it out thoroughly before shampooing as you normally would. ✉ Connie F., CA

MAYO FOR YOUR MANE. To moisturize my extra-dry hair, I condition it every month or so with mayonnaise. I slather it on damp hair, then wrap my head in plastic wrap and leave it on for 30 minutes. I rinse out the mayo, then shampoo my hair. The result? Nice, shiny hair that's oh-so-soft to the touch! ✉ Kathy T., MI

GOOD FOR WHAT ALES YOU. The next time you shampoo your hair, give it a finishing rinse with a can of beer. Just pour the beer right over your head, wait one minute, then rinse it out with cool water. The beer will make your hair really shine, so bottoms up! ✉ Carol B., IL

SODA SENSE. Add a little baking soda to your shampoo to remove greasy buildup and other gunk caused by hair products and hard water. Baking soda won't harm your hair, but it does have a lightening effect, so limit your use to every three days or so if you want to stick with your natural color. ✉ Candy S., IN

QUICK FIX

It's easy to add soft shine to your dull and lifeless hair. Just sprinkle a few drops of rosemary oil onto your hairbrush. Then every time you brush your hair, you'll perk it up and stimulate your scalp.

TAKE 5

Here are five natural ways to take care of your hair:

1 Puree three raw carrots in a blender, and apply the mush to your scalp for 15 minutes to absorb oil without overdrying.

2 Skin and mash a ripe avocado, apply it to your hair, and leave it on for 15 minutes to add moisture.

3 Peel and puree two cucumbers in a blender, massage the mix into your hair, and leave it on for 15 minutes to soothe your scalp and add shine to your hair.

4 Mix ½ cup of olive oil into ½ cup of boiling water, let it cool to warm, and apply the mixture to your hair. Cover your hair with a shower cap, and leave it on for 30 minutes so the treatment can deep-condition your hair.

5 Brew a cup of chamomile tea, let it cool, then use it as a rinse after you shampoo to add natural highlights to any color of hair.

GO FOR OATS. When I don't have time to wash my hair, I dry-shampoo it with oatmeal. All it takes is about a handful of oats. I simply work the dry cereal through my hair with my fingers, and then brush it out. The oats remove all the oil and leave my hair clean and shiny. ✉ Cynthia L., MO

EGG CONDITIONER. Here's a natural way to have healthier hair. Whisk two eggs in a bowl, and slather them onto your wet tresses. Wrap a warm, wet towel around your head, and leave it on for 20 minutes. Then rinse out the eggs, and shampoo thoroughly. The eggs will give you a smooth and shiny look, and repair any damaged hair. ✉ Carol N., OK

A HONEY OF AN IDEA. Honey is nature's perfect hair conditioner. Here's how I use it: I mix ½ cup of honey with ¼ cup of olive oil, and work a small amount at a time through my hair until my entire head is coated. I cover my hair with a shower cap and leave it on for 30 minutes. Then I shampoo, condition, and style my hair as usual. Try it—you'll love the results! ✉ Amanda M., SK

DETANGLING DOS AND DON'TS. There's no need to waste good money on expensive hair detanglers. Instead, reach into your kitchen's pantry for the olive oil. Just rub a few drops of the oil between your fingertips and work it through your hair, concentrating on the ends and avoiding the roots. You'll put a stop to tangles and get a nice salon shine for only pennies. ✉ Kathie B., OR

FIGHT THE FRIZZIES. To tame frizzy hair, give JELL-O® a try. Just dissolve 1 teaspoon of lemon JELL-O powdered mix in a small amount of water. Dip your comb into the liquid, and run it through your hair, section by section, rolling each section onto a roller as you go. After your hair dries, comb it out, and you'll have no more frizzies. ✉ Diane K., HI

READY, SET, CURL. Forget those pricey hair-setting solutions—make your own at home! Here's how: Mix 1 part sugar with 2 parts warm water, making enough to fill at least three-quarters of an old mayonnaise jar. Allow the sugar to dissolve, then dip your comb in

ANOTHER GREAT IDEA!

GEL WITH GELATIN

Before you spend another dime on hair gel, try this homemade alternative: Mix a box of unflavored gelatin with half as much water as the instructions specify, and use it as you would regular hair gel. You'll be glad you did!

the solution and run the comb through your hair before setting it with curlers. ✉ **Elaine C., SC**

HOME-STYLE HAIR SPRAY. I stopped buying hair spray years ago after trying this sun-kissed recipe: Squeeze the juice of one lemon or orange into a cup of water and mix well. Pour the mixture into a handheld sprayer bottle and spray it on your hair for a style-setting spray that's got a nice zesty twist. ✉ **Lori F., IL**

JAZZ IT UP WITH JELL-O. You can have fun with colors by temporarily dyeing your hair with JELL-O®. Mix the gelatin powder in a bowl with enough hair conditioner to make a mayonnaise-like consistency. Apply the mixture to your hair and cover it with plastic wrap or a shower cap. Leave it on for at least an hour. The color will last through 7 to 10 washings. If you want to get rid of it sooner, wash your hair with a whitening toothpaste. It may take a few toothpaste washings and rinses to get back to your natural color, but once you do, you can shampoo and condition as usual. ✉ **Nancy C., AZ**

Ask Jerry

Q: My hair is so oily. Even though I shampoo every morning, by dinnertime, I look like a greasy mess. Is there anything I can do?

A: You bet there is! The next time you shampoo, follow up with a rinse of vinegar or lemon juice. That'll tone down the oil and leave your hair nice and shiny. Just be careful—lemon juice and vinegar are both astringents, which means overuse will dry out your luscious locks. So don't use this treatment every day.

ERASE YOUR MISTAKE. The last time I dyed my hair, I really couldn't stand the new color. So I washed my hair with liquid laundry detergent, which helped strip a lot of the unwanted color out. I lathered it in as I would shampoo, rinsed it out, then followed up with my usual shampoo and conditioner. I had to do this a few days in a row before my normal color came back. ✉ Colleen R., AK

BE A THRIFTY BLONDE. To lighten your hair on the cheap, use hydrogen peroxide. Fill a handheld sprayer bottle halfway with 3% hydrogen peroxide, and top the bottle off with water. Spritz and comb the mixture through damp hair. Keep it in place for 10 to 15 minutes, then rinse it out thoroughly and condition your hair (peroxide dries it out). You may need to experiment with this treatment and repeat the process if you didn't get it light enough the first time. And be careful! If hydrogen peroxide is left on your hair for too long, it can damage your tresses. ✉ Larry M., CA

DOWN WITH DANDRUFF. Here's how I keep the dandruff flakes away: After lathering up with my usual shampoo, I rinse my hair with a solution of 1/2 cup of vinegar and 2 cups of warm water. It really helps clear things up. ✉ Jennifer L., MI

SWEET DANDRUFF SOLUTION. I use those pink packets of sugar substitute with my shampoo to get rid of dandruff. Just mix the two together in your hand, lather the concoction into your hair, then rinse and condition as usual. ✉ Carolyn F., UT

Jerry's Handy Hints

RED WINE'S A WINNER

➜ To tame blonde hair that's turned green from overexposure to chlorine, use a clean sponge to dab some red wine on the strands. The tannic acid in the wine will neutralize the pool chemicals, and you'll be back to your natural (?) shade of blonde in no time at all.

Grandma Putt's Wisdom

My teenage years included bouts with dandruff. But my Grandma Putt had a surefire cure—a lemon juice hair rinse. Try it yourself: Dilute the juice with enough water (say 2 ounces of juice to 1 quart of water) so you don't feel a burning sensation on your scalp. It'll leave your hair shiny and squeaky clean. Rinsing or dabbing this weak acid directly onto your scalp helps remove dandruff flakes, too.

MINTY FRESH ... HAIR? If you suffer from an itchy scalp as a result of eczema or dermatitis, you can get some relief with mouthwash. After you shampoo, use your fingertips to massage some antiseptic mouthwash into your scalp, then rinse thoroughly with clear water. It'll help put a stop to the itch and irritation just like that. It works for me! ✉ Karen M., OH

GET OUT, GUM. Got some icky, sticky gum in your hair? Don't reach for the scissors—save your hair by reaching for the peanut butter instead. Put a glob on the gum and work it into the mess with your fingers. After about 15 minutes, you should be able to pull out the gum; then wash it out with shampoo for oily hair and condition as you normally would. ✉ Nancy R., IN

FIGHT LICE WITH MAYO. No matter how clean you keep yourself and your hair, sometimes you just can't avoid head lice, especially if you spend a lot of time around school-age kids. Over-the-counter remedies for lice are extremely harsh and smelly, so why not try a natural remedy that works just as well? Grab a jar of mayonnaise and slather mayo by the handful over the entire scalp of the affected person, making sure you cover every strand of hair. Then cover the head with either a shower cap or plastic wrap, and let the treatment sit. After two hours, shampoo the mayo out in the shower, and follow that up with a vinegar rinse. Finish by going through the hair with a fine-toothed nit comb to remove dead nits or any live ones that survived the treatment. Then continue to comb through the hair with the nit comb every day, checking the roots until all of the nits are gone. ✉ **Brandi C., TN**

GROW HAIR WITH ONIONS. This trick sounds crazy, but it works for me. I finely dice half an onion, and add the pieces to my shampoo bottle. I put the cap back on, and let it sit for a week. Then I shampoo with my homemade mixture every other day to slow hair loss and promote regrowth. ✉ **Maribel H., CA**

TELL 'EM APART. When you buy the same brand of shampoo and conditioner, the bottles are often identical, which means it's easy to grab the wrong one when you're in the shower with water in your eyes. Here's what I do to tell them apart: I place a couple of rubber bands around the shampoo bottle. That way, I know which bottle I need by glancing at it quickly or simply feeling for the rubber bands. ✉ **Elaine S., DE**

CLEAN YOUR COMBS. Hair products and oils can build up on your combs and brushes. So get them super-clean by periodically dropping them into a sink filled with hot water and 2 tablespoons of ammonia. Let them soak for 10 minutes, then rinse them thoroughly, lay them on an absorbent towel, and allow them to air-dry. ✉ **Karen G., IN**

BAKING SODA BATH. Bubble away dirty buildup on your combs with good ol' baking soda. Just fill your sink with a few inches of hot water and pour in 1 cup of baking soda. Submerge the combs and let 'em soak for half an hour, wipe off the grime, and rinse them thoroughly. ✉ **Vince M., RI**

QUICK FIX

Don't panic when paint ends up in your hair—just pour some baby oil onto a cotton makeup-remover pad, wrap the pad around your painted locks, and wipe the paint right out. Repeat the treatment if needed, and then shampoo your hair to remove the slick residue the baby oil leaves behind.

Smooth Hands and Feet

OLIVE MASSAGE. Olive oil is a rich, natural moisturizer that can't be beat. So massage a drop of it into your fingernail cuticles once a week to soften them and the surrounding skin. It works just as well as those fancy store-bought cuticle moisturizers, at a fraction of the cost. ✉ **Nancy R., VA**

A BRIGHT IDEA. Here's a neat trick I learned from my mom: Use whitening toothpaste on a soft toothbrush to clean and brighten your fingernails. Scrub them daily with the paste, and you'll have great-looking, healthy nails. ✉ **Jane G., PA**

HARD AS NAILS. To harden soft, splitting nails, treat them with garlic slices. Just take one clove and slice it thinly. With your hand lying flat (palm down) on a table, lay a garlic slice on each nail and let the slivers sit for 5 to 10 minutes. Then repeat the process with your other hand. This garlic treatment also helps even out ridges as it strengthens the nails. ✉ **Nelsa V., CT**

QUICK-DRY YOUR POLISH. Need to dash before your fingernail polish has time to dry? Don't risk smearing and smudging—just

Grandma Putt's Wisdom

Soothe your sore, cracked cuticles and hangnails the way my Grandma Putt did—by rubbing castor oil into the skin around your nails. Follow this routine every night before going to bed, and in no time you'll see and *feel* an amazing difference.

spritz a little cooking spray on your nails. The spray will make the polish dry in no time flat. ✉ Suzanne O., FL

TAKE IT OFF. Instead of using cotton balls to remove your fingernail polish, use a piece of nylon from an old pair of panty hose. The fabric is soft on your nails, and because it's not absorbent, more remover will get on the nail where it belongs.
✉ Katherine M., OH

FOIL FUNGUS. I've got a surefire cure for fingernail fungus. I just put a capful of bleach in a tall glass of water, and soak my fingernails in the solution for about a minute every day. It usually takes only a few days until the fungus is gone. ✉ Annetta C., TX

ROUGH AROUND THE EDGES. Frigid winter temperatures can roughen up even the toughest hands. To moisturize them—and get rid of any rough spots—rub them with a tablespoon of mayonnaise that's got a teaspoon of sugar mixed in it. Wipe your hands dry with a paper towel, and make sure you wear gloves the next time you spend any time outside. ✉ Virginia V., NH

CIDER FOR LOVELY HANDS. To soothe my dry hands, I pour a splash of apple cider vinegar into my palms and rub them together as though I'm putting on lotion. Then I rinse off the vinegar, and my hands are oh-so-soft, just like that. ✉ Patti C., MO

Jerry's Handy Hints

SOAK AWAY THE STAIN

→ If you've been wearing dark nail polish for a long time and now want a more natural look, you may notice that your nails are discolored. You can erase the stain by soaking your nails for 15 minutes in ¼ cup of water with two denture-cleaning tablets dissolved in it. Then brush them gently with a nailbrush, rinse, and dry them completely before applying a lighter polish.

GARDENER'S FRIEND. Hands that have gotten grimy and rough in the garden can be restored with a mix of equal parts cooking oil and sugar. Simply rub the mixture on your hands, making sure to get it under your nails, too. Rinse with cool water, and your hands will be soft and free of rough spots—until the next weeding session, that is! ✉ Donna F., CA

GLUE BEGONE. Got stubborn, sticky glue stuck between your fingers? Here's a quick way to remove it: Simply rub salt between your fingers. Sprinkle a generous amount in the palm of your hand, then rub your hands back and forth against each other, working the salt into every nook and cranny. That should solve your sticky situation right quick. ✉ Maureen K., PA

ANOTHER GREAT IDEA!

GO AWAY, BROWN SPOTS!

Nothing can turn back the hands of time, but you *can* diminish the appearance of brown spots on your hands with this regimen: Apply vitamin E to the spots daily. Then at night, follow up by applying castor oil. The spots will begin to fade after a few weeks.

SPLINTER S.O.S. The next time you have a splinter, don't reach for the tweezers until you try this trick: Place a fatty bit of bacon over the splinter and hold it in place with an adhesive bandage. After a day or two, the bacon fat will draw the sliver to the skin's surface, where you can painlessly wipe it away. ✉ Sally B., IA

PEEL AWAY SPLINTERS. I've found the perfect way to remove splinters easily and painlessly. I simply paint a thin layer of all-purpose white glue over the sliver and let it dry. Then when I peel off the glue, the sliver comes right out! ✉ Brenda C., VA

MOVE IT WITH MARSHMALLOW. You can use marshmallow ointment to coax a stubborn splinter to the surface of your skin. Just dab some ointment (available at health-food stores) on the site, bandage it, and leave it alone for a few hours. When you remove the bandage, the splinter will have inched close enough to the surface so that you can easily pluck it out. ✉ Ron L., AL

EASY FOOT SMOOTHER. Here's a great two-for-one trick I discovered: Sprinkle a handful of baking soda on your shower stall floor or on the bottom of your bathtub before showering. When you get in, move your feet around and the soda will soften the rough, patchy skin on your heels and soles and, at the same time, it'll deep-clean the shower floor or tub bottom, too. Now that's what I call a smooth solution! ✉ Roberta G., CT

THE PLANE TRUTH. Do you have a microplane in your kitchen to finely grate hard cheese and zest lemons? Then you know it works like a charm on even the toughest ingredients. And believe it or not, it will also work wonders on the hard calluses on your heels! I picked up a second one to keep in my bathroom. I've been using it on my feet regularly, and now I have soft, smooth, callus-free feet, just like that. ✉ Christine A., WA

Ask Jerry

Q: Jerry, my heels are so cracked that they hurt! And sandal season is right around the corner. Can you help?

A: I sure can! Slather the cracked areas with petroleum jelly, then wrap your heel in plastic wrap. Pull on a sock so the jelly stays in place all day, and before you know it, your heels will be baby soft and smooth.

EASE THE OUCH. It's hard to believe such a little thing can cause so much pain, but ingrown toenails do just that. You can get relief by putting a slice of milk-soaked bread in a plastic storage bag, then placing the affected foot in the bag and pressing the bread around the swollen toe. Keep your foot in the bag for 30 minutes, and repeat as necessary. ✉ Christie S., VT

Grandma Putt's Wisdom

My Grandma Putt used pineapple to soften a callus. To try this, apply a piece of pineapple rind to the callus, cover it with an adhesive bandage, and keep it on overnight. In the morning, the callus will be soft and practically pain-free. Although Grandma didn't know why this worked, we do now—it's bromelain, an enzyme in the pineapple rind, that does the trick.

SUPER SALT SOAK. When I have an ingrown toenail, I use an Epsom salts soak to draw out the pain and fight infection. I fill a basin with warm water, add a cup of Epsom salts, and soak my foot for about 30 minutes. I repeat this treatment twice a day until the pain is gone and there's no longer any sign of swelling or infection. ✉ Tom L., MI

NO MORE CORNS. Here's an old-fashioned way to get rid of ugly corns on your feet. All you have to do is tape a moist, used tea bag to the spot for 30 minutes every day. Follow this procedure, and your corn will be gone in about two weeks. ✉ Mildred R., NY

RUB IT IN. Say good-bye to rough, cracked skin on your feet with this soothing solution: Combine 1 tablespoon of almond oil, 1 tablespoon of olive oil, and 1 teaspoon of wheat germ, and store the mixture in a bottle with a tight-fitting cap. Shake it well before using, then rub the softener generously into your clean, dry feet, paying particular attention to your heels and wherever else your feet are rough. After just a few days of this rich treatment, you'll see and feel the difference. ✉ **Karin P., VA**

FEEL THE HEAT. Are you one of those people whose feet quickly get cold outdoors? I am, and I found this great way to heat things up: I sprinkle a little cayenne pepper in my socks before I put on my shoes and head out the door. It's an easy way to keep my feet warm, even on the coldest winter day. ✉ **Wendy H., NC**

Luscious Lips

IT'S TEATIME. Before you spend time in the sun, you slather yourself with sunscreen to keep your skin from burning, but what about your lips? If you've neglected them, and now they're sore from sunburn, soothe them with tea. Simply wet a tea bag in cool water until it's soaked through, and hold it on your sunburned lips for 15 minutes, four times daily. And next time, apply a lip balm that's got sunscreen in it before you head out the door! ✉ **Vicki A., NC**

LIP RUB. I use Vicks® VapoRub® as a lip balm whenever I'm suffering from dry, chapped lips. In addition to soothing my lips, it clears out my sinuses at the same time. If you give this a try, just don't eat or drink anything while the Rub is on your lips; you might ingest some—and it's for external use only. ✉ **Terri D., ON**

BABY YOUR LIPS. When my lips are cracked and dry, I rub a small amount of baby oil on them. It makes my lips smooth and healthy looking, just like that. ✉ **Susan G., OK**

SAY HELLO TO JELL-O. For long-lasting lip color, I stain my lips with red JELL-O® instead of lipstick. It's easy to do—just dip the end of a dampened cotton swab into the gelatin powder, and apply it to your lips. Be careful not to go outside your natural lip line, or that area will end up stained, too. ✉ *Anita B., SC*

PEARLY WHITES. You don't have to buy expensive tooth-whitening kits when you can make this effective solution with stuff you've already got at home. Mix a teaspoon of baking soda with a teaspoon of salt, and add just enough water to make a paste. Brush your teeth with this once a week, and you'll notice your teeth whitening up in no time. ✉ *Mary D., TN*

Rx FOR RETAINERS. If your kids or grandkids wear orthodontic retainers, a weekly super-cleaning will keep the appliances fresh

Ask Jerry

Q: Why, oh, why do my lips get so chapped in the winter?

A: Your lips don't produce any oils on their own, so once they're chapped, it's up to you to heal them by bringing them much-needed moisture. Here's how to prevent them from chapping again:

1. Slough off flaky, rough skin with a clean, damp washcloth.

2. Rub in a coating of .5% hydrocortisone cream twice a day.

3. Seal in the moisture with a lip balm that contains a protective wax (like beeswax) and sunscreen (check the label).

and free of bacteria. Just soak the retainers in a bowl of vinegar for about an hour, then rinse and brush them as usual before putting them back into service. ✉ William B., NC

ANOTHER GREAT IDEA!

GO GREEN

You may not see the connection, but eating green vegetables is a great way to keep your lips in the pink. That's because greens are rich in zinc, essential fatty acids, and riboflavin—everything your lips need to retain moisture and stay healthy. So eat plenty of greens every day!

The Skin You're In

MEGA MOISTURE. Why waste big bucks on pricey cold cream, when you can reach into your pantry for shortening instead? Use it to moisturize your face and neck, and rub a bit on your heels, elbows, and knees to get rid of any rough patches. ✉ Mary T., CA

OLIVE, OOOH. I massage olive oil into my skin to lock in moisture and keep it soft and supple. Olive oil works as well as any of those fancy body lotions and, the best part is, it's gentle enough to use on a baby's skin. ✉ Amy M., OH

IT'S IN THE BAG. Believe it or not, Bag Balm® is as healing for people as it is for their pets. Try rubbing some into the tough, rough skin on your elbows and knees, and you'll see what I mean—it really works! Bag Balm can be purchased at drugstores or pet-supply stores. ✉ Michael B., PA

FADE AWAY. Don't resort to costly and possibly painful solutions to get rid of those annoying brown spots on your skin that are caused by too much sun or hormonal changes—give this tip a try first. Pour some apple cider vinegar onto a cotton ball, and dab it on the darkened areas twice a day. The spots will fade within a matter of a few weeks. ✉ Phyllis F., MO

Jerry's Handy Hints

KITCHEN PASTE FOR DRY SKIN

→ Here's a simple solution to dry skin problems, and you can find it right in your own kitchen. Mix ordinary table salt with vegetable oil in a small plastic bowl to make a gritty paste. In the shower, use it to scrub dry, rough trouble spots: knees, elbows, hands, face . . . you get the idea. Rinse the areas well, then pat your skin dry with a soft towel. You'll be lookin' and feelin' smooth, moisturized, and fresh!

SOMETHING FISHY. To prevent or remove dry, scaly skin on my legs, I turn the tables and use fish scales. I place wet fish scales in cheesecloth and rub the cloth over my skin until it is smooth, silky, and soft. Then I wash my legs using a nice scented soap to take the lingering fishy smell away. ✉ Elena K., BC

A REAL JUICE JOINT. You can whiten and soften up rough elbows by using your joint as a juicer. Simply cut a lemon in half and rub it directly on your bent elbow. Mush your elbow right into the fruit as though you are trying to juice the lemon with it. Use the leftover half for your other elbow, then rinse the pulp and juice off with warm water. ✉ Florence C., FL

SHOWER WITH SUGAR. Make a terrific exfoliating scrub by mixing granulated sugar with liquid soap. Scrub the mixture into your skin while you're in the shower after a long day in the garden. It'll soften and exfoliate your skin, while getting rid of the grittiest grime—even on rough hands and feet. ✉ Lisa E., CO

MORE MOISTURE. Here's a simple solution to revitalize skin and even soothe eczema: Use a humidifier in your home during the long winter months when your furnace is busy warming you up—and drying you out. It really helps keep your skin healthy. ✉ **Mark D., CA**

JAVA SCRUB. Before your next shower, mix 1 cup of hand lotion with 3 tablespoons of coffee grounds in a plastic bowl. Bring this mixture with you into the shower, and after wetting your skin, scrub your entire body with it. It's an excellent exfoliant! And don't worry—after you rinse, you won't smell like a cup of joe. ✉ **Constance S., MI**

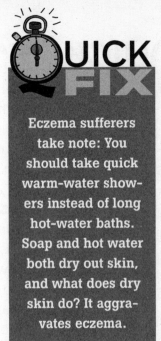

QUICK FIX

Eczema sufferers take note: You should take quick warm-water showers instead of long hot-water baths. Soap and hot water both dry out skin, and what does dry skin do? It aggravates eczema.

SPICY SOAK. A nice hot bath opens the pores and helps rid your body of toxins. So here's how I add some spice to my soak: I grate 4 tablespoons of fresh ginger (about ¼ cup) and add it to my bathwater while the tub is filling. It makes the water—and me—smell great and also promotes perspiration, which is the skin's way of eliminating some of the poisons our bodies have absorbed from the environment. ✉ **Sheila V., WI**

SUPER-DUPER SOLUTIONS

A RESTORATIVE SOAK ● Make a batch of this soothing bath oil, and reach for it anytime you need to relax and refresh after a long, hard day. Mix 1 egg, ¼ cup of milk, ½ cup of baby oil, ¼ cup of vodka, and 2 tablespoons of honey in a blender for 45 seconds. Fill your bathtub with water and pour in the mixture. Then jump in, sit back, and say, "Aaahhh!" Store any leftovers in an airtight container in your fridge.

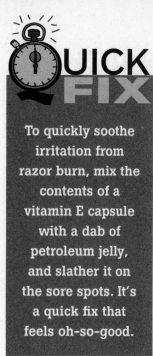

QUICK FIX

To quickly soothe irritation from razor burn, mix the contents of a vitamin E capsule with a dab of petroleum jelly, and slather it on the sore spots. It's a quick fix that feels oh-so-good.

GET A LEG UP. Make your legs extra smooth and silky by treating them to a great-smelling conditioner before shaving. Just add a few drops of your favorite essential oils to a splash of castor oil. Rub the oils together in your hands, then slather the mixture on your wet legs before taking a razor to them. ✉ Judy D., LA

CONDITION YOUR LEGS. Don't bother keeping shaving cream (or foam) in your shower—who needs another product cluttering up the shower stall when you can just use hair conditioner instead? Apply a thin coat of conditioner to your legs and then shave away. You'll not only save space, but also get silky smooth legs in the process. ✉ Sheryl C., CA

OH, BABY. I use baby oil instead of shaving cream to shave my legs when I'm taking a shower. It gives me a nice close shave, and my legs end up soft and smooth. ✉ Irasema K., NY

FACE THE FACTS. Believe it or not, you can use mayonnaise to clean your face. Apply a layer as you would any deep-cleansing facial soap. After 15 or 20 minutes, wipe the mayo off and rinse your face thoroughly. The oils and salt in the mayo will remove any impurities and restore moisture to your skin. ✉ Sharon R., OH

HOMEMADE BEAUTY. I don't spend much money on beauty products because I make my own. One of my favorite recipes is for an egg facial that's super-easy to whip up: Whisk one egg and pat it onto your clean face. Let it sit for 15 minutes, then wash it off. I guarantee your skin will feel refreshed and renewed like never before! ✉ Elizabeth H., OR

MARVELOUS MASK. Baking soda makes a great facial mask because it neutralizes the pH of your skin and draws out and kills bacteria. Prepare the mask by mixing ½ cup of baking soda with just enough water to form a paste, then smooth it over your face. Let it dry, then wash it off with warm water. Gently pat your face dry with a soft, clean towel. ✉ **Donna S., MI**

LOVE THAT LITTER! You can make a wonderful facial mask in your own home with pure-clay cat litter (make sure the label says

TAKE **5**

Here are five not-so-common health and beauty uses for baking soda:

1 Bathe in baking soda the next time you have a close encounter with poison ivy; just dump ½ cup into lukewarm bathwater and soak for a good long while.

2 Zap tooth stains by pouring a little baking soda in your hand, adding a drop or two of water, and brushing with a wet tooth-brush that's been dipped into the powdery paste.

3 Zing a bee sting by making a paste with a handful of baking soda and water. Smear it on the sting, and leave it in place for at least 20 minutes.

4 Remove hair spray or oil buildup from combs and brushes by soaking them for 15 minutes in a tub of warm water that's got 3 tablespoons each of baking soda and bleach added to it. Rinse with cold water and air-dry.

5 Clear up a persistent case of gingivitis with a paste made of 1 teaspoon of baking soda and a drizzle of hydrogen peroxide. Work it gently under the gum line with your toothbrush, leave the paste on for a few minutes, then rinse your mouth.

it's 100 percent natural clay). Mix a handful of clean litter with 3 tablespoons of lukewarm water. Combine them well, and apply the wet litter to your face and neck. Let the mask dry, and then wash it off after about 15 minutes. Aaahhh . . . refreshing! ✉ **Sheri M., GA**

AND I MEAN CLEAN. I've found that the Mr. Clean® Magic Eraser® sponge can clean my face as well as it cleans my walls and cabinets. I cut a 1-inch square from a sponge, then wet it and make one *very gentle* pass over my entire face. All of the gunk that was clogging up my pores and dulling my face disappears. I use the sponge just once a week for noticeably fresher, cleaner skin. ✉ **Stephania G., OK**

"Y" NOT YOGURT? Try smoothing plain yogurt all over your face to soften your skin and lighten the appearance of sun discolorations and dark spots. After your usual face-washing routine, rub the yogurt on, let it sit for a few minutes, then rinse it off with warm water and pat your face dry with a soft towel. ✉ **Kate H., WY**

A MILKY MASK. Here's a quick and easy facial mask that's made to order for oily skin: plain old milk of magnesia. Spread the liquid over your face, and let it dry. After leaving it on for 10 minutes, rinse it off with warm water and pat your face dry with a soft, clean towel. You'll feel refreshed, and your skin will be smooth and soft. ✉ **Debra C., TN**

LOTS OF LEMON. I fight oily skin with lemons. After washing my face, I rub it

Jerry's Handy Hints

IT'S FOR YOU

→ Knock, knock! Who's there? A wake-up call for your face! It's no joke: This mini facial will stimulate circulation while washing away dead skin cells. Mix 1 tablespoon of honey with ½ teaspoon of ground nutmeg, and then massage the mixture into your skin. Leave it on for 20 minutes, while lightly tapping your face with your fingertips. Rinse with a warm, water-soaked washcloth, and gently pat your skin dry.

Grandma Putt's Wisdom

Grandma Putt would often hand me a thin slice of potato to put on a pimple to help dry it up. She knew it worked, but she didn't know why—white potatoes contain natural chemicals that seem to help pimples and boils drain. To try this remedy, just thinly slice or grate a potato and apply it directly to the area. Leave it on for 10 to 20 minutes, then wash the area well and pat dry. Repeat once or twice a day until the blemishes are history.

with a slice or two of fresh-cut lemon. The citrus cuts through skin oils and helps tighten my pores. I finish up with a rinse of lukewarm water and pat my face dry with a soft, clean towel. ✉ **Sonia F., SC**

PAMPER WITH PAPAYA. Is your face dry with patchy skin and uneven tone? Then thinly slice a fresh papaya and lay the slivers on your face—avoiding your eyes—for about five minutes. The papaya will dissolve dead skin cells at the surface and leave you looking fresh and evenly toned. ✉ **Kelly B., MD**

NUTMEG FACIAL. Give yourself a facial with this fabulous formula: Add a teaspoon of freshly ground nutmeg to one beaten egg white. Brush the mask on your face, let it dry completely, then rinse it off and pat your face dry. This is an especially effective treatment if you're prone to pimples. ✉ **Robin P., PA**

PAINLESS PEEL. Whatever you do, don't resort to chemical peels that can irritate or damage your skin. Instead, try my quick-and-easy technique that's kind to your skin: Paint all-purpose white glue on your face. Allow it to dry, then peel it off. You'll be amazed to see all of the dead skin, blackheads, and other gunk that come right off with it. ✉ **Jane R., WI**

SMOOTHING SODA SOLUTION. I use baking soda to exfoliate the skin on my face. It's easy—just pour about a teaspoon of baking soda into your hand, then add a little water and gently massage it into your skin. Rinse it off with cool water and pat your face dry with a soft towel. I use this treatment about three times a week, and when my elbows, knees, and heels are feeling rough I use it there too! The best part is that baking soda is so inexpensive, and it works just as well as, if not better than, high-end, store-bought products. ✉ Shawn M., SC

PART WITH PIMPLES. You can get rid of a pimple overnight by dabbing it with a little white toothpaste (not gel) before going to bed. In the morning, the pimple will be noticeably smaller and less red. For large zits, you may need to repeat the treatment a few nights in a row. ✉ Mary Jane N., MA

BYE-BYE, BLEMISHES. I use cod liver oil to help draw out impurities and heal blemishes. I apply the oil to my skin with a warm washcloth, leave it on for several seconds, and then rinse it off. If you use this treatment every evening, you'll soon see a noticeable difference in your skin. ✉ Maria S., GA

ANOTHER GREAT IDEA!

GO BANANAS!

To really add some a-peel to your complexion and wipe out blemishes at the same time, try this overnight treatment. Use a spoon to scrape off the insides of a very ripe banana, and apply the pulp to any trouble spots on your face. Keep the banana mush in place by covering the area with gauze that's secured with surgical tape. The sugars and enzymes in the banana pulp will draw out dirt, pus, and oils from your pores. In the morning, you can just gently wipe it all away and your face will feel invigorated!

PART 3

Lawn and Garden

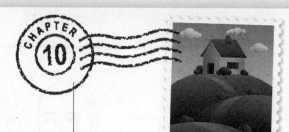

CHAPTER **10**

Green Acres

In the Beginning . . .

I SAY HAY. Instead of covering your newly seeded lawn with straw, use hay. It won't blow around like straw, and it'll provide a little sustenance to the grass. Best of all, water goes through hay like it goes through a tea bag—giving the grass seed the nourishment it needs to get off to a great start. ✉ **Lloyd M., IN**

A GREEN SCREEN. When it's time to patch bare spots in your lawn, be sure you have an old window screen on hand. Paint the screen green, then go ahead and sprinkle seed in your lawn's bald spots. Tamp the seed down, and cover the area with the screen. The green color will camouflage the patch, and the screen will protect the seeds from thievin' varmints! ✉ **Eileen H., PA**

WIRE YOUR GRASS. I cover any newly planted areas in my lawn with good old-fashioned chicken wire. It keeps dogs, cats, birds, and other animals away from the tender young grass; protects my new turf; and reminds me of where I need to water. ✉ Carl B., IL

PUT MUD TO GOOD USE. If rain is washing away newly sprinkled grass seed before it has a chance to take root in your lawn's bare patches, try this trick: After the next good rain, scatter the seed on the bare spots, and stomp it into the mud. It'll be so embedded into the ground that water from the sprinkler or rainfall won't wash it away. ✉ Kelly W., TN

MADE FOR THE SHADE. Why go through the frustration of overseeding your lawn every 20 days—forever—just to get a little grass under your shade tree? Instead, switch to a shade-loving groundcover like myrtle. Then you can relax and enjoy your beautiful shady oasis. ✉ Cecil R., TX

HIGH-TEST GRASS SEED. I can't count the number of times I've seeded bare patches in my lawn, only to have spotty results because much of the seed didn't germinate. Then I discovered your fantastic formula: Mix ¼ cup of baby shampoo and 1 tablespoon of Epsom salts in 1 gallon of weak tea water. Drop the grass seed into the container, and stash it in the refrigerator for at least 24 hours. Spread the seeds out on your driveway to dry, then sow them. Since I started

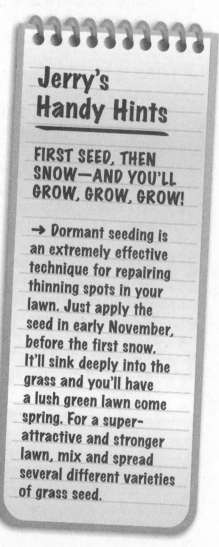

Jerry's Handy Hints

FIRST SEED, THEN SNOW—AND YOU'LL GROW, GROW, GROW!

→ Dormant seeding is an extremely effective technique for repairing thinning spots in your lawn. Just apply the seed in early November, before the first snow. It'll sink deeply into the grass and you'll have a lush green lawn come spring. For a super-attractive and stronger lawn, mix and spread several different varieties of grass seed.

TAKE 5

Here are five not-so-common materials that make great lawn and garden fertilizers:

1 Ashes: Apply at a rate of 1 pound per 10 to 20 square feet of garden area.

2 Bones, a.k.a. bonemeal: Apply a bucketful of ground-up bones to 200 row feet in a garden.

3 Coffee grounds: Sprinkle a generous handful around acid-loving plants once a year.

4 Eggshells: Soak crushed shells in water for 24 hours, and use the mixture to water your plants.

5 Hair: Work either human or animal hair into the soil for outstanding results.

using this technique, I've gotten almost 100 percent germination every time! ✉ Jerome R., MD

DOWN THE DRAIN. If you're watering your grass daily but still can't keep it thriving over the summer, you probably have a drainage problem—either too much or too little. I solved my lawn's drainage issues by first applying gypsum at the recommended rate to condition the soil. Then I followed up every two weeks with a soapy water bath I made with 1 cup of dishwashing liquid and 1 cup of ammonia in my 20 gallon hose-end sprayer. That did the trick! ✉ Don L., NH

SUPER SPRINKLER. When I have a not-so-big area of lawn to fertilize, I use an old Parmesan cheese canister. It's the perfect size for storing small amounts of fertilizer, and the lawn food sprinkles right out through the holes in the lid. ✉ Norah C., SC

SNACK ATTACK. Before you fertilize your lawn, remove a few scoops of the fertilizer and store it in an old margarine tub or deli container with a lid. Label the tub, and reach for it anytime a special shrub or other plant needs an extra snack. ✉ Philip R., OH

Great Groundskeeping

MOW, MOW, MOW THE MOAT. If you border your flower beds with edging, you're going to have to do a lot of grass trimming. So make it easier on yourself and dig a 5- to 6-inch-deep "moat" next to the edging, and fill it with gravel. Then when you're mowing, simply run your mower along the moat, and it'll trim right up to the edges, just like that. ✉ Kathleen K., OK

SPRAY AND MOW. I make cleaning up after mowing a real breeze. I just spray nonstick cooking spray underneath my mower before I begin. Then when I'm done mowing my lawn, I wash away any stuck-on grass with a garden hose. The green gunk washes right off! ✉ Christa C., WV

DRINK UP. Mowing on a hot summer day can be a real draining experience, so you need to keep your cool by staying hydrated. Here's how I handle the heat: The night before I mow, I place two bottles of Gatorade® in the freezer. The next day I take out both bottles, and bring one outside with me when I start to mow. I drink it as it thaws, and by the time I'm done with the front yard, the first

ANOTHER GREAT IDEA!

KNOW WHEN TO MOW

It's best to cut your grass after 7:00 p.m. Why? Because it's more comfortable for you and more comfortable for the grass. A lawn that's cut at sundown will recover from the shock of the cut, restore chlorophyll manufacturing, and cauterize itself in dew time a whole lot faster than in hot daytime. You'll also sleep sounder after mowing and bathing in the evening.

bottle is empty. Then I get the other bottle, which has since thawed, and drink it while I mow the backyard. When I'm all done, I go inside and enjoy a nice cool shower. ✉ Lianne L., GA

LET IT SLIDE. Hate to clean the underside of your mower? The next time you clean and dry the bottom, apply a heavy coat of silicone spray. The cut grass will slide right off on its own, which means no more messy cleanups for you! ✉ Ferne S., IN

A CLEAN CATCH(ER). Your lawn mower will continue to work in top form if you keep the grass-catcher bag clean. After every other mowing, use a stiff-bristled or wire brush to remove all grass clippings that are plugging up the openings in the bag. That way, things will keep running smoothly, and you'll never have to worry about dropping fresh-cut clipping clumps on your lawn. ✉ Mike G., MI

LET'S TALK TURKEY. Anyone who lives in an area where freezing temperatures are the norm knows that to protect your mower you must remove all the gas at the end of the mowing season. I've discovered an easy way to get most of the gas out quickly. I simply use a large turkey baster (reserved just for this purpose) to draw out the petrol and empty it into a gas can. When I've got as much gas out as I can, I run the mower until it conks out, which clears out any remaining fuel and the fuel lines. ✉ Vickie Z., IL

WATER WIDELY—AND WISELY. If you have a lot of ground to cover when it comes time to water your lawn, do what I do and

---

SUPER-DUPER SOLUTIONS

WIPE IT AWAY ● When your lawn mower ends up splattered with grease, oil, or some kind of mystery gunk, reach for the baby wipes. They'll clear the mess away lickety-split without harming your mower's paint job.

use Y adapters for your main feeder hose. Doing this allows me to fit up to four 10- to 15-foot hose ends with spot sprinklers. And to make sure I'm not wasting any water, I put clear deli containers next to the plants being watered so that as they fill up, I can tell just how much each lawn area is getting and adjust my sprinklers accordingly. ✉ **Barbara S., WI**

MAKE IT 50/50. Is your usual routine to water each area of your lawn for 30 minutes at a time? Well, then, take my advice and split that half hour into two 15-minute sessions spaced 20 to 30 minutes apart. You'll get better results because the shorter soaking time gives the water a chance to seep into the soil, which means more water for your grass and a lot less runoff. ✉ **Rita L., FL**

The War on Weeds

CAN IT. To kill weeds that are growing where you can't use weed killer, cut them back until their stems are 6 or 8 inches long. Then cover the stems with an empty, clean metal soup can, pushing the can into the earth so that it can't be dislodged. The weeds will die because they can't grow around or out of the metal can. ✉ **Paul B., NE**

BEAT 'EM WITH BORAX. Borax is great to use as a weed killer for vigorous, invasive lawn weeds like creeping Charlie. For every 1,000 square feet of lawn area you have, dissolve 10 ounces of borax in 1/2 cup of warm water in a bucket, then dilute it with 2 1/2 gallons of water. Fill your 20 gallon hose-end sprayer with this solution, and spray it on your yard once a year. The results should last for the entire growing season. ✉ **David S., IA**

SHOOT WEEDS DOWN. I use vinegar to kill the weeds in my yard. It's safe, easy to use, and effective. Just fill a handheld sprayer

Ask Jerry

Q: How can I get rid of creeping Charlie in my lawn?

A: This one's easy: Simply add 1 teaspoon of dishwashing liquid to any broadleaf weed killer, and apply as directed. Then wave and say, "Good-bye, Charlie!"

bottle with nothing but white vinegar, take aim, and fire away! ✉ C.J. F., MO

PROTECT YOUR PUPS. I hate seeing weeds sprout up in my lawn, but I also hate to use any type of weed killer that may harm my beloved dogs. If you, too, have been search-ing for a pet-friendly solution to your weed problem, I've got the perfect recipe: Mix 1 capful each of vinegar, baby shampoo, and gin in a quart of warm water, pour the mixture into a handheld sprayer bottle, take aim, and shoot those weeds down. ✉ Bonnie L., DE

BLEACH BLASTER. Here's what I use to kill poison ivy and other broadleaf weeds—ordinary household bleach. I pour some into a handheld sprayer bottle and add a few drops of liquid hand soap. I give it a good shake, then go out and blast those yard invaders but good. ✉ Rita W., TX

VINEGAR ON THE VINE. If you find poison ivy on your property, you need to get rid of it pronto. First, pour a large bottle of vinegar over the entire plant, leaves and all. The next day, put on gloves, long sleeves, and long pants, and roll a wheeled garbage can out to the spot. Put a plastic garbage bag over each hand, grab the wicked weed by the root, and yank the whole thing out, pulling the plastic bag down over it while it's still in your hand. Then place it in the garbage can. Look around for any dead but still-rash-producing leaves lying about and remove them with the bag trick, too. When you get back inside, wash your hands and arms with soap and water as a precaution to thwart any poison ivy oils that may have come in contact with your skin. ✉ Andie W., MO

A DANDY SNACK. Instead of yanking out the dandelions in my lawn and tossing 'em in the yard-waste bag, I use the flowers to make delicious snacks. Simply remove the blooms and soak them in salt water for 10 minutes, rinse them twice, and set them on paper towels. Whip up a batter using pancake mix with an extra whisked egg added. Then dip the blossoms into the batter, and either deep-fry or pan-fry them in canola oil until they're light brown and crispy. *Note:* Only use dandelions from lawns that haven't been chemically treated. ✉ Orville F., OR

SWEET WEEDS. After you've spent the day pulling dandelions from your yard, it's time to make honey from those weeds. Here's my recipe: Boil 350 dandelion flowers and 3 sliced lemons in 2 cups of water until the water is gone. Add 1 cup of hot water, and strain the mixture through cheesecloth. Add 3¼ pounds of sugar to the liquid, and cook for 30 minutes to get delicious golden honey. Let it cool, and pour it into jars. Then enjoy some on tomorrow morning's toast! *Note:* Only use dandelions from lawns that haven't been chemically treated. ✉ Marie V., ON

SUPER-DUPER SOLUTIONS

A-MAIZING WEED STOPPER ● Applied to your lawn in mid-spring, corn gluten is an all-natural, chemical-free way to stop weeds before they even think about showing their ugly heads. It actually prevents crabgrass, dandelions, and other weed seeds from sprouting, too. Best of all, the powdery material is a by-product of corn processing, so it's safe for kids and pets to play on your lawn right after it's been put down. You can find corn gluten at your local feed store, or order it from suppliers that specialize in natural pest controls.

THE SALT OF THE EARTH. When there's no rain in the forecast, it's the perfect time to tackle your dandelion problems. Pull out the center of each weed (bud, flower, and stem), and fill the hole that's left behind with table salt. It'll kill the dandelion—taproot and all—and it's safe, quick, and environmentally friendly! ✉ **Nancy W., MA**

TAKE 5

Here are five not-so-common uses for salt in and around the yard and garden:

1 Kill weeds by adding a little salt to boiling water and pouring the mixture over sprouts growing in sidewalks.

2 Melt snails and slugs into a biodegradable, slimy goo by sprinkling them with salt.

3 Boost your cleaning power by adding 1 teaspoon of salt to your regular laundry soapsuds.

4 Derail ant trails by dusting troublesome indoor ants and their trails with a little salt.

5 Cool hot embers in your barbecue grill by scattering them with salt when the cooking's done for the day.

GIVE TAILS A TRIM. Don't fight a losing battle with cattails in your backyard pond—instead, cut 'em down to size. Use clippers to cut the cattails below the waterline. These nuisances take in air through their stems, so keep cutting them as shoots come up, and they'll eventually die out. ✉ **Tony M., OH**

BY THE LIGHT OF THE MOON. My grandfather passed along this old-time bit of wisdom on how to get rid of cattails on your property: Just whip 'em down on the day of the last full moon in August. Give it a try! ✉ **Emma A., MI**

LOSE THE MOSS. Here's the quick and easy technique that I use to kill moss in my yard: I mix equal parts of clear ammonia and water in a handheld sprayer bottle, and fire away! It couldn't be any simpler, and it really does the trick. ✉ **Robert B., MO**

MOVE ALONG, MOSS! Moss is quite harmless to trees, but in your lawn, it could be a sign of poor drainage, lack of sunlight, or acid buildup in the soil. If you want to remove it, mix up a solution of ½ cup of bleach and ½ cup of dishwashing liquid in 1 gallon of warm water. Apply it lightly several times until the moss dies. Then improve the soil by applying a mix of 50 percent lime and 50 percent gypsum in late fall or early winter. That should put an end to your moss misery. ✉ Gary P., MA

Calling All Composters

A SIMPLE PROCESS. Use an old food processor to puree all of your non-meat kitchen scraps—vegetable and fruit trimmings, banana peels, eggshells, coffee grounds—then dig a small trench in your compost pile. Drop the slop into the trench, and cover it. It will break down quickly, which means you can put your compost to work sooner! ✉ Robin R., AZ

PUT IT IN A POT. If you don't have room on your property for a compost pile, I've got a great solution that will give you enough "black gold" to enrich the soil of a small garden: Fill a large clay pot with a 3-inch layer of potting soil and place it in a sunny corner on your patio. Then, in a plastic bucket with a tight lid, collect vegetable, fruit, and other food scraps (no meat or dairy products), until you have enough to make a 3-inch layer on top of the soil. Continue alternating soil and food scraps until the pot is full, then cover it with plastic or cardboard. Turn the mixture with a garden fork every few days, adding water as needed. After six weeks, you'll have nutrient-rich compost that's ready to be worked into your garden soil. ✉ Rita B., MI

FEED YOUR PILE. This is a tip for all livestock owners: Don't toss out that livestock feed supplement just because it's past the expiration date. Even though it may no longer be suitable for your animals to eat, it contains minerals that make wonderful additions to your compost pile, garden, or lawn. As I always say, "Waste not, want not!" ✉ **Bonnie B., IN**

LET THERE BE LINT. The next time you wash and dry 100 percent cotton clothes, towels, or linens, don't toss the lint that ends up in the dryer screen. Instead, recycle it by adding it to your compost pile, where it counts as a "brown" material to balance out the food scrap and grass clipping "greens." ✉ **Helen B., NH**

BE A GOOD EGG. I always buy eggs in biodegradable cardboard cartons. That way, I not only have eggshells to add to my compost bin, but I also can recycle the container for compost. I simply soak the carton in hot water until I can easily tear it into small pieces, then toss them onto my compost pile. ✉ **Diana J., MA**

TURN UP THE HEAT. A compost pile must generate heat in order to break down into the nutrient-rich food your garden needs. You can speed up the process by placing a few bricks in your bin. Start by setting the bricks out in the sun for a full day so they get nice and warm. Then bury them in the pile, where they'll give off heat, helping your compost to break down more quickly. ✉ **Amy C., MI**

Ask Jerry

Q: Is it safe to add weeds to my compost pile?

A: Yes, you can add weeds to your compost pile, as long as they're not in the seed-formation stage. By the way, it's not a good idea to use any weed killer–tainted clippings for composting for at least six weeks after the application. After that, you should be okay.

READ ALL ABOUT IT. If your compost pile contains plenty of green matter, but not a whole lot of brown matter, start shredding the news! Shred your old newspapers, phone books, and other non-glossy paper, and add 'em to the heap to even things out. ✉ Martha C., VT

MOVE THE MANURE. It's not a good idea to put a load of fresh manure in your garden—by doing so, you could introduce hundreds of garden thugs and provide more nitrogen than most plants need. The best way to handle fresh manure is to compost it. Layer it about 8 inches deep, and soak the layer with Jerry's All-Season Clean-Up Tonic, which is made by mixing 1 cup each of baby shampoo, antiseptic mouthwash, and tobacco tea (see page 201 for the tea recipe). Top the pile with a little sawdust. It'll soak up some of the excess nitrogen as the manure rots, help keep moisture and odors under control, keep bugs out, and allow rain to come in. ✉ Byron B., NH

THE NEED FOR SPEED. Not sure what to do with the thatch you've removed? What about grass clippings and leaves? Yard wastes like these can be hard to compost and slow to break down. But the process will go a lot faster in the pile if you add a layer of garden soil over every 8 inches of yard waste, and spray the entire mound with half a can of beer

TAKE 5

Here are five not-so-common uses for onions around the yard and garden:

1 Create great compost by adding onion skins to your pile or bin.

2 Control moles by placing pieces of onion in their runs.

3 Wipe out whiteflies by grating a small onion and steeping it overnight in 2 cups of water. Strain, add 1 quart of water to the remaining liquid, and spray once a month.

4 Stop bugs in their tracks by blending equal parts of onions and garlic into a puree. Soak overnight in 2 cups of warm water, strain, and then spray away.

5 Plant sprouting onions in a pot and grow them in a sunny window. Cut off the tops and eat 'em like green onions.

or Coke® (that's been shaken) every two weeks. That'll get your compost going. ✉ Steve R., PA

IT'S IN THE BAG. I don't have much time or energy to maintain an outdoor compost bin, and living alone, I don't have many food scraps to contribute. But that doesn't stop me from composting. I simply keep a black plastic trash bag on my back porch and fill it with my vegetable scraps, eggshells, tea bags, and so on. Once a week I turn the bag upside down to mix things up. In no time, I've got compost ready for use in my small flower garden. ✉ Cicely R., MD

DOWN BY THE SEA. Whenever I vacation at a saltwater beach, I collect buckets of seaweed and bring them home. Then I chop up the seaweed and mix it into my compost pile along with my lawn clippings and other organic waste. My garden loves it! ✉ Joan F., OH

IT'S TIME FOR TEA. Give your garden a treat with some of Jerry's famous compost tea. Just put a shovelful of compost in a burlap sack and tie it shut. Then put the sack in a large bucket of water, cover it, and let it steep for several days. Remove the sack and spread its contents throughout your garden. Apply the remaining "tea" water to the soil around your plants every two weeks during the growing season. ✉ Gerald M., IL

ANOTHER GREAT IDEA!

CAN IT!

You don't need a big yard to start composting. In fact, you can begin with just a small piece of ground and a garbage can (it doesn't matter if it's plastic or metal). Simply cut away the bottom of the can and add your materials. To speed things up, drill some air holes in the sides and a couple of drainage holes near the bottom. Then you'll have the perfect compact composter!

Gather Your Gear

LET'S TALK TRASH. I use a wheeled trash can with a lid to conveniently store my small garden stakes. I simply roll the can out to the garden when the stakes are needed and return it to my garage when I'm finished. The lid keeps the stakes dry and at the ready, regardless of the weather. ✉ Donna F., CA

MESH TAMES THE MESS. To keep my tools neatly stored but still within easy reach, I nailed chicken wire between the exposed two-by-four upright supports in my garage. Now I can slide the handles of my rakes, shovels, brooms, and other long-handled tools right behind the wire mesh. These large tools no longer take up valuable floor and wall space, and I can quickly find and grab the one I need. ✉ Robert M., TX

FORE! Here's a super way to make good use of an old golf pull cart: Turn it into a handy garden-tool caddy. Use duct tape to join a cluster of PVC pipes, capped on one end. Strap the cluster onto the cart with the capped ends on the bottom, slip your long-handled tools into the open ends, and voilà! Roll the caddy out to the garden and have at it. ✉ Betty K., NH

READY, SET, RETOOL. If you have an old set of fireplace tools, recycle the shovel (used for removing ashes) by using it in your garden. It'll quickly become your favorite tool for mixing potting soil, transferring mulch, and cutting away small weeds. The short handle makes it easy to control, and the shovel holds a lot more than an ordinary trowel. ✉ Eileen C., CA

DON'T PICK ON ME. Many home gardeners use a hand pick as a gardening tool, but I've found that the ones available for sale are usually too light for heavy-duty gardening use. Instead, I cut down the handle of an old pointed hoe so that it's a comfortable size (about 24 inches long for me; you may need to start there and cut it down more for a perfect fit). Now I have a hand pick that's heavy enough, strong enough, and sharp enough to easily dig into even the hardest clay soil. ✉ **Deanna A., CA**

TAKE

Here are five not-so-common ways to use duct tape in your yard and garden:

1 Prevent blisters by wrapping a long piece of duct tape around the palms of your hands.

2 Remove a tick by sticking a piece of duct tape onto it and giving the tick a quick jerk; it should come right out.

3 Secure garbage cans and keep critters out by taping the lids shut with duct tape.

4 Mend rubber boots or garden clogs by putting duct tape over any holes, worn spots, or tears.

5 Give old plant labels a new lease on life by taping over the outdated info.

OH, THE STRAIN. A handheld kitchen strainer is just the ticket for applying powdered fertilizer to your garden. It works great—just scoop up or pour in the fertilizer, and shake it right over each plant. Just remember to keep separate strainers for kitchen and garden use, and mark the garden one with a dab of nail polish or permanent marker before storing it with your other garden supplies. ✉ **Mary G., MO**

HOE, HOE, HOE. I found an ideal use for an old disc blade that was cluttering up my workbench: I turned it into a garden hoe! Using a cutting torch, I cut the disc blade into five equal pieces, setting four aside. I then drilled a hole into the narrow end of the remaining piece (this would become the hoe blade). I cut the head off a ¾-inch hardened bolt and sharpened the end, put the hoe blade on the bolt, and secured it tightly between two nuts and lock washers. My last step was

Ask Jerry

Q: What exactly is a 20 gallon hose-end sprayer that you talk about?

A: A 20 gallon hose-end sprayer is simply a quart jar with a sprayer head on top of it that attaches to any garden hose. Pay attention to the label on your sprayer, though, because you don't want to confuse a 20-gallon sprayer head with a 6-gallon sprayer head. The sprayer jars themselves are both 1 quart, but the sprayer heads draw the contents out of the jar and mix them with either 6 or 20 gallons of water from your hose. And be sure to clean the sprayers well after using them. Let the heads sit in hot, soapy water overnight, or it may take twice as long to cover your lawn next time.

to hammer the sharp end of the bolt into a long wooden handle from on old broom, and my hoe was complete. ✉ Gerald M., IL

THE SOFT TOUCH. If you find yourself wishing your garden tools had soft rubber handles, don't go out and buy all new equipment. Instead, purchase some foam rubber slide-on pipe insulation. It's already split, so it'll slide easily onto any rake, shovel, or other tool handle and can be easily cut down to size. Best of all, those soft handles ensure no more blisters! ✉ Denise L., IN

OIL ALL HANDLES. A lot of folks paint the wooden handles of their garden tools. But in no time at all, the paint is peeling and chipping, and you've got to clean 'em up and do the job all over again. I have a better idea: Instead of painting your tool handles, treat them with boiled linseed oil. It'll keep the handles strong, and they'll last a long time with no threat of dry rot. ✉ Charles C., PA

THERE'S THE RUB. Keep your wooden tool handles in good shape by rubbing them every now and again with a mixture of 2 parts mayonnaise and 1 part lemon juice on a soft cloth. The wood will stay smooth, clean, and free of cracks. ✉ Tom D., IL

SOAK AWAY RUST. You can save rusty garden tools from the trash heap by giving 'em an occasional bath in apple cider vinegar. Put the tools in a bucket or tub, pour in enough vinegar to completely cover them, and let them soak overnight. The next morning, wipe them dry with a clean rag and enjoy working with your shiny "new" tools! ✉ Anita B., MO

SUPER-DUPER SOLUTIONS

WINTERIZE YOUR TOOLS ● Before you put your shovels, hoes, and other garden gear away for the season, rub down the metal parts with a little petroleum jelly on a soft, clean cloth. It'll keep your tools rust-free and ready to go when duty calls in the spring.

BE CAGEY. When you need to dry out your gardening gloves, use a tomato cage. Just turn the cage upside down, and use plastic clothespins to hang your gloves from the wire. This setup can be used indoors or out to quickly dry as many pairs of gloves as you'd like. ✉ Gina D., CA

TEAR AND TOSS. I use disposable latex gloves instead of cloth garden gloves to do my planting. That way, I can easily wash mud off the gloves, but my hands stay dry. And when I wear a hole through one of the fingers, I simply throw that glove away and grab another one. ✉ Laura K., ND

Grandma Putt's Wisdom

Every once in a while, I'd become forgetful and leave my leather gardening gloves out in the rain. Of course, by the time I found them and dried them out, they were stiff as boards. But Grandma knew just what to do. She'd dip them in a sink full of warm water, squeeze them dry in a towel, and then rub a little castor oil into the leather. The result? Gloves as soft as the day I bought them!

SMOOTH MOVES. Cut the fingers off rubber dishwashing gloves and slide them onto your fingers before putting cloth gardening gloves on. This'll give extra-strength fingertip protection to the gardening gloves, not to mention your fingernails, too! ✉ Sara J., IA

PERFECT PADDING. I've found a quick and easy way to make the perfect kneeling pad. The next time you buy topsoil, carefully cut open the bag along the top seam. Empty the bag, clean the inside, and thoroughly dry it in the sun. Then buy a piece of foam padding that's about the size of the bag, cut it to fit, slide it in, and staple the bag shut. Now you can use it to sit, kneel, or even lie on while you're doing your gardening chores. It's lightweight, waterproof, and comfy. ✉ Shelly A., MN

TAKE 'EM ALONG. Here's an idea for a kneeling pad that you won't have to pick up every time you move to a new position in your garden: Sew pockets over the knees of your old gardening pants. Then insert a piece of foam-backed carpeting into each pocket pouch, and you've got kneeling pads that move when you do! ✉ Kristel W., MI

YOU'VE GOT MAIL. Don't fumble with your gloves, hand tools, and seed packets every time you head outdoors to get some work done. Instead, decorate a mailbox and place it in your garden as an attrac-

QUICK FIX

tive (and convenient) place to store those garden essentials. The mailbox will keep the items dry, and they'll be within easy reach whenever you need them. ✉ **Lois B., SD**

GET A GRIP. Here's a way to help you hold on to your tools more easily, even when your hands are sweaty: Just wrap some adhesive tape around the handles. Overlap the tape by about half its width, and use as many layers as it takes to get a firm, comfortable grip. Then get to work! ✉ **Susan L., WY**

IT'S A WRAP. I can't always bring all of my terra-cotta pots inside to protect them from winter's freezing temps because some of 'em are just too darn heavy! So I must leave them outside, which until recently meant risking the chance that they would crack in the cold. Then I hit upon this great idea: I wrap Bubble Wrap® around the outside of all the pots I can't bring in. It creates a cushion of air that protects them from the deep freeze, and they stay intact year after year. ✉ **Sandy S., ND**

INFORMATION, PLEASE. When I'm out working in my garden, I keep seed packets, notes, and other info close at hand by simply attaching spring-clip clothes-pins to my garden stakes. The stakes not only mark my rows, but also identify the plants and hold cards containing information like special feeding or watering instructions. It's the next best thing to having another pair of hands in the garden! ✉ **Bill P., MI**

MARK MY WORDS. Don't pitch those old mini blinds when you redecorate your house. Instead, put 'em to good use in your garden by recycling them into durable plant markers. Just cut each slat into 6-inch lengths, mark them with a permanent marker, and you're good to go. ✉ **Mary R., NV**

BAMBOO BONUS. If you have bamboo growing in your yard, you know how quickly it spreads. And that means you've got plenty of spare bamboo you can use to make a trellis. Cut the stalks down to size, fit them together into a trellis pattern of your choosing, and tie them together securely with nylon string. Then set the trellis in your growing bed, and push the supports 6 inches into the ground. Plant tomatoes, beans, or other climbers next to the trellis and watch 'em grow. ✉ **Gerald M., IL**

SUPER SOAKER. Save your empty, clean plastic milk jugs and use them to water newly planted trees and shrubs. Puncture

TAKE 5

Here are five not-so-common uses for Bubble Wrap® in the garden:

1 Create a deer deterrent by placing sheets of Bubble Wrap around your garden (deer won't walk on it). Weigh 'em down with boards, bricks, or rocks.

2 Make handy knee pads by taping sheets of doubled-over Bubble Wrap to each of your knees for more comfortable, low-down ground work.

3 Stuff a scarecrow—make yours as skinny or as plump as you want by filling it with strips of Bubble Wrap.

4 Mulch with sheets of Bubble Wrap in your veggie garden. Cut appropriate-size holes in each sheet to set the plants in, and keep it in place with boards, bricks, rocks, or water-filled milk jugs.

5 Protect pets and people from sharp garden stakes. Simply tape cut-to-fit pieces of Bubble Wrap around the tops to avoid unfortunate accidents.

three nail holes in the bottom, set the jug next to your tree trunk or shrub base, and place a few clean rocks inside the jug to keep it from blowing away. Then fill the container with water—it'll drip out of the bottom slowly with no runoff, and save you from watering chores. ✉ Beth L., OH

GET THE HANG OF IT. You say you don't want to save old milk jugs because you don't have space? Here's my space-saving solution: Simply tie a long rope to the handles of the jugs, one after the other, then hang them from the ceiling of your garage or basement; or string them clothesline-style from one wall to another. When it's time to place them in your garden, unhook the entire rope and drag the jugs to wherever you need them. ✉ Linda O., MN

SECOND LIFE FOR BOTTLES. Here's how to get the best use out of empty, clean 2-liter soda bottles. First, remove the cap and

Grandma Putt's Wisdom

When it was time to clean out the closets and attic in Grandma's house, we weren't allowed to toss anything until she'd checked it out first for potential garden use. Here's just a sampling of things that she put back into circulation as sturdy plant stakes to keep her floppy flowers and veggies on the up-and-up:

- Curtain rods
- Golf clubs
- Hockey sticks (sink the blade end into the soil)
- Pool cues
- Posts from badminton and volleyball nets
- Ski poles
- Stakes from a croquet set
- Walking sticks

ANOTHER GREAT IDEA!

DOUBLE-DUTY DETERGENT BOTTLES

The large, sturdy, waterproof plastic bottles that hold laundry detergent sure do come in handy in the garden. For example, you can turn a thoroughly washed and dried giant-size bottle into a garden-tool caddy. Here's how: Cut a big hole on the side of the bottle opposite the handle. Then insert your trowel, pruning shears, dibble, and other small hand tools into the bottle through the hole, and use the handle to tote it around. That's all there is to it!

label, and then cut the bottle crosswise into three pieces. Use the top as a funnel in your garden or kitchen. Use the middle as a protective collar for your fragile seedlings. Save the bottom to use as a container for small items like nuts and bolts, sewing doodads, or paper clips. That way, nothing goes to waste! ✉ **Ed B., MI**

BOTTLE BASICS. I make handy garden helpers from plastic gallon milk jugs. After washing a jug, I cut off and discard the bottom third. Then I replace the lid and use the remaining handled section to scoop materials like sand, peat moss, and fertilizer at planting time. These scoops are also great for handling cat litter and sidewalk salt. ✉ **Susan M., MO**

Tonic Talk

TOO HOT TO HANDLE. If you're using hot-pepper sauce in your garden tonics, strain it first to get rid of any chunks that might clog up your hose-end sprayer. Filtering it through the toe of an old pair of panty hose will do the trick. Just remember to wear rubber

Many lawn and garden tonics call for the use of a hose-end sprayer. But what if water restrictions in your community don't allow the use of a hose? No problem—just put the same solutions in a watering can or pressurized sprayer at a ratio of 1 teaspoon per 1 quart of water, 1 tablespoon per 1 gallon of water, or 1 cup per 20 gallons of water used.

gloves while you're handling the hot stuff, and keep your hands away from your nose and eyes. ✉ **Darlene B., TN**

NOW AND LATER. Recipes for garden tonics sometimes make a larger amount than you need for a single application. When I find myself with leftover tonic on hand, I store it in an empty liquid laundry detergent bottle. I just clean the bottle, then add the tonic, screw the lid on, and save it for later use. ✉ **Karen S., WA**

PUREE POWER. If a tonic recipe calls for finely chopped onions and garlic, don't waste your time chopping—just toss the ingredients into a food processor and liquefy them in a snap. And don't discard the leftover, strained-out solids. Spread them over any infested plants to drive the bugs up to the surface. Then whip out the tonic and spray 'em on the spot. ✉ **Jennifer P., CA**

MEASURE FOR MEASURE. Save metal cans, 2-liter bottles, and other sturdy containers to use as measuring cups when you're mixing garden tonics. Mark the outsides with a permanent marker to show 1/4-cup, 1/2-cup, and 1-cup increments. That way, you won't need to dirty up your good measuring cups, and you can easily reach into the recycling bin to find replacements. ✉ **Adrianna F., OH**

QUICK CRUSH. When garden tips and tonics call for crushed eggshells, I stick the shell halves in my blender and hit the puree button. It smashes 'em up in a flash. ✉ **Charlotte W., TX**

WHAT A GRIND. Use your coffee grinder to crush eggshells for use in the garden. Just zap 'em in the microwave for two or three minutes first, then break them up to fit in the grinder. Store the ground shells in a clear glass jar so you can identify them at a glance when you need to perk up soil or potting mix. ✉ Janine C., IN

CATCH THE CLOGS. Before I fill my hose-end sprayer with a tonic, I make sure to filter out all of the ingredients' solid chunks first. An easy way to do this is with a Scotch-Brite™ pad. I pour the fluid through the pad and into a clear measuring cup (so I can see if I've missed any chunks), then I add the filtered liquid to my sprayer. Since I started using this technique, I've had no problems with clogging. ✉ Darlene D., WA

A FINER FILTER. Even when you strain out the solids you use when making your garden tonics, you can still end up with clogs in your hose-end sprayer. Try attaching a filter from an airless paint sprayer to the hose-end sprayer's suction tube—the liquid solution will get through just fine, and the filter will remove any remaining solids. ✉ Adrienne M., PA

CLEAN UP THE MESS. I've found that some tonics leave clumpy messes behind in my hose-end sprayer. So after each use, I remove the sprayer jar and rinse off the applicator end. Then I aim the suction tube away from my body, cover the applicator end with my hand,

TAKE 5

Here are five not-so-common uses for eggshells around the yard and garden:

1 Feed your landscape by soaking eggshells in water for at least 24 hours to make a great liquid fertilizer.

2 Start seeds by poking a hole in the bottom of an eggshell, filling the shell with soil, and planting the seeds in it. Then plant the seedling, eggshell and all, in your garden.

3 Supercharge soil by drying and crushing the eggshells and then adding them to any planter mix.

4 Make great compost material by adding eggshells to your compost pile.

5 Sweeten acidic soil by adding crushed eggshells to it.

and turn the water on for 15 to 20 seconds. This flushes the mixing chamber and ensures that nothing's gonna stick around to plug up the works. ✉ Byron B., NH

FAST FUNNEL. To keep your hose-end sprayer from clogging, all you need is a plastic funnel and a nylon knee-high. Wet the knee-high and thread the toe through the small end of the funnel. Then stretch the ribbed end over the large end of the funnel and insert the small end of the funnel into a 2-liter pop bottle. After mixing a tonic, pour it through the funnel/stocking and into the bottle. You've just filtered out any lumps, bumps, and other debris. Using this method will also cut down on foam from beer and dishwashing liquid. Rinse and wash the knee-high after each use, and you'll be able to use it again and again. ✉ Vincent C., MO

AN APPLE A DAY. Whenever I eat an apple, I save the peels and core in a plastic-covered container in my fridge. When the container's full, I boil its contents, strain out the juice, and pour it into an ice cube tray. (I keep the remaining solids for later use.) Then I stick the tray in the freezer until the juice is frozen solid and put the cubes into a plastic freezer bag. I take out only what I need for my garden tonics (most ice cube trays hold 1/8 cup in each compartment), and keep the rest frozen. In the meantime, I gather the solids I strained from the juice and scatter them on all of my flower beds. ✉ Joannie O., IL

Jerry's Handy Hints

THE TOO-MUCH-SOLUTION SOLUTION

→ When a tonic calls for more liquid than the hose-end sprayer jar can hold, just mix the solution in a separate container and let it sit for a while until the suds go down. Then pour it into the sprayer jar and spray, spray, spray. The quantities of ingredients in the tonics that I recommend, when applied with a 20 gallon hose-end sprayer, should cover approximately 2,500 square feet.

MAKES NO DIFFERENCE TO ME. If you're shopping for ingredients to use in lawn and garden tonics, keep in mind that there really isn't much of a difference between the ammonias you'll find on the grocery store shelves, with the exception of the additives in them. I like the brands that have soap and lemon scent added because they can do three jobs at once: wash, feed, and scare flying bugs away. I've also found that brands of Epsom salts and corn syrup are pretty much the same, so I buy the cheapest ones I can find. ✉ Leslie R., RI

A BETTER BREW. Here's how I whip up batches of tobacco tea to use in garden tonics: I brew it in an old coffeemaker! Just add a pouch of tobacco to a clean coffee filter, fill the machine with water, and brew as you would coffee. When you're done, store the tea in a jar with a tight lid until you need it for a tonic. ✉ Pamela S., FL

TOBACCO, PLEASE. It pays to know the manager at your local convenience store. When the expiration date passes on loose tobacco products, ask if he or she would be willing (or legally able) to give you a can or pouch at a discount rather than trash it. Just explain that you're using it strictly for your garden, and you may get a break. ✉ Dennis M., IA

Ask Jerry

Q: A lot of your tonics call for tobacco tea. Just exactly how do you make tobacco tea?

A: This one's easy. To make tobacco tea, place half a handful of chewing tobacco in an old nylon stocking, and soak it in a gallon of hot water until the mixture is dark brown.

Grandma Putt's Wisdom

Some of my Grandma Putt's neighbors were hesitant to use tobacco tea in their garden because they were afraid it would infect their plants with tobacco mosaic virus. Maybe you've got that same concern, too. There's no need to worry, and I'll give you the same explanation Grandma gave to her neighbors: Tobacco mosaic starts when the virus is exposed to intense heat from a burning cigar, a lit cigarette, or burning pipe tobacco. Burning is the culprit, and the disease attaches itself to your hand and face and is then transferred to the plant. Fresh-leaf tobacco, made into a tea, is never a threat. So brew some tobacco tea and let your plants reap the benefits!

SOLAR POWER. Steep your tobacco tea in a large glass jar in the sun just as you would brew sun tea. When the solution is ready to use in one of your garden tonics, plug the opening of the jar with a nylon scrubber to strain out any solids that are floating around and could clog up your sprayer. ✉ Frank D., MI

ALTERNATIVE FOR TEA. I usually don't have any old panty hose lying around to use for making tobacco tea, so I use coffee filters instead. I simply fill a filter with the loose tobacco and tie it shut with a twist tie. It works just as well. ✉ Al B., IL

DOUBLE STRAIN. Keep your hose-end sprayer from clogging when applying tobacco tea by double-straining the liquid first. Start with a large, clean glass bottle that's got a tight-fitting lid. Punch several holes in the lid with a nail, then stretch the foot of a panty hose leg over the jar opening, and screw on the top. Make your tobacco tea, then carefully pour it through the jar lid strainer to be sure that it's perfectly clear. ✉ Faith B., MI

America's Best
Practical Problem Solvers

CHAPTER
11

Lush Landscaping

Setting the Scene

BEST IDEA ON THE BLOCK. The next time you plant a tree, try this method: Dig a large hole and put gravel in the bottom, then place half of a cement block on top of the gravel. Put the tree in the hole with the roots on top of the block. Then fill in the hole with planting soil and water well. I've used this technique with all of my trees, and have found that the block keeps the roots from getting waterlogged and rotting. ✉ **Dina E., WA**

IT'S A TIE. When I plant trees on my property, I use strips of old panty hose to tie the saplings to their stakes. The panty hose is soft and stretchy, so it doesn't cut into the young trunks as the trees grow. ✉ **Marie B., MI**

HOSE HELPERS. Every time you stake a newly planted sapling, you run the risk of damaging the tree's tender bark with wire or rope ties. To make sure they don't do damage, cover the ties with pieces of old garden hose. Your tree will thank you for the TLC by growing straight and tall. ✉ Ellen P., NY

SPUD STARTERS. When you're planting or transplanting a tree, do what I do and line the hole with baking potatoes. They'll help to hold the moisture that your young tree needs to get started. And as they decay, the potatoes provide nutrients for your tree to grow on. ✉ Carl O., DE

DOUBLE YOUR SHRUBS. If you'd like to add a new flowering shrub to your property, consider growing a new bush from one you already have. Simply select a long branch at the bottom of the plant, bend it, and bury the end next to the plant. By the following spring, it will have developed new roots of its own, and you can cut it away from the original shrub, dig it up, and replant it in a new location. ✉ Veronica R., KY

Jerry's Handy Hints

BOY MEETS GIRL

→ You say your holly bush isn't producing berries? Well, for starters, you need more than one plant for the—ahem—reproduction process to take place. So purchase at least one small male and one small female tree, then let nature take its course for beautiful results.

CURTAIN CORRAL. When it's time to trim your trees and shrubs, bring along an old shower curtain or a large sheet of plastic. I place one right under the tree when I'm trimming, and use it to catch the branches, leaves, and other debris. Then I just roll it up and drag it to my compost pile. I find that it's a whole lot easier than hauling a heavy wheelbarrow around. ✉ Jill G., GA

Tree and Shrub TLC

DRINK UP! It can take a L-O-N-G time to satisfy the thirst of a tree or large shrub. So I enlist the aid of empty 2-liter soda bottles. First I cut off the bottoms, saving the hard plastic bases. Then I use a nail to poke holes in the bottle caps and put them back on the bottles. I dig holes around my trees and shrubs that are deep enough to cover about half the height of each bottle when it's pushed upside-down into the hole. Then, with the caps on, I fill the bottles with water and set them cap-down into the holes, putting the bases on as lids. The water seeps slowly through the perforated caps and my thirsty trees and shrubs drink it up! ✉ **Sally P., WA**

IT'S IN THE CAN. To water trees and shrubs, try this: Cut off both ends of several large coffee and juice cans. Then dig a hole every few feet around the base of your trees and shrubs. Set a can into each hole with the rim at or just above ground level, then fill each can with small-size gravel. Every time you water, fill the cans right up to the brim. The water will seep down through the gravel, slowly giving the tree and shrub roots the drink they need. ✉ **Don L., IN**

BET ON BUCKETS. Don't throw away that old leaky bucket! It'll make an excellent slow-watering system for your trees and shrubs.

TAKE 5

Here are five not-so-common uses for buckets around the yard and garden:

1 Make a hose holder by attaching a 5-gallon pail to your house (near a faucet) and wrapping your hose around it for handy storage. Tuck watering attachments inside, and you're all set to grow.

2 Create a potato planter by drilling several drainage holes in the bottom of a 5-gallon bucket, filling it with planting soil, and planting your spuds. When it's time to harvest, simply turn the bucket upside down to empty it out.

3 Attract birds to your birdbath by creating a steady drip, drip, drip sound. Poke a tiny hole in a small bucket, and add water. Cover the bucket (to keep debris out), and hang it from a branch above your birdbath.

4 Hang a bucket full of hand tools from a tree branch near your garden, and you'll never have to run back and forth to the garage or shed again. Plus, the tools won't get drenched by your sprinkler, and they're out of reach of small children.

5 Store birdseed in a 5-gallon bucket that's got a tight-fitting lid. It'll keep the birdseed dry and safe from varmints.

Just fill up the holey bucket, set it near a tree, and let it do its work, slowly seeping water into the soil. ✉ George C., IN

THE GREEN SCENE. For greener shrubs, I mix 1 tablespoon of Epsom salts with 1 gallon of water in a bucket. Then I fill my 20 gallon hose-end sprayer with the solution and spray my shrubs once a month. They turn extra green just a few days after the first treatment—and stay that way! ✉ Wendy L., WV

SHRUB REVIVAL. If you have an old shrub that's starting to look its age, give it a new lease on life with this Jerry Baker elixir: Mix 1 can of beer, 1 cup of ammonia, ½ cup of dishwashing liquid, and ½ cup of molasses in a 20 gallon hose-end sprayer. Drench the shrub thoroughly, including the undersides of the leaves. If you have any leftover mixture, use it on your young shrubs, too. ✉ Paul M., NY

GET GROWING. If it's been some time since you topped and trimmed your large trees, and you still haven't noticed any new growth, stimulate them with a mixture of equal parts of liquid seaweed and ginger ale. I feed my trees this drink at their weep lines between mid-March and the beginning of April, and it really gets 'em growing. ✉ Denise Q., TX

DON'T PINE AWAY. I have lots of evergreens on my property, and boy, they sure do drop a lot of needles! But I don't let the needles go to waste. I rake 'em up and use 'em as winter mulch for all of my acid-loving plants. It saves me a small fortune in mulch costs, and it's easy to rake up come spring. ✉ Robert B., MO

Jerry's Handy Hints

WEEP NO MORE

→ You should always feed trees at the weep line (out at the tips of the longest branches). But for young trees whose roots haven't grown that far yet, start at the outer edge of the planting hole, and then feed them 6 inches farther out. That'll get the nutrients to them in the right place at the right time.

RING AROUND THE TREES. To protect my young trees from the cold winter weather, I give them a "hug" with this trick: Cut enough chicken wire to make a large cylinder, and connect the ends. Place the wire cylinder over the sapling, with the sapling as close to the center as possible. Then loosely place dry grass and leaves all around the tree, filling the cylinder. Come spring, you can remove the cylinder and reuse the leaves as mulch. ✉ John D., OK

IT'S A WRAP. Wrap 1-foot-long pieces of 4-inch corrugated black plastic drain tile around the trunks of your newly planted trees. The plastic will protect them from wind and critters, and the black material absorbs the sun's heat, helping to keep the baby trees warm all winter long. ✉ David S., IL

SAPLING SAVERS. I give my precious saplings winter protection with recycled 1-gallon vinegar jugs. I simply cut the jugs about 2 inches up from the bottom, and place one over each of my young trees, working the cut jug bottoms into the soil a bit so the wind can't blow them away. The jugs protect my baby trees until I remove them in spring. ✉ Edith L., WY

QUICK FIX

Before winter sets in, wrap the trunks of your shrubs and young trees loosely in aluminum foil to a height of between 18 and 24 inches. The glittering, rattling surface will send varmints looking elsewhere for their winter chow!

PAPER SHIELD. To protect the trunks of your young trees from bark-munching rabbits and deer, cut brown paper bags into strips about 6 inches wide. Then wrap the strips in spiral fashion up the trunk, overlapping as you go, fastening the ends with masking tape. If rabbits are your main concern, you can stop wrapping about 2 feet above the ground. But if you're trying to deter deer, continue wrapping up to the height of the tree's lowest branches. ✉ Carol B., NJ

DAMAGE CONTROL. Ice storms can really do a number on trees—bending branches and splitting limbs. After the ice melts, I repair the wounds by

WHEN LIGHTNING STRIKES

If lightning strikes a tree, it'll tear off a big piece of bark, and then the tree will begin to die. If this happens to one of your trees, you can bring it back to life by painting the zapped zone with three coats of interior latex paint as soon as you can after the damage has been done.

drilling holes and inserting carriage bolts and nuts across any splits. Then I gently tighten them up. To try this technique, cut the excess bolt lengths down to the nut, and fill the crack with silicone to keep out pests and moisture. As the tree heals, it'll push out the silicone and cover over the bolt heads and nut ends, leaving behind a normal scar. It's amazing what Mother Nature can do with a little help! ✉ Dick K., IN

Keeping Up Appearances

QUICK CLEANUP. Bring a large rectangle of cardboard with you the next time you trim your small shrubs. Cut a notch in the long side of the cardboard, and slip it around the bottom of the shrub. The clippings will fall on the cardboard, making cleanup a snap. All you have to do is remove the cardboard and carry it to your compost pile, where you can deposit it, clippings and all. ✉ Stacy H., IL

STOP THE SPREAD. Whenever I'm pruning a diseased tree or shrub, I do everything I can to keep the diseases from spreading. Here's how: In a bucket, mix ¼ cup each of antiseptic mouthwash, ammonia, and dishwashing liquid with 1 gallon of warm water. Pour the solution into a handheld sprayer, and drench all the pruning cuts on your plants, as well as your pruning tools. ✉ **Gene R., MT**

PUT THE SQUEEZE ON. When you need to apply sealer to pruning cuts on your trees and shrubs, nothing beats an old bottle of white glue. (Just rinse the bottle out well before adding any sealer to it.) The pointed tip provides great control for getting the sealer into small cuts. For larger wounds, squeeze the sealer on the area, then spread it around with a disposable foam pad. ✉ **Connie S., WA**

TWIN YOUR TREE. To take a cutting from a tree, I make a slit in a branch about one-third of the way through, then wrap the cut area with several layers of fabric to pad it. I hang a slowly leaking bottle from another branch, just over the site, to keep it supplied with water. After some time, a root forms, and I cut off the rooted branch and plant my new tree. ✉ **Gerald M., IL**

IT'S A STRETCH. When I root cuttings in water, I stretch a piece of aluminum foil across the top of a container filled with water and poke holes in the foil. Then I insert the cuttings through the

---

SUPER-DUPER SOLUTIONS

PRUDENT PRUNING ● I've found that there's rarely a need to prune my trees. But there are a few cases in which it might be beneficial, such as when you need to:

- Encourage strong branching patterns or a particular shape in young trees.
- Remove branches that cross, grow very close together, or grow at crazy angles.
- Eliminate limbs that have been damaged by wind or disease.

Other than these instances, the only parts that really need to be removed regularly are the twiggy "suckers" that sprout at the base of the tree.

holes. The foil holds the stems securely in place, and it keeps the water from evaporating as it would from an uncovered container. ✉ Herb L., OH

SIMPLE SEAL. After you've grafted a cutting to a tree, seal the union by wrapping the grafted area with strips of latex balloons instead of using rubber bands or grafting wax. Cut the balloons into 1/2-inch-wide, 6-inch-long strips, and wrap them around the graft, making sure you overlap the layers. The strips will disintegrate after a few months, long after the grafting site has healed. ✉ Greg M., IL

DON'T BE STUMPED. There's no need to remove tree stumps from your yard—just cut them to ground level. They make great surfaces for standing your potted plants and garden statues on. ✉ Fred W., MI

Jerry's Handy Hints

FALL RIGHT IN

➔ Fall is the best time of year to take cuttings from your plants. Just bundle your cuttings in groups of eight, and bury them 18 inches deep in soil for the winter. Then uncover them in early spring to graft or root them to your favorite stock.

PERFECT PLANTERS. You can avoid the hassle of removing a tree stump from your yard—if you keep it right where it is and turn it into a planter. Just cut a 3- to 6-inch-wide hole into the stump, and fill it with rich soil mixed with compost. Transplant a few annuals into it, water them well, and watch them grow. ✉ Susan R., MA

LET IT BE. Rather than struggle with taking down an old dead tree, I left mine in place. Since it wasn't in any danger of falling on my house or on my neighbor's property, I figured it wouldn't do any harm. And since I've left it standing, I've watched with delight as woodpeckers feast on the insects living in the dead wood, and other birds nest in the holes left behind. My dead tree contributes to the circle of life! ✉ Margaret K., PA

Ask Jerry

Q: About 20 years ago, I planted two fruit-less mulberry trees. I cut them down a few years ago, but the roots continue to run everywhere in the yard and the stumps continue to sprout. How can I get rid of them for good?

A: If you're not too keen on trying some of the previous tips (see "Don't be stumped" and "Perfect planters" on page 211), then all I can tell you is to dig, pull, chop, and pray!

RE-ROUTE ROOTS. When you must cut exposed roots in your lawn or planting beds, don't use clippers to do the job. Instead, dig the soil away from the roots and use a short-handled saw. Then make sure you seal the cuts with 8 ounces of interior latex paint mixed with 1 tablespoon of antiseptic mouthwash. That'll get the job done right. ✉ Jack R., CT

EASE WITH OIL. There's no need to wrestle with the ground when you're root-pruning. Instead, simply rub a light coat of motor oil on your shovel before plunging it into the ground. Apply a new smear before each cut, and your root-pruning chores will be a real breeze! ✉ Hazel M., KS

RAG TIME. Before I transplant a tree into a windbreak, I always tie a rag on a north-pointing branch. That way, when I replant the tree, I know exactly how to position it so that the branch with the rag on it is pointing north again. ✉ Robin H., WY

SMOOTH SHOVELING. You can save your back with this transplanting tip: Before you head out to dig up a shrub or small tree, grab a can of nonstick cooking spray. Lightly spritz your shovel with the oil before each use to make digging in the dirt a snap. ✉ **Joseph B., OH**

IT TAKES TWO TO TRANSPLANT. I learned this lesson the hard way—don't try to transplant a tree or large shrub on your own. If you recruit a helper, you'll get the job done a whole lot faster. While one of you gently pulls and jiggles the plant to the correct planting depth, the other can shovel in the soil and follow up with the water. Then both of you can stand back and admire your teamwork! ✉ **Bob E., NJ**

DIG DEEP AND WIDE. Most gardeners know that when it comes to planting trees, you should dig a hole that's deep and wide enough for the roots. But what you may not know is that it pays to dig another hole in the center of the first, as deep as you can, with a post-hole digger. Fill this second hole with a planting mix consisting of 5 pounds of compost, 2 pounds of gypsum, and 1 pound each of dry dog food and dry oatmeal. Then plant your tree. Believe you me, the roots of all trees will benefit from this bit of extra soil prep, so it's well worth your effort. ✉ **Betsy M., CO**

Don't Forget Your Fine-Feathered Friends

SIMPLY SUET. One of the simplest ways to feed your backyard birds is to make a suet feeding station. Find a thick fallen tree branch, drill 1-inch holes into it, and hang it from a tree. Fill the holes with suet (heating the suet will make it easier to pack) and you're good to go. Make sure to keep the suet coming after your feathered friends have flown in for a snack. ✉ **Frances S., MI**

PEANUTS AND PINE. Birds love pinecones stuffed with peanut butter. Here's how to make your own: Gather several good-sized pinecones and tie a 2-foot-long string or ribbon to the top of each. Spread peanut butter all over the cones, as deep as you can, and on the edges, too. Roll the sticky cones in sunflower seeds, and hang 'em with the string or ribbon in your backyard trees. Then you can sit back and watch the birds enjoy their treats. ✉ **Marie B., ON**

SQUIRREL BUSTER. Feeding birds in your backyard can be difficult if squirrels and raccoons get to the feeder first. I had critter problems until I hit upon this idea: I mounted my feeder on a pole made of PVC pipe, and placed it at least 10 feet away from any trees, shrubs, and branches. Not long afterward, I spotted some pesky squirrels trying to climb the pipe, but they quickly got frustrated and gave up. Problem solved! ✉ **Stacy H., IL**

BIRD ON A WIRE. I always hang a wire clothes hanger near my hummingbird feeder. The reason? Hummers love resting on it after filling up at their drinking station, so they linger a bit longer near the feeder. ✉ **Brad T., MO**

SWEET TREAT. Don't waste your hard-earned bucks on store-bought hummingbird nectar because it's very simple to make some at home. You'll need 1 part granulated sugar to 4 parts water. Heat the water almost to the boiling point, remove it from the heat, and stir in the sugar until it's completely dissolved. Once the mixture is cool, pour it into your feeder and watch the hummers come a-buzzin'! ✉ **Denise R., WA**

DON'T BE A DRIP. I find it to be very inconvenient to fill my hummingbird feeders outside, and carrying a full nectar feeder from my kitchen to the yard leaves a sticky trail of drips along the way. So

ANOTHER GREAT IDEA!

BE FRUITFUL

You can attract birds to your backyard by planting trees and shrubs that have the fruit, seeds, or berries they love. Mountain ash, wild cherry, mulberry, blackberry, honeysuckle, hawthorn, and crabapple are just a few of the many attention getters. While these natural foods will bring birds to your yard, if you want them to linger, be sure to include these in your landscape:

* BIRDHOUSES. These will attract bluebirds, chickadees, nuthatches, purple martins, swallows, woodpeckers, and more. You'll find houses at bird-supply, discount, and hardware stores, and online. Buy sturdy, well-made birdhouses. They'll cost a bit more, but will outlast their skimpy cousins.

* FEEDERS. Even though you've planted bird-attracting trees and shrubs, having a few feeders in your yard will bring even more fine-feathered friends. If you position your feeders so that you have a good view from your house, you'll have the pleasure of watching the birds come and go each day. Buy feeders that are practical and easy to use and clean, as well as convenient for the birds. Make sure that there's room for at least a dozen birds to perch at one time, that the feeder holds enough seed so that you don't have to refill it more than once a day, and that it's well made.

* BIRDBATHS. Birds will drink from just about anything when they're thirsty. But to really make them happy, set up a birdbath that's at or near ground level. The bath should have places for birds to perch, such as molded faux rocks beside the water and protruding from it, like the stones in a stream, and the surface should be rough, so birds can get a grip. If the water depth is shallow, birds will feel safe when using your birdbath. Two inches of water is perfect for jays and robins; smaller birds need shallower water. Look for baths that have multiple depths to attract a wider variety of birds.

my solution is to hold a dishcloth below the full feeder when I head out the door. It stops the drips and also comes in handy for wiping up any wayward spills that occur on my way to hanging the feeder. And since it's only sugar water, cleanup is a snap. I just give the towel a quick rinse in warm water and hang it out to dry.
✉ Sandra L., DE

CLEAN SWEEP. The birds love visiting my backyard feeders, but they sure leave a big mess behind! I've discovered a handy way to clean up all the spilled seed, empty hulls, and overflow in a snap—with my wet/dry vac. It's a quick and easy way to tidy things up in a hurry. ✉ Doris L., NY

NIGHT SOAK. Here's how to keep your backyard birdbath in tip-top shape. After the birds have gone to bed for the evening, empty your birdbath, fill it with white vinegar, and let it soak. In the morning, wipe it clean using a cloth or a soft brush, then rinse it out thoroughly before filling it with fresh, clean water. Your feathered friends will give you a good housekeeping seal of approval! ✉ Laurie F., OH

EASY CLEAN. Want a simple way to clean your birdbath overnight with absolutely no scrubbing involved? Then put a couple of denture-cleaning tablets in the old water before you go to bed; there's no need to empty the birdbath first. In the morning, all you have to do is dump the dirty water out, wipe up any residue, and fill 'er up with clean water. ✉ Diane P., MI

QUICK FIX

You'll easily attract hummingbirds to your backyard if you hang out a hummingbird feeder—but you'll attract plenty of ants and yellow jackets, too. So switch to a smaller feeder, and as soon as it's empty, wash it thoroughly before refilling it and hanging it back outside. And keep in mind—hummers love the color red. So if you plant plenty of bright red flowers, you'll create your own heavenly hummingbird hangout.

CHAPTER
12

Beautiful Blooms

Off to a Good Start

BEAT THE HEAT. When you want to grow hydrangeas and other colorful shrubs in a hot climate where the soil is sandy and doesn't hold water, you need to specially prepare the planting holes. Here's what I do: I start by digging a hole twice as deep and wide as the original plant pot. Then I put a 2-inch layer of clay on the bottom, add a layer of pine needles, and cover it all with dirt. I put the plant in the hole, then mix the sandy soil I dug out with pine bark mulch, and fill the rest of the hole with that mixture. I finish with another thick layer of pine bark mulch, and water deeply. Try it—you'll be rewarded with beautiful, colorful flowers. ✉ Deborah B., TX

SIMPLE SEED SOAK. Before planting morning glories, soak the seeds in water overnight. Then place the seeds on a damp paper towel and seal them in a plastic bag for several days. Once the sprouts appear, use tweezers to transplant them directly into the warm garden soil. Then step back and get ready for glorious morning glories! ✉ **Monica S., WI**

PROTECT THOSE PANSIES. If you get the gardening itch early—when temps are warm during the day, but still dip below freezing overnight—go ahead and plant your pansies, but keep a paper bag handy. Put the bag over the colorful blooms as soon as the sun goes down, and take it off after sunrise the next day. With this helping hand, the pansies will grow well and keep producing new blooms. ✉ **Rhonda M., OR**

A QUICK CLIP. The best trick for helping your perennials look their best and bloom their longest is also the easiest: Simply remove the spent flowers every few days so they don't set seed. And the best tools for this task are a good pair of garden clippers and a basic 5-gallon plastic bucket. You can often find these buckets for free, or for just a buck or two, at fast-food restaurants, delis, and bakeries. ✉ **Adrienne C., OH**

EASY INSPIRATION. You can get terrific ideas for long-lived perennials by visiting old cemeteries or abandoned home-steads in your area. You'll see plants there that have been thriving for years without any special care whatsoever, so you know they'll do well in your garden. ✉ **Ryan M., IL**

PORTABLE POTS. When I plant my flower garden, I always place some of

Jerry's Handy Hints

MAKE YOUR BED

➔ Prep your planting bed just right for grow-ing annuals and you'll be sure to get ample root growth for a summer filled with fabulous flowers. Here's how: For each 100 square feet of garden, spread six bags of shredded leaves, two bags of grass clippings, ¼ cup of sugar, and 1 cup of Epsom salts, and spade them all in well. Then plant your flowers and watch 'em grow!

MADE IN THE SHADE ● Prepare the soil for a shady flower bed by drilling holes 4 inches deep and filling them with professional potting soil. Then plant your shade-loving seedlings. New Guinea impatiens are one good choice—they're a beautiful, low-maintenance, shade-happy favorite.

my choices in pots and set them among the flowers I've planted in the ground. This way, I can rearrange my flower beds as needed for maximum color and height. ✉ **Bootsie H., WI**

ROLL 'EM, ROLL 'EM, ROLL 'EM. Do you have trouble getting anything to grow in your shady garden? If so, here's an idea that will work for you—put your garden on wheels! Make a movable bed out of an old toy wagon. Drill drainage holes in the bottom, add a thin layer of gravel, top it with soil, and plant lots of shade-loving flowers and foliage. When the plants start looking a little spindly from the lack of light, just wheel them into a brighter spot for a few days, then roll 'em back to the shade. ✉ **Amory R., VA**

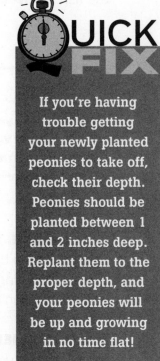

A BIT OFF THE TOP. I always cut the top third off my impatiens immediately after planting them. It encourages the plants to spread out more fully, without becoming tall and leggy. The result? I have large, bushy impatiens with lots of beautiful blooms. ✉ **Kristin H., NC**

JUST A PINCH. Give your autumn-flowering perennials a pinch in early to midsummer. Snipping or pinching the top few inches off each

QUICK FIX

If you're having trouble getting your newly planted peonies to take off, check their depth. Peonies should be planted between 1 and 2 inches deep. Replant them to the proper depth, and your peonies will be up and growing in no time flat!

stem tip will delay blooming by a few weeks, so you'll have fabulous flowers to enjoy just when you want 'em. ✉ Anthony B., MI

INDOOR/OUTDOOR PREP. Just before you set out your indoor-grown annual transplants, water them with a solution of ¼ cup of baking soda per gallon of water. This will temporarily stop their growth and increase their strength, so they'll shrug off the tougher conditions that await them outdoors. ✉ Lucy G., IN

SOMETHING FISHY. Here's an old-time trick that really works for me: I drop a medium-sized perch or trout into the soil wherever I'm going to plant a rosebush. This natural fertilizer makes the flowers grow like wildfire! ✉ John V., WA

ANOTHER FISH TALE. If you want truly amazing rose blooms, try this: After a fishing trip, save the fish innards and plant them under and around your roses. Your roses will be gorgeous, all thanks to the fish. ✉ Wendy D., KY

ANOTHER GREAT IDEA!

SMELLING LIKE ROSES

If the roses you've planted don't have any fragrance, try another variety. A few of the more modern types have little or no fragrance as a result of breeding. So seek out heirloom varieties for more aromatic results.

A CUT ABOVE. Cut your first rose blooms off just above a five-leaf cluster, and do the same for all of the surrounding blooms. This selective pruning will ensure that you'll have bunches of beautiful roses all season long. ✉ Carol R., WI

DON'T BUG ME! I spread cedar mulch around my roses and other flowers to help keep destructive bugs away. It works like a charm,

Grandma Putt's Wisdom

Roses in my Grandma Putt's garden were for more than just bouquets. She used the fragrant petals along with other ingredients to make a potpourri that could perfume an entire room. Grandma Putt had all sorts of recipes for potpourris; as a matter of fact, anything that smelled good was a candidate—flowers, sweet herbs, fragrant grasses, vanilla, lemon and orange rinds, walnut leaves, and so on.

To make her favorite potpourri, she started with a pint-sized glass jar with a lid and added these ingredients: 4 lightly packed cups of fresh rose petals, 3 tablespoons of mixed spices such as ground cloves and allspice, and 1 tablespoon of powdered orrisroot (which she bought at the drugstore). She air-dried the rose petals on paper towels until they were crisp; about three days usually did it. After she put the petals in the jar, she sprinkled the other ingredients over them, stirring gently, and then put the lid on the jar. Then she would open the jar whenever she wanted the wonderful fragrance to escape.

and I never have to use toxic chemicals to keep pests out of my flower garden. ✉ **Tammy W., NJ**

JAVA JOLT. Sprinkle used, unflavored coffee grounds around your rosebushes, working them loosely into the soil. You'll grow beautiful, healthy roses with a bonus: Insects are repelled by coffee, so the grounds will also keep your roses pest-free. ✉ **Deborah R., LA**

SMELLS LIKE . . . GLUE? If your rosebushes are flowering beautifully but lack the typical scent, I've got the solution for you: Dig a hole under the bush, right down to the roots, and drop in a teaspoon of powdered glue (found at craft-supply or hardware stores). I've done this and believe it or not, before too long, my roses started smelling like, well, roses! Try it and you'll see. ✉ **Arlene K., NH**

DARLING DAHLIAS. Mark your dahlias using tongue depressors and a wood-burning tool. Burn the name of the dahlia on one side of the depressor, and the color and variety on the other. Drill a small hole in the top of the depressor, and tie a string to it at planting time. Push the depressors into the soil to identify each planted flower. Then when it's time to dig up and store your tubers for the

TAKE 5

Five uses for chopsticks in your yard and garden include:

1 For perfect planting every time, use a chopstick or two to make the right size holes when you're sowing seeds. Simply poke, drop, cover, and move on.

2 After taking cuttings and planting them in starting flats, stick several chopsticks in the soil, then place a clear plastic bag over the whole shebang. The plastic helps keep the cuttings moist, while the chopsticks keep the plastic off the cuttings and the soil.

3 The next time you cover your garden bed to protect it from the wind, weather, or hungry varmints, keep the row cover in place by using chopsticks to pin it to the soil.

4 If you're using those green plastic berry baskets to protect newly planted sunflower, melon, or cuke seeds, anchor them in place with a chopstick or two.

5 Use chopsticks and twist ties as stakes to support smaller branches and leaves on any floppy plants.

Ask Jerry

Q: I've tried sowing wildflower seeds in my yard, with no luck. Very few of them ever come up, let alone bloom. What's the secret to growing these beauties?

A: Packets of wildflower seeds can lead to beautiful beds of flowers, but you'll have a much better chance of success if you follow this advice: Mix the seeds with a little soil and put them to sleep in the fridge for a week prior to planting them as early in the spring as possible. It works every time. By the way, any of the wildflower mixes that you can buy through gardening catalogs or Web sites are perennial mixes. So what's the secret to keeping them producing year after year? Mow 'em down to 3 inches in the fall, and let the cut stems lie on the ground over the winter.

winter, remove the depressor from the ground and tie it to the tuber. That way, you'll always know what's what! ✉ **Charles W., MI**

A PERFECT PAIRING. I plant spring-blooming bulbs in between my hostas. The bulbs come up and bloom before the hostas do, and by the time the bulbs' flowers start to fade, my hostas are big and leafy enough to camouflage the browning bulbs. ✉ **Lois B., SD**

BAMBOO FOR YOU. Leave bamboo stakes in the ground to re-mind you of where you planted your lilies. In the spring, tie three to four strips of soft material to the bamboo, so when the lilies shoot up, you'll have plant ties at your fingertips. ✉ **Shirley H., CA**

SUNNY SUPPORT. Don't get rid of sunflower stalks in the fall; you can make a trellis out of them next year. After harvesting the flowers, strip the leaves from the stalks, and let the stalks dry for a few weeks. Then chop them down and keep them protected in a safe spot over the winter. Next spring, assemble the stalks in the shape you want, and tie the cross pieces together with string. Now you're ready to grow! ✉ Gerald M., IL

TIDY TRELLIS. If you have a big, blank, boring section of siding outside your house, cover it with climbing flowers. Start by making a string trellis—simply pound a few nails into the house siding, and tie string from one nail to the other in a sunburst pattern. Plant a flowering vine like morning glories, and let the vines grow and fill in the blank spot with beautiful flowers. In the fall, collect all the seeds and divvy them up into fancy little jars. They make the perfect stocking stuffers for your gardening friends. ✉ Sherry D., WI

THINK OUTSIDE THE PHLOX. Here's one sure thing I've learned about planting phlox: It's best to wait until spring to plant the seeds in a sunny location with good drainage. Then I wait until July before I feed them. I'm not sure why this works, but after much trial and error, I've found that if I follow this schedule, I end up with a bed full of beautiful flowers, complete with butterflies fluttering by to check 'em out. ✉ Robert W., NY

Blossom and Grow

SLOW THE FLOW. It's hard to control the flow of water from a watering can that doesn't have a sprinkler head, and too much water at once can drown young plants and delicate flowers. Here's how I solved the problem: I stretched the foot from a pair of panty

Grandma Putt's Wisdom

My Grandma Putt was very particular about what her flowers drank. She said that plants would choose rainwater over plain old drinking water any day. So she'd leave several large buckets outside during a storm. Afterward, she'd warm the water by setting the buckets in the sun for a few days. Finally, before pouring the water on her plants, she'd soften it by dissolving a little washing soda (sodium carbonate) in the buckets. She'd use about 1 ounce of washing soda to 12 gallons of water. The soda helped rid the water of excess minerals, making it clean and safe for her flowers.

Believe me, if you give your flowers the water they want, you'll be rewarded with happy, healthy bloomers. That's what Grandma Putt did, and she always had the biggest, bestest flowers around!

hose over the spout of my watering can. That way, I can give my flowers a gentle drink instead of a big gulp. ✉ **June D., OH**

NO MORE NUMB THUMBS. If you don't have a spray nozzle for your garden hose, you probably water with your thumb over the tip of the hose to disperse the water flow. And I'm guessing that your thumb gets pretty chilled using this technique. Next time, slip on a rubber finger cover (available at office-supply stores, they're intended to help you sort papers and count paper money quickly). The thick rubber will keep your thumb from chilling out! ✉ **Kay J., CO**

BOTTLED WATER. I use old soda bottles to automatically water my flower garden. I start by cutting the end of an 8-inch-long piece of 1-inch-diameter PVC pipe at a 45-degree angle, and sinking the angled end of the pipe several inches down into the garden's soil. Then I take a clean, empty 2-liter soda bottle with a cap and fill the

QUICK FIX

bottle almost to the top with water. I pound a small nail hole into the center of the cap, then screw the cap onto the bottle. Out in my garden, I turn the bottle upside down and insert the cap end into the PVC pipe. The water slowly drips into the soil, giving my flowers the drink they need. Use several of these "watering spikes" throughout your gardens, and you won't have to spend hours each day standing there with a hose or watering can. ✉ Joanna S., TX

MAKE IT WARM. I've heard that plants prefer to be watered with warm water. That's fine with me, but I don't bother running up my water-heating bill by giving my flowers and plants hot tap water. Instead, I fill my buckets with cold water, let them sit in the sun for most of the day, then use the nice warm water to quench my plants' thirst. ✉ Wilma R., MN

GOT MILK? After you've poured out the last drop of milk, don't rinse out the carton. Instead, fill it to the top with water, and use the milky solution to water your outdoor flowering plants. It'll make 'em lush and green. ✉ Nancy R., OR

A FINE FILTER. I bury used coffee filters in my garden soil after the grounds dry. The grounds give my acid-loving plants the jolt they need, and the filters help keep moisture in my garden soil between waterings. ✉ Verla V., TX

BOTTLE-FED FLOWERS. When I water my tender flower seed-lings, I use a sports bottle that's got a pop-top cap. It lets me control the water flow better than when I use a regular watering can, so I don't drown my baby plants. ✉ Meredith H., WA

SLO-MO WATERING. Poking holes in the bottoms of plastic milk jugs and using them to water your plants is a great idea that really works! Bury each holey jug up to its neck near a plant, and fill it with water. The liquid will slowly seep out, keeping your garden moist and well watered. ✉ Lisa G., MO

IT'S A/C FOR ME! If you're tired of high water bills, but can't stand to see your garden dry up in summer's oppressive heat, then it's time to get creative. You're probably running your air conditioner around the clock, and it's producing lots of condensation, so take advantage of all that free water. Place buckets under window units to collect the condensation, or dig a hole under the pipes of outdoor compressors so you can place buckets there to collect any runoff. Then water your thirsty plants, and enjoy your beautiful, blooming garden. ✉ Laurie W., VA

PUMPING IRON. To add much-needed iron to your garden, water it using an old, rusty coffee can. Your plants will drink the iron-laced liquid right up! ✉ Jack B., IN

Ask Jerry

Q: I've been told that my plants would do better if I didn't water them with tap water. If this is this true, then what should I use?

A: Go ahead and use tap water, but add an ounce of hydrogen peroxide per gallon. And if you have conditioned water—which can be salty—either use the water before it enters the softener system, or set out a rain barrel and gather water naturally.

TANKS A LOT. Don't dump the old water when you clean your fish tank. Instead, use it to water your flowering plants. This nutrient-rich drink will help them really thrive. ✉ Andrea G., IL

IN A PICKLE. This sounds a bit crazy, but every time I finish a jar of pickles, I dump the remaining pickle juice on my gardenias. I don't know just what it is about the briny water that these flowers love, but boy, do they ever, and they reward me with beautiful blooms. Try it and you'll see! ✉ Michael L., MD

STEP RIGHT UP. Even if you have a large garden, you can water it easily by using a stepladder. Simply attach a sprinkler to your hose, tie it to the top step of the ladder, and let 'er rip. You'll cover a lot of ground in no time at all. ✉ Tom L., MI

SUPER SOAKER. If you have an old, leaky hose lying around, don't toss it out! Just turn it into a soaker hose instead. All you have to do is straighten the hose on the ground and punch holes all the way through using an ice pick, spacing the holes about 12 inches

---

SUPER-DUPER SOLUTIONS

WATER WISDOM ● Not sure when it's the right time to water your flower garden? Listen to your plants—they'll tell you! Here are some signs that indicate your flowers are thirsty:

- Leaves droop slightly during the heat of the day, but recover once the sun goes down.
- Leaves are duller or grayer than normal.
- The foliage of fleshy-leaved plants shrivels slightly or feels soft to the touch.

But before you go hog wild with watering, check the soil to make sure the ground isn't waterlogged. Plants that have too much moisture may also show these same symptoms.

ANOTHER GREAT IDEA!

SEASONAL SOLUTION

Soaker hoses snaked through your flower beds don't simply make watering a snap—they also keep your water bill in check! That's because they deliver water directly to the plants' roots and minimize evaporation. Cover them with mulch and leave them in place year-round, and your watering woes will be a thing of the past.

apart. Then tie 6-inch strips of rags around each punched area, screw one end of the hose to the faucet, and put a hose end cap on the other end. Lay the hose in your garden bed, turn the water on low, and let your garden beauties soak. ✉ Ginny M., IL

HOSE CONTROL. When you drag a hose through the garden to water your flowers, it's hard to keep from knocking over the precious plants at the edges and corners of the beds. So control your garden hose by pounding an 18-inch metal pipe, PVC pipe, or stake into the ground at each corner of the bed. Then cut a hole in a few old tennis balls, and stick one on top of each stake. The pipe keeps the hose off the plants, and the tennis balls keep you from tripping over the nearly invisible stakes. ✉ Donald G., IA

A BLOOMIN' BREW. If you can't get your rhododendrons and other acid-loving plants to bloom, start feeding them leftover coffee and coffee grounds. In no time at all, they'll be thanking you with loads of beautiful blooms. ✉ Gretchen H., MN

TREAT THEIR FEET. For terrific spring blooms, I give my rhododendron a "pedicure" in the fall. I root-prune it, then pour ¼ cup of sugar into the cuts. Afterward, I water it well and mulch heavily with shredded cedar bark. My fall primping guarantees fabulous flowers the following spring. ✉ Linda R., CT

WAGE WAR ON WEEDS. Don't let ugly weeds spoil the beauty of your flower gardens. Stay on top of the rascals by pulling up weed seedlings as soon as you spot them. If you've got older, more stubborn weeds to contend with, do as I do and use a well-sharpened, long-handled shovel to do battle without having to bend over. Use it to dig 'em up at the root, then scoop 'em up and toss 'em into your garden waste bin. ✉ Jo Ellen H., NE

FORK IT OVER. Sometimes there are so many weeds growing in my garden that my regular tools seem useless. That's when I reach for a kitchen tool instead—a 12-inch, two-pronged kitchen fork. It makes for easy weeding in tight spots. I just position the tines around the base of a weed and rotate the fork. It brings up the whole weed, roots and all, in a hurry. ✉ Richard H., VT

WEED WIPEOUT. When weeds start their march across your flower beds, stop 'em dead in their tracks with this lethal weapon: Mix 1 tablespoon of gin, 1 teaspoon of apple cider vinegar, and 1 teaspoon of dishwashing liquid into 1 quart of very warm water. Pour the mixture into a handheld sprayer bottle and use it to drench weeds to the point of runoff. Just be sure not to spray any of your flowers with this powerful potion. ✉ Kim L., OK

PILE ON THE PILE. Carpet pile, that is. I cut up old carpeting and rugs into strips, then lay them down in my garden between the rows. They keep the weeds down and act as mulch around my plants. ✉ Mary C., CO

Jerry's Handy Hints

SINGIN' IN THE RAIN

→ Whenever I see Gene Kelly dancing to "Singin' in the Rain," I always think about weeding. Yep, we always weeded in the rain or, to be more precise, after a rain. That's because weed roots come up easier when the soil is moist, so that's the best time to attack them. And singin' while you're weedin' makes the work go that much faster!

TRIM TIME ● After a hard frost hits, you won't have to worry about weeding your garden, but you do have to turn your attention to cleanup. Pull out dead annuals and cut back perennials, except for the ones that provide winter interest (like ornamental grasses), or food for birds (like asters). Add the trimmings to your compost pile—unless the plants were bothered by pests or diseases; in that case, just toss 'em in the trash.

GIVE 'EM A BREAK. Protect your rhododendrons and other fragile plants with windbreaks before winter arrives. Start by pounding precut lengths of two-by-two lumber, or branches that have fallen in your yard, into the ground in front of each plant. Then, using a staple gun, attach a length of burlap between the posts. You'll have an effective and inexpensive windbreak in no time. ✉ Perry N., IN

CAGED HEART. After my bleeding heart plant has died back for the winter, but before it starts to grow in the spring, I place a tomato cage over it. The cage supports (and protects) my prized perennial until it gets growing again. ✉ Kay W., WA

DIVIDE AND MULTIPLY. If your impatiens get leggy, simply cut off the tops and replant the cuttings in small pots. Put them in a sunny spot and keep them watered. In a few weeks, you'll have plenty of new plants. ✉ Melissa H., FL

BEAT THE FROST. Be sure to clean up your spent impatiens and begonias before the first frost. Why? Because once they're nipped by Ol' Jack Frost, these juicy-stemmed plants turn into a slimy mush that's no fun to handle! ✉ Garrett B., OH

THIN TO WIN. Thinning crowded seedlings is a must, but if you hate the thought of killing all those healthy little sprouts, here's a solution: Instead of pulling out or snipping off the extra baby plants, carefully lift them out with a spoon or tiny trowel, and pot them up or plant them in the corner of your veggie garden. Then when you need color to fill a bare spot in your flower garden later on, simply pop in the extras where you need them. That way, your beds and borders will look as lush and lovely in fall as they do in early summer! ✉ **Wyatt R., CO**

PROTECT YOUR ROSES. In the fall, put a layer of leaves all around your roses and perennials. When spring arrives, you can easily sweep away (or blow out) the leaves, and you won't have to pull up any weeds. ✉ **Helen B., PA**

FOREVER ROSES. I keep my roses alive over the winter by giving them some TLC—I mound oak bark shavings around the cut-back rose branches. Then during the first week of October, I mix dirt with ½ cup of a sulfur-potassium-magnesium product and apply it in and around the roots of each bush. My roses stay healthy right on through to summer! ✉ **Julia K., WI**

ROSE ROUNDUP. Roses need to be "toughened up" if you want them to make it through the winter. Just follow these steps, and

Ask Jerry

Q: I am growing a 'Royal Highness' hybrid tea rose, and it's very winter sensitive. What winter protection do you suggest that'll keep this beauty alive?

A: Before I mulch, I wrap my sensitive roses with cheesecloth and then cover them with foam rose cones (available at garden centers). That should do the trick for you, too.

there'll be no need to cover your roses, even in the coldest areas. First, don't overwater them during the summer months. Second, never fertilize after August. Third, don't prune in the fall or cut after September (it'll encourage weak, late growth). And fourth, dump a quart of dirt on the center of the plant in late fall. That's the game plan to get your roses through the winter months and have 'em blooming beautifully next summer.
✉ Kathy W., MI

DOUBLE-DUTY DUST. I protect my roses from winter's freezing temps by covering the ground around the bushes with 6 to 8 inches of sawdust. In the spring, I clean the sawdust off the ground quickly and easily with my wet/dry vac. Then I empty the canister into a bag and save the sawdust to use the following winter. ✉ Donna Z., WI

SHELTER YOUR MUMS. Don't be in a hurry to tidy up your mums after a hard frost. Cut off the dead flowers if you want, but leave the stems standing; they'll help insulate the crown from cold temperatures. For additional protection, cover the clumps with evergreen boughs, leaves, or 6 inches of loose straw toward the end of November. Then in early spring, remove the mulch and trim off the dead stems. ✉ Owen V., IA

LET 'EM BREATHE. I don't smother my perennials with a thick layer of mulch every winter. Instead, I lay old cornstalks or some

Jerry's Handy Hints

LOVIN' LILACS

→ If lilacs are allowed to grow too tall (over 8 feet) or too thick, or if they develop long, straight shafts called suckers, they'll never bloom. So cut any old, thick canes that don't produce; cut out all suckers level with the ground; cut back healthy bloom stock to 6 feet high; and root-prune the bushes in the fall, pouring ¼ cup of Epsom salts into the cuts to stimulate blooms come spring. After they start producing flowers, trim them only in June, after they've bloomed.

woody brush over my beds. That way, I don't have mulch resting right on the plants, and my perennials are able to breathe under their warm winter blanket. ✉ Nora R., MO

BUFFER WITH BRANCHES. After Christmas, I recycle our holiday tree by sawing off the branches and laying them over my sleeping perennials. I arch the branches over the plants to protect them from snow, frost, and damaging winds. Best of all, the branches are easy to lift up and replace whenever I want to check on my sleeping beauties. ✉ Jeannie L., KS

SUPER-DUPER SOLUTIONS

CLEVER CLEMATIS ● Clematis are generally low-maintenance plants, so even if you notice drying leaves and browning stems, it's okay to leave them alone because they'll do just fine. And if they don't bloom every year, not to worry—sometimes clematis just skip a year. If yours tend to bloom late, cut 'em back in the spring. If they're early bloomers, cut 'em back in the fall. After cutting them back, root-prune them and sprinkle a handful of Epsom salts into the cuts.

HIYA, CINTH! Don't cut off hyacinth foliage until it has yellowed and begun to die back. The leaves are needed to provide food to build up the bulb so it can bloom again next year. Once the foliage yellows, you can cut it back all the way to the ground. The bulbs will be dormant until next spring, when they'll grow again and flower. ✉ Chuck L., DE

SAFE STORAGE. You can store your bulbs in Styrofoam® coolers for the winter, but check the coolers first to see if they are completely waterproof. If they are, then you can leave 'em outside and your bulbs will be protected from all kinds of wild winter weather. ✉ Maria H., WA

TAKE

Here are five not-so-common uses for ice chests in your yard and garden:

1 Old coolers are perfect as mini rain barrels, catching (and holding) water as it comes pouring out of your downspout.

2 If you've got any grass seed left over after sowing, keep it high and dry in a foam cooler. It'll protect the seed from temperature fluctuations and, more importantly, keep it from spilling all over the place.

3 Use an old cooler (with its lid, of course) as a portable potting bench and a convenient place to keep your potting supplies all together. The lid makes an excellent work surface, and if it's sturdy enough, you can even use it as a seat when you're working in your garden.

4 Recycle old foam coolers by stacking several of them on top of each other and using them as planters. Place the first on the ground with a long side facing you. Then stack a second on top of it with a short side facing you. Alternate long and short sides as you stack them. Cut a hole in the center of the bottom of each cooler, and thread a hose (that's already got holes punched along its length) through the top cooler all the way to the bottom one. Fill them with potting soil, put plants in the corners of the lower coolers and all across the top one, and you're good to go!

5 Old foam coolers make excellent winter protectors for roses and other tender shrubs. Cut a couple of small vents in the bottom, and invert the cooler over the plant. Then anchor it in place with a handy rock or two.

QUICK FIX

BOX YOUR BULBS. Here's how I protect my treasured flowering bulbs from pesky bulb eaters: I start by making boxes out of ¼-inch vinyl-coated hardware screen. I simply cut six appropriately sized pieces for each box, fasten the bottom and sides together with twist ties, and set aside the top pieces. After I dig the planting holes, I lower a box into each hole, filling it with ½ inch of soil. Then I place my bulb on top of the soil, secure the top piece to the box, and fill the hole with the remaining soil. My precious bulbs are then safe from predators, but there's still plenty of room for the plant to grow through the mesh on top of the box. ✉ Charlotte S., WI

TENDER TREATMENT. Most tender bulbs like gladiolus and tuberous begonias can be kept from year to year with a bit of TLC. As soon as their leaves start to turn color in the fall, dig them up and set them in a shady spot to dry for a few days. Then pack them in paper bags or boxes filled with dry peat moss or vermiculite, and keep them in a cool, dry place until spring. ✉ Clara R., RI

BABY THOSE BULBS. When you dig up gladiolus and other tender bulbs for winter storage, treat 'em like babies. Simply dust them with medicated baby powder, drop them into a panty hose leg, and hang it up in a cool, dry place. ✉ Michelle N., DE

LIVELY LILIES. To keep your daylily plants healthy and blooming year after year, dig up and separate the bulbs each fall. Unearth the clumps and separate them by hand, or use a pitchfork or shovel. Discard any old, withered, or dying plants before replanting the healthy ones. That's all there is to it! ✉ Denise F., PA

Flower Power

SPUD SECURITY. Want to help your cut flowers stay fresh longer? Then do what I do and use a potato. Simply cut slits in a white potato, and push the stems of the flowers into the slits, making sure they are secure. Then place the spud in the bottom of an opaque vase. If you place the vase out of direct sunlight and away from heat sources, the potato will help keep your flowers looking good for up to two weeks. ✉ Delia E., WA

FRESH FORMULA. Freshly cut flowers are a beautiful, cheerful way to bring the outdoors inside, but they never seem to last. To keep 'em at their blooming best, I mix 1 part lemon-lime soda and 3 parts water to make a quart of solution. Then I add ¼ teaspoon of bleach and pour the mixture into a vase. I add another ¼ teaspoon of bleach about every four or five days. Try it, and you'll be amazed at how long your flowers stay nice and pretty. ✉ Thelma K., IN

PEBBLE POWER. To hold freshly cut flowers in place in a wide-mouthed vase, use plastic pebbles (the kind used for stuffing toys; available at craft-supply stores). A few handfuls will float on top of the water and form a layer through which the stems can move easily, but the pebbles will give some stability to the arrangement. You can reuse the pebbles for future bouquets by simply rinsing them in a light bleach solution and then drying them thoroughly. ✉ Polly W., PA

Jerry's Handy Hints

CLOUDY WITH A CHANCE OF CLEARING

→ To get rid of the cloudy haze in your favorite vase, let it soak in vinegar for a few hours. Then rinse it and wipe down inside it with a soft sloth. It'll look as good as new!

Grandma Putt's Wisdom

When my Grandma Putt wanted to add daffodils to a cut-flower arrangement, she picked her daffs when they were about half open. Then she'd make a 1-inch-long slit up through the base of each stem and stand the flowers in water up to their necks for several hours before putting them into an arrangement. Why bother with this extra step? Because Grandma knew that daffodil stems are full of sticky sap that clogs the stems of other flowers. Treating them this way prevents that problem and lengthens the vase life of all the other flowers in the bouquet.

PERFECT PANSIES. The next time you're arranging pansies you cut from your garden, put them in a flower bowl that's half filled with sand. Add water after the pansies are inserted and your flowers will remain standing tall. ✉ Patricia B., KS

SUPPORT WITH STRAWS. Try this quick trick to boost your cut blooms and make your short-stemmed flowers a whole lot taller. Simply slide the stems into plastic soda straws and arrange them in an opaque vase. Then stand back and admire your beautiful blooms. ✉ Carol P., NJ

IF I HAD A HAMMER… When I want to display woody-stemmed flowers in indoor arrangements, I first crush about an inch of the cut stems with a hammer. This allows the fibers to better soak up water, and that means my lilacs, roses, honeysuckle, and other beautiful blossoms will last longer. ✉ Jill S., WI

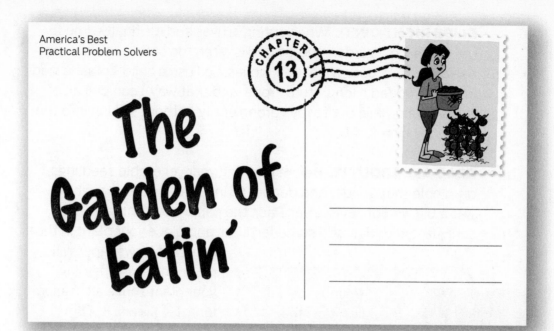

America's Best
Practical Problem Solvers

CHAPTER
13

The Garden of Eatin'

Plot Preparations

FEED THE BIRDS. When I'm laying out a new garden, I outline the plot with birdseed or pieces of stale bread instead of using a garden hose. Once I'm satisfied with the shape, I cut along the outline with a spade. Then I go relax on my deck and watch the birds and squirrels feast on the treats I've left behind. ✉ Patricia W., PA

LOOK OUT FOR SHADE. If you lay out your garden plot before your trees are filled with leaves, you may be in for a surprise come summer. That's because those bare-limbed spring trees will become leafy shade-producers in a few months. So choose your planting area with great care and pay attention to how your yard will look in every season. And don't forget to take note of which trees in your neighbors' yards will grow to shade your future garden area. Then plant accordingly. ✉ Sam M., LA

SLIDE RIGHT OVER. When spring arrives and it's finally time for me to start my garden, the ground is often too soft to use a wheelbarrow to haul out my heavy supplies. So I use a child's plastic sled instead. I added a long, sturdy rope, and that way, I can pull all of the paraphernalia out to my garden easily, without sinking into the muck. ✉ Patsy C., AZ

READ ALL ABOUT IT. Before planting your vegetable seedlings, dig a hole that's wider and deeper than usual, then thoroughly wet a big wad of newspaper. Pack the paper down into the hole, sprinkle it with dirt, add some fertilizer, and place your plant in the hole. The newspaper will retain moisture, helping your plant thrive all season long. ✉ Roberta H., TN

Ask Jerry

Q: When is the best time to start working the ground in my garden?

A: Start as soon as you can get the shovel into the soil and half of Iowa doesn't stick to it!

LOVE THAT LINT! I save the lint from my dryer and till it into the soil before planting my vegetable garden. It really helps retain moisture in the soil—even in our hot, dry climate—so my veggies get the water they need. ✉ Verla V., TX

PINEY PATHS. Gather up pine needles from your property and use them to cover your garden paths. They smell good, add color, and help keep your feet dry and clean—even after it rains! ✉ Ellen C., OR

NO-MUSS, NO-FUSS MULCH. Here's a neat trick I learned that saves me time and makes less of a mess in my garden. I lay down mulch after I prepare the soil, but *before* I plant. It takes a lot less time to spread the mulch when I don't have to be careful around

Whether it's straight off the sheep's back or in the form of an old rug, wool makes great garden mulch. Just cut or tear the wool into strips, and place it around plants and in between garden rows.

tender young plants. Then when I'm ready to plant, I simply push the mulch aside, dig a hole, put in my plant, and gently push the mulch back in place. ✉ Phyllis M., WI

NEW WORK FOR WALLS. Don't toss leftover drywall or gypsum—instead, use it as mulch for walkways, or as a soil additive in your garden. Soak it with a hose to make it soft, then cut it with a sharp knife and use it wherever you wish. ✉ Gerald M., IL

CLEAN FEET. Put down carpet padding between the rows in your vegetable garden. Water will soak right through the padding, but it'll keep your feet from getting muddy while you work in the beds. At the end of the season, hose it off, let it dry, then roll it up and store it until the next growing season. ✉ Jennifer C., NE

ROUNDABOUT TOMATOES. I plant my tomato seedlings in a circle, dig a hole in the center of the circle, and fill it with aged manure. Then every time my tomatoes need a drink, I water through the center hole. It keeps my tomatoes well nourished throughout the season, with no extra work on my part. ✉ Dabney C., OH

TRY TOMATO TIRES. Here's a great tip for growing terrific tomatoes: Find a good, sunny spot, and stack up three or four old tires per plant. Fill the space

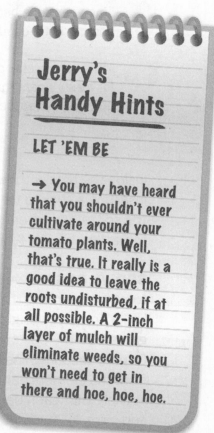

Jerry's Handy Hints

LET 'EM BE

→ You may have heard that you shouldn't ever cultivate around your tomato plants. Well, that's true. It really is a good idea to leave the roots undisturbed, if at all possible. A 2-inch layer of mulch will eliminate weeds, so you won't need to get in there and hoe, hoe, hoe.

TAKE 5

Here are five not-so-common uses for carpet scraps:

1 Lay strips of carpet scraps between garden rows instead of using mulch.

2 Use old carpet scraps to cover your cold frame. You'll lock the heat in, and keep the cold out.

3 Nail carpet scraps to the walls of your garden shed where you hang tools. The tools will rest against the carpet instead of the wall, protecting your shed and tools from possible damage.

4 Line your pet's bed or kennel with carpet scraps to make the flooring extra comfy.

5 Trace the insoles of your boots and cut carpet scraps to match for toasty liners that'll keep you warm on ice fishing trips or other cold-weather adventures.

inside the tires with rich garden soil, then plant your tomatoes, inserting a stick to tie the plant to as it grows. The tires will help the soil retain water for days, and you'll end up with beautiful, juicy tomatoes. ✉ Rita C., CA

BROWN BAG IT. I've found a great way to grow healthy, delicious tomatoes—I plant them in paper bags. It's simple: For each plant, I bury an open, upright brown paper bag about 6 inches deep in my garden, fill the bottom of the bag with planting soil, and plant a tomato seedling. The bags really help protect the young plants from the elements and hungry insects. And when frost is expected, I simply shut each bag with a clothespin to keep my plants warm and snug. ✉ Sandy M., MI

Ready, Set, Grow

A SWEET SHAKE. To get your seeds off to a disease-free start, sprinkle some lemon JELL-O® powder on them with a saltshaker, then continue feeding your young plants JELL-O even after they become established. The gelatin helps retain water, the sugar feeds the soil, and the lemon helps repel bad bugs. ✉ Judith L., MN

DOUBLE-DUTY DELI. I recycle clear plastic deli containers and use them to start my seeds. I just fill each container halfway with potting soil, plant my seeds, give them a little water, and snap the lid shut. Before long, the little plants start coming up, and they stay nice and moist in their miniature hothouses. When they've grown almost up to the lid, I know it's time to move them to new digs. ✉ Lynda P., MN

SEED TEA. Germinate seeds quickly with this easy trick: Steep five chamomile tea bags in a gallon of water for 30 minutes. Then soak a paper towel in the tea, and set it on a plate. Sprinkle your seeds on the paper towel, then fold it over to cover the seeds. Cover them with an inverted plate to keep the seeds moist, warm, and dark.

SUPER-DUPER SOLUTIONS

SOAK YOUR SEEDS ● There was a time when seed starting was not much of an issue because you knew precisely where the seeds came from and how they were stored. Nowadays, we're not so lucky. So here's a little trick that produces wonderful seed-starting results. It requires the making of "manure tea." Just fill a bucket with a mixture of half well-dried manure and half water. Let it steep for a day, strain away the residue, and dilute with more water until the liquid is a light amber color. Then soak your seeds in the brew overnight before planting them.

After five days, take a peek. Most seeds that usually need two to three weeks to germinate will already be growing! And when it comes time to plant the seeds, you can go ahead and plant the paper towel right along with them. ✉ **Shannon V., MI**

ANOTHER SEED SOLUTION. To improve the germination rate of woody-coated seeds like nasturtium, parsley, parsnip, and beets, soak the seeds overnight in a mixture of 1 cup of vinegar, 2 cups of water, and a squirt of dishwashing liquid. In the morning, remove the seeds from the mixture, rinse them off, and plant to your heart's content. You'll be happy with the results! ✉ **Julia C., MN**

SODA POP PLANTERS. Here's a great way to recycle those 2-liter plastic soda bottles and save money on gardening supplies at the same time. Simply cut rinsed-out soda bottles into three sections. Then use the bottom section as a starter pot for seedlings, use the middle section as a collar to protect tender outdoor plants from the elements, and save the top section to use as a funnel. ✉ **Ruth T., WI**

TERRIFIC TUBES. Whenever I need containers to start my seeds in, I use the cardboard tubes from toilet paper and paper towel rolls. I just cut them to size, fill them with soil, and plant my seeds. They hold together well, retain moisture, and can be planted right in the garden along with the seedling. ✉ **Robert F., MA**

PAPER POTS. Recycle your newspapers by turning them into seedling pots. Tear a 3-inch strip from a newspaper page and loosely roll it around a soup can, leaving a little overlap at the bottom. Crimp the overlap, and press it firmly into the bottom of the can. Slide the newspaper "pot" off the can, fill it with seed-starting mix, and plant the seed inside. When the seedling grows to 4 inches or so, plant it in your garden, newspaper pot and all. ✉ **Jane R., PA**

SET UP A SEED SPA. Here's a great way to get your seeds off to a fast start. Place your seed trays in a 48-quart cooler, leaving about 5 inches of space open in the center. Then fill a large ziplock plastic

TAKE 5

Here are five not-so-common uses for newspaper in your yard and garden:

1 Keep your newly sown bean seeds safe and sound from marauding birds by laying long strips of newspaper on top of the rows. To keep the strips in place, lay several sticks and/or stones on top of the paper, removing them once the seeds begin to sprout.

2 Make a quick cold frame by stacking bundles of newspapers around tender young plants, and laying a piece of glass or plastic on top of the bundles. Voilà—instant frost protection!

3 Protect your tender plants from old Jack Frost with a handy paper row cover. Just staple together several sheets of newspaper and place them over the plants. Secure them in place with sticks or stones. Once the newspaper is in tatters after several uses, recycle it in your compost pile.

4 Protect small trees from snow and ice damage with this nifty setup: Put tomato cages around the trees, line the cages with newspaper, and fill 'em up with leaves. Your treasured trees will be snug as a bug in a rug all winter long.

5 Trap moisture-loving insects (like sow bugs, millipedes, and earwigs) by crumpling up several sheets of newspaper and moistening them with water. Then place the sheets in areas where the pests are doing their damage, leaving them out overnight. First thing next morning, pick up the traps and throw 'em in a bucket of soapy water. Wait an hour or so, and you can toss the whole kit and caboodle on your compost pile.

bag with hot water, seal it, and set it in the open space. Close the cooler's lid and let the heat from the bag warm the seeds for six to eight hours. Change the water three or four times a day to keep it hot, and your little seedlings will be showing their heads in no time at all! ✉ Mark K., IN

A CLEAR ADVANTAGE. If you've got any clear plastic shoe boxes with lids lying around your house, put them to work as mini greenhouses. Start by separating the box from its lid and placing the lid upside down on a table. Plant your seeds in small peat pots, lightly water them, and line up the pots on the upside-down lid. Then cover the lid with the overturned plastic box, making sure the box and lid snap shut tightly. Your soon-to-sprout seedlings will be happy in this home until planting time. ✉ Sheri P., CA

DON'T PICK ON ME. Some seeds are so tiny that they're hard to plant with your hands. Instead, tap some seeds onto a sturdy index card, and with a slightly wet toothpick, pick up each seed one by one, and place it just under the soil. ✉ Melanie H., MI

SAVE YOUR BACK. When my back was acting up, I found it painful to bend over and plant seeds in my garden. That's when I came up with the idea of making a planting tube to extend my reach. I

ANOTHER GREAT IDEA!

KEEP 'EM COOL

If your future plants need chilly moisture to help them germinate, follow this routine: Put a coffee filter inside a small ziplock plastic bag, pour 3 tablespoons of water on the filter, and add your seeds, spacing them out on the filter. Then zip the bag closed and stash it in the fridge until the seeds sprout.

SUPER-DUPER SOLUTIONS

A REAL JUG-LING ACT ● You might be surprised at how many ways you can put an empty plastic milk jug to good use around your yard and garden. Here are just a few ideas:

- Protect tender young plants from the weather and varmints by cutting the bottoms out of milk jugs and placing the tops over all of your newly planted seedlings.
- Make cutworm collars by removing the tops and bottoms from milk jugs, and pushing the remaining tube into the ground around tomatoes and peppers to discourage those pesky grubs and cutworms.
- Fashion a birdseed scoop by cutting off the bottom of the jug, turning the top half upside down, and filling it with birdseed. Then unscrew the cap and let the seed flow through the opening like a funnel to fill your bird feeder.
- Prevent root rot and keep pesky mites away from melons by cutting milk jugs in half and placing the halves under your ripening melons.

started with a length of PVC pipe that I then cut so that it touched the ground when I was standing comfortably. Then I pushed one end of the pipe into the soil at the appropriate planting depth, and dropped my seeds into the pipe from the top. The seeds easily slid down the tube and into the soil, right where I wanted 'em. ✉ **Debbie H., IL**

SIMPLE SPROUTER. I've discovered a foolproof, no-fuss way to germinate seeds—by starting them in a mini greenhouse. First, I rinse out a plastic milk jug and cut across the lower section of the jug to get a 4-inch-deep base. Then I punch drainage holes in the bottom. Next, I fill the perforated base with soil, plant my seeds, and water carefully. Now here's the neat trick: The last thing I do is slip a plastic bag under the base, gently pull it up and over, and blow it up like a balloon, tying the top tightly. I set my greenhouse in a warm, sunny window, and wait for the seeds to sprout—no watering needed! ✉ Tony R., GA

CARTONS FOR THE GARDEN. Egg cartons make great mini pots for starting seeds. They're the perfect size, and if you use the cardboard kind, when it's time to transplant, you can just cut the sections apart and plant the whole shebang in your garden. ✉ Malynda M., AR

I'VE GOT A CRUSH ON YOU. If you have trouble getting your beet seeds to germinate, spread them between two pieces of wax paper, and roll over them with a rolling pin. The seed husks will be crushed, and all your seeds will come up. ✉ Betsy L., NJ

QUITE A STIR. I save plastic coffee stirrers (the ones with the little paddles on the end), and use them whenever I'm working with delicate seedlings. They're the perfect gentle "garden spades" to use around any tiny, tender plant. ✉ Margaret H., WA

PERFECT PITCH. There's more than one way to use pitchforks in the garden—put 'em to work as row markers. After planting seeds in your garden, mark the long rows with two pitchforks—one at each end, prongs down into the dirt—with a wire stretched tight between them and wrapped around each handle. ✉ Alison H., MI

YARN MARKS THE SPOT. Don't forget where you planted all those seeds! Make a garden marker by tying brightly colored yarn around one plastic fork for each row of seeds. Stick the fork in the ground in front of each row, and you'll immediately know where to look for those little green shoots. ✉ Polly K., NY

TRACK YOUR TRANSPLANTS. Don't lose track of the new plants you've put into an existing garden. Save a few green mesh baskets that berries come in, and cover the newbies with them. The mesh will allow your baby plants to get plenty of light, air, and water, and the bright color will help you find them. ✉ Betty N., MI

TERRIFIC TOMATOES. You'll be amazed by the wonderful tomatoes you'll have if you feed your plants rabbit food. All you have to do is mix a few handfuls of the pellets into the soil all around the tomato plants, and voilà—plump, juicy tomatoes come harvest time! ✉ Caroline H., TX

IT'S A WRAP. When you're ready to plant your tomato seedlings, loosely wrap a banana peel around the roots of each plant before placing it in its hole. As the peel rots, it'll release potassium into the soil, and that's great for your tomatoes. ✉ Celia S., WI

ANOTHER GREAT IDEA!

EASY AS PIE (PANS)

Here's a permanent solution to the age-old problem of how to keep track of which crops you've planted where: pie pans! Just cut strips from the base of clean, used aluminum pie pans, then use a ballpoint pen to "engrave" the name of the crop into the metal. Thumbtack each strip to a stick to mark the rows in your garden. These tags practically last forever, and best of all, they're free!

A PINCH IN TIME. Here's a trick I learned that helps my tomato plants produce a bumper crop. I remove any shoots that appear between the main stalk and side branches. Then I cut or pinch the top of the plant, keeping it low and full. ✉ **Hal K., NJ**

TIE A YELLOW RIBBON . . . Instead of tying your tomato plants to stakes with plant ties, use a ribbon, and hold it in place with an alligator clip. With no knots to untie, it's quick and easy to reposition the ribbons along the stakes as your plants grow bigger and bigger. ✉ **Fred W., PA**

STOP THE ROT. Are you fretting over blossom-end rot on your tomato plants? Then reach for an antacid. No, not for you, for your plants! Just crush two antacid tablets, spread the powder around each plant, and water well. ✉ **Sheri S., CA**

SUPER-DUPER SOLUTIONS

TOMATO, TOMAH-TO? ● Tomatoes tend to crack when they grow rapidly during their ripening stage. This usually happens when a heavy rainfall follows a drought, and the inside of the tomato plumps up faster than the outer skin can grow. You can thwart this problem by watering your tomato plants regularly to keep the soil's moisture even. And next year, consider planting varieties that are crack tolerant, such as Avalanche, Bragger, Early Girl, Glamour, Jet Star, and Roma.

THE CLIPPINGS CURE. You can stop tomato plant flowers from turning brown, wilting, then dropping off (blossom-end rot). How? By simply adding 6 to 8 inches of grass clippings on top of the soil when you plant them. ✉ **Douglas P., NC**

A FLICK OF THE FINGER. Here's an easy way to head off blossom-end rot: Flick off the blossom from the bottom of the fruit

Ask Jerry

Q: My garden is doing great—except for the tomatoes. They started to grow nicely until they bloomed, then the leaves shriveled and turned black. All I had left were the stems and ugly, cracked tomatoes. What's the problem?

A: Sounds like a soil problem to me. As soon as the temperatures get above freezing, spray the soil with a mixture of 2 tablespoons of bleach and $\frac{1}{2}$ can of Sprite® in 5 gallons of water per 100 square feet of garden area. That should do the trick.

with your finger. It costs nothing and works if you do it before the rot has a chance to get started. ✉ Florian B., IL

TOMATOES BY THE BUSHEL. I've had bad luck growing tomatoes, so now I grow 'em the old-fashioned way, in bushel baskets. I just sink the baskets halfway into the ground, then fill them with 50 percent professional planter mix and 50 percent "strange" soil (from my neighbor's yard). Then I set in my plants and watch 'em grow like crazy! ✉ Dom L., NY

COLD-WEATHER TOMATOES. You can grow vine-ripened tomatoes, even in the winter, by following this technique: Start by pruning pencil-thick branches from your best plants just before the first frost in the fall. Strip the leaves from the bottom third of each branch, and remove any fruits and buds. Then bring the branches inside and place each one in a clay pot filled with potting soil. Water each pot and insert tomato cages, then cover the whole shebang with plastic. When new growth appears, remove the plastic and add fertilizer. Stick the pots in a sunny window, and you'll enjoy ripe, juicy tomatoes all winter long. ✉ **Bill Z., IL**

AW, SHOOTS! When planting broccoli, I set my plants just 8 inches apart. This makes the side-shoot population explode, and gives me a much bigger harvest. There's only one drawback—with this close planting, I get fairly small central heads. So if your objective is big main heads, then make your plantings 18 to 24 inches apart instead. ✉ **Charlene C., NJ**

BETTER BROCCOLI. Pruning broccoli the right way will give you a double crop. When you cut the first head, cut it high on the stalk, leaving as much of the stem and as many leaves on the plant as possible. Then destroy the buds at the base of all but the bottom

Grandma Putt's Wisdom

My Grandma Putt was always looking for ways to extend the growing season. Besides planting frost-resistant veggies like Swiss chard, broccoli, kale, and others that she harvested well into winter, she took good care of her garden to increase her harvest. What was her secret?

First off, starting in late summer, she removed any buds that weren't going to have enough time to mature before they would be claimed by the cold. This increased the size and growing power of the veggies that were left on the vine. Then, when cold weather moved in, she covered her plants at night with glass jars, cardboard boxes, blankets, and newspapers. If Jack Frost snuck up on her without warning, Grandma Putt was able to save her veggies by giving them a fine spray from the hose as soon as Ol' Sol peeked his head over the horizon the following morning.

leaves by inserting the point of a knife and twisting where each leaf joins the main stem. The undeveloped buds that are lower on each stem will send up strong shoots. These will form secondary heads as large and tender as the first. ✉ George L., MI

BROCCOLI BASICS. I always start my broccoli indoors. I use a large container and fill it with loose peat. Then I plant the seeds at least 1 inch apart and at least ½ inch deep. I set the container where it gets plenty of bright light, and water it regularly. Best of all, I'm never disappointed with the results! ✉ Kathleen M., MT

Jerry's Handy Hints

STEP ON IT!

→ Want to know how to grow large onions? You're standing on the answer—your feet! When your onions are about twice the size of your thumb, simply step on them, pressing them down deeper into the soil. That's all there is to it!

SHOO, FLIES. If you notice a lot of little flies buzzing around your onions, head for your fireplace, gather up some ashes, and sprinkle them around the base of your onion plants. The ashes discourage flies from laying their eggs near your onions. This same trick works great against cabbage root maggots, too. ✉ Nancy L., PA

AIN'T THAT SWEET? I always started my onions from sets, but I wanted a change of pace from the usual pungent-flavored bulbs. That's when I decided to try growing my onions from seed. I found that I had a much wider selection of varieties to choose from, including those sweet types I'd been craving. So if you're looking for sweet onions, give seeds a try. ✉ Ellen P., OR

EASY GROWS IT. It's easy to grow garlic—the secret is to plant fresh, fertile cloves from the seed department, not the cloves you buy from the produce section of the grocery store (which are treated with anti-sprouting chemicals). Plant at the end of March, placing the cloves 6 inches apart and 1½ inches deep. By the way, garlic will grow anywhere onions will. ✉ Deb R., WV

MIX IT UP. When you're planting carrot seeds, mix in several radish seeds. Radishes sprout much faster than carrots—so you'll know where you planted your carrots that much sooner. And you can enjoy both veggies in crisp, crunchy salads. ✉ Mike F., MI

SEED SPACER. It can be tough going when you try to grow radishes because it's easy to plant them too close to each other; then you end up losing plants when you have to thin them out. So try this trick: Spoon ½ teaspoon of flour into a saucer, then add just enough water to make a paste, and sprinkle your radish seeds in it. Using tweezers, pull out the seeds, and place them on a sheet of toilet paper, spacing them 1 inch apart. The seeds will dry and stick to the toilet paper. After you've prepared your garden rows, lay out the toilet paper where you want the radishes, and sprinkle soil on the seeds through a ¼-inch wire soil sifter. Shake until the toilet paper is completely covered. As the paper breaks down, the radishes will take root, and before too long, you'll be enjoying the fruits of your labor. ✉ Jeannine M., PA

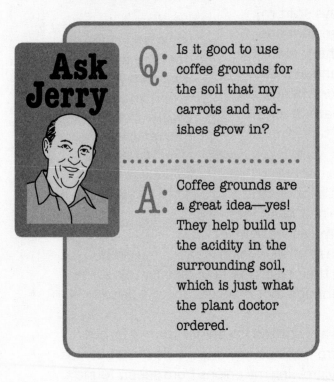

Ask Jerry

Q: Is it good to use coffee grounds for the soil that my carrots and radishes grow in?

A: Coffee grounds are a great idea—yes! They help build up the acidity in the surrounding soil, which is just what the plant doctor ordered.

RAPID RADISHES. I get my radishes off to a speedy start by soaking them for 24 hours before planting. Then I put them in a brown paper bag and set the bag in the sun. Within a day, the seeds have sprouted, and they're ready to set into the ground and get growing. ✉ Marlene B., MA

RADISH DECOYS. You'll grow a great crop of mustard and turnip greens if you mix in a packet of radish seeds when you're planting. I find that this trick helps keep the aphids away from my tasty greens. ✉ Jaye H., TN

CARRY A BIG STICK. I don't know just why this works, but it does: When I plant peppers, I put a stick that is 6 inches taller than each plant into the ground next to it, and the birds leave my pepper plants alone. ✉ Leota C., IA

PERENNIAL PEPPERS. You can keep the peppers poppin' if you just dig the plants up in September and transfer them to 5-gallon pots that you've lined with compost. Keep the containers next to a window in a 60°F basement, and water the plants weekly. At the end of May, replant your peppers in the garden, and enjoy a fresh crop of zesty veggies! ✉ Mark L., RI

GO-GO OKRA. Get your okra off to a quick start by soaking the seeds in a little bleach (just enough to cover them) for about 15 minutes

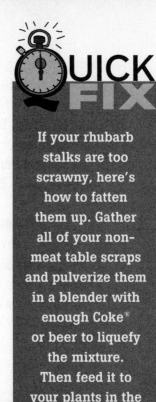

QUICK FIX

If your rhubarb stalks are too scrawny, here's how to fatten them up. Gather all of your non-meat table scraps and pulverize them in a blender with enough Coke® or beer to liquefy the mixture. Then feed it to your plants in the winter. Come summer, you'll be mighty proud of the results.

ANOTHER GREAT IDEA!

BED PREP

For the best garlic crop around, you've got to start with the right planting bed. Dig a hole about a foot across and a foot deep, and fill it with equal parts of garden soil, professional potting soil, and builder's sand. Plant your garlic in it, and you'll soon be savoring the results.

before planting. The bleach dissolves the outer layer of the seed, which speeds up germination. ✉ Teresa W., FL

BEAN THERE, DONE THAT. Whenever I plant green beans, I place a wire cage over each seed. As the plant starts to grow, the vines go right between the wires, and that keeps my beans off the ground. ✉ Lisa R., MN

SAY IT IN PUMPKIN. Here's a fun trick: When your pumpkins are still in the green stage, carve your name in a few. I use a pocket-knife, and just pierce the outer skin. The cut will heal over, and as it does, the name will rise up, creating your own personalized pumpkin. ✉ Bette E., AZ

Safeguarding the Garden

WARM AND COZY. A 2-liter plastic soda bottle with a few inches removed from the bottom makes a fantastic mini greenhouse and frost protector for a plant. Just place the bottle, cut-end down, over your plant and press the cut bottom edge down into the soil to keep the bottle in place. Remove and replace the screw-on cap as needed to regulate the heat. ✉ Pattie K., NH

A BETTER BOTTOM. If you use plastic milk jugs for mini greenhouses for your vegetables in the spring, don't cut the bottoms completely off. Instead, leave one side attached to make a flap. Then when you cover each plant with a jug, fold the bottom flap out and place a rock on top of it. This will keep your protective greenhouse from blowing away. ✉ Linda O., MN

QUICK COLD FRAME. Here's a simple cold frame that doesn't take any carpentry skills. Stack two layers of straw or hay bales for

Grandma Putt's Wisdom

Ah, strawberries. "Plant enough for thee and me," the robin may be heard to say. To make sure we always got our fair share, Grandma Putt had me cover the beds before the berries began to color because once the wise robin had a taste, he was persistent. We didn't drape regular bird netting loosely over or along edges of a strawberry patch, though; instead, we built an 8-inch-high frame around the bed, and stretched netting over the top, looping it over nails for quick removal at picking time.

the back of the frame and one on each side, to form a slope. Put bricks on the bottom and against the back wall for extra heat retention. Then cover the front with a sheet of plastic. ✉ Gerald M., IL

DOWN THE DRAIN. I protect my tomatoes, peppers, and other plants in my vegetable garden with pieces of 4-inch corrugated black plastic drainpipe. I cut the pipe into 6-inch lengths and place a piece around each plant to give it protection from nibbling animals, destructive cutworms, and the wind. ✉ David S., IL

LINE 'EM UP. After you've planted your vegetable garden, here's how to make sure it's safe from harm. Cut plastic water line and bend it to create arches over wide beds. Then use these as supports for floating row covers. This will keep your crops safe and sound from cold nights and pesky insects. ✉ Jenny V., PA

TOTALLY TUBULAR. You can guard your baby tomato plants with cutworm collars made from paper towel or toilet paper tubes. Cut each tube into short sections and make a slit in one side of each section. Then wrap it around the stem of your tomato after planting it. ✉ Victoria Z., IL

METALLIC MAGIC. I wrap copper wire around the base of my tomato plants. For whatever reason, it actually protects them from slugs and blight. Give it a try—you'll be amazed by how many tomatoes you'll grow this year. ✉ **Sharon M., IL**

CUTWORM CONTROL. Instead of wrapping your vegetable plant stems to ward off pesky cutworms, just stick several 3-inch-long twigs in the ground next to the main stem. I've been doing this for years, and I haven't lost a plant yet! ✉ **Thomas S., VA**

FOILED AGAIN. Once a tomato seedling grows to about 2 inches, make a collar for it that'll give it some extra warmth and protect it from blight. Cut an aluminum foil pie pan from the edge to the center, then cut a 1-inch circle in the center. Use the pan as a collar by placing it on the ground and spreading the pan open at the slit to fit around the plant stem. ✉ **Margaret H., WA**

WIPE OUT WIND. Here's a way to protect your tomato plants from gusty spring winds: Create a windbreak by placing water-filled 2-liter bottles in a ring around each of your plants. If you get a sudden drop in temperature at night, you can simply lay a cover over the top of the bottles to keep your plants warm. ✉ **Lydia O., MN**

SUPER-DUPER SOLUTIONS

STOCKING(S) UP ● Here's a surefire way to prevent bad bugs from taking a bite out of your harvest—cover up your crops! There's no need to buy special protectors, though; old pairs of panty hose make perfect crop covers. Just snip off the legs and slip 'em over the plant parts you want to protect, such as whole heads of cabbage or cauliflower, or individual fruits on eggplants, peppers, and tomatoes. The nylons are stretchy, so they expand easily as your crops mature. And pests can't get through, so you'll get a picture-perfect harvest every time!

ANOTHER GREAT IDEA!

ELEVENTH-HOUR SAVE

Has this ever happened to you? The weather takes an unexpected cold turn during the night, leaving your uncovered veggie crops to Mother Nature's mercy. If it happens again, don't panic and rip out what's left of your garden. You may be able to revive hardy crops like chard, collards, and mustard. Simply sprinkle the plants gently with water from your garden hose *before* the sun shines on them. That may be enough to prevent damage so you can keep on harvesting.

BAR NONE. Most folks tie their tomatoes to stakes or wooden cages, but I find those can be tipsy, even on days with just light wind. So I make sure my tomatoes are secure by using a strip of 60-inch rebar base mat (used in cement work), held up with metal stakes. I plant tomatoes on both sides of the mat, and since the plants grow up, up, up this extra-tall support, I use less garden space, leaving plenty of room to grow other goodies. ✉ Arlie S., CO

Cream of the Crop

TOMATOES BY THE DOZEN. As soon as you know the first frost is right around the corner, pick the rest of your cherry tomatoes and put them in an empty egg carton, one tomato per "cup," to store until you're ready to use them. The tomatoes won't be touching each other, the cartons are stackable, and your tomatoes will be handy whenever you want to eat them! ✉ Debbie L., OH

GET A LEG UP. When you dig up your onions, place them in old panty hose legs, one at a time, and tie a knot above each bulb. Hang

Jerry's Handy Hints

EVENING SERENADE

→ I always pick my vegetables in the early evening, just before suppertime. That's because during the day, the sun burns up a lot of the vitamins and minerals stored in the plant leaves. As soon as the sun starts to set, the plants begin to replenish and refortify themselves. And I never keep vegetables in the hot sun after they've been picked, because Old Sol will diminish their nutritional value even after they've been brought in out of the hot garden. So once you're done picking, get your harvest into the shade where it's cool.

the hose in a cool, dry location. Then whenever you need an onion, just cut below the lowest knot, and leave the rest hanging where they are. ✉ Nancy F., IN

SINK OR SWIM. After picking cherries, I use this trick to separate the good ones from the bad. I place the fruit in a bowl and fill the bowl with cold water. If any cherries float, I pitch 'em because it's a good bet they're wormy. ✉ Donald M., MI

CROP BASKET. As you're harvesting your garden's crop, place your veggies in a plastic laundry basket. Then you can clean them easily with a garden hose, rotating and gently shaking the basket as you spray. ✉ Reggie R., AL

SHINY STORAGE. Here's how I keep my celery and iceberg lettuce lasting longer: After harvesting my crops, I wash them, shake off the excess water, and wrap the lettuce and the celery separately in aluminum foil. They keep for almost two weeks in my fridge without wilting. ✉ Katherine B., CO

HOW UN-A-PEELING. Don't waste your time peeling fresh-from-the-garden carrots. Instead, gently scrub them with a clean pad of nonsoapy steel wool, then rinse and dry them before storing in the fridge. ✉ Gretchen M., MI

KEEP 'EM COMING. As your mustard, turnip, and kale begin to go to seed, here's how to get a second harvest out of them. Just mow over the entire patch with your lawn mower, then water the patch thoroughly, and follow up with a good dose of compost. In no time at all, you'll be picking tender greens again. ✉ **Tim O., ON**

BURIED TREASURE. If you don't have a cool, dark basement where you can store your harvested fruits and vegetables, here's a simple solution. Just bury a barrel or a galvanized garbage can on a well-drained site, leaving about 4 inches of container above the ground. Then place your produce in sacks or perforated bags, and put them in the can. Put the lid on, cover it thickly with straw, and then top it off with a waterproof canvas or plastic sheet. Your produce will stay fresh through the winter. ✉ **Sam G., OK**

Ask Jerry

Q: How do I know when my pumpkins are ready for picking? And once I pick them, what's the best way to store them?

A: Pumpkins are ready for picking when they've reached full color and have hardened. To avoid damaging the vine, cut them free with a sharp knife. Then carry them in your hands—not by the stems. Wash them in a mild chlorine solution (1 cup of chlorine to 1 gallon of water) to kill any bacteria. Be sure to let them dry off completely before storing them away. But don't keep them on cement floors—they tend to rot there. They'll store best if you set them on a board or piece of cardboard in a cool, dry, dark place. With the proper precautions, you'll have fresh pumpkins through the fall and even into the winter.

CHAPTER **14**

Potted Potential

Healthy Houseplants

TAKE YOUR VITAMINS. After boiling or steaming your vegetables, don't dump the water down the drain. Instead, let it cool, and then water your houseplants with it. They'll love the vitamins and minerals from the veggies that have leached into the water. ✉ **Karen F., IN**

HERE'S THE SCOOP. Every winter, I scoop up snow and put it in buckets in my garage. Once the snow melts, I use it to water my houseplants. It's way better for them than tap water, which can contain harmful chemicals. ✉ **Laurel H., VT**

HOME BREW. Help your houseplants retain water the cheap and easy way by substituting used tea bags for those water-absorbing crystals in your houseplant containers. The bags retain water to help keep your plants moist, and they also provide fertilizer as the tea leaves break down. ✉ **Anna Y., WI**

TEA-RIFFIC TREAT. Here's a simple treat I mix up to keep my houseplants happy. I pop a used tea bag into a quart of warm water and add 2 drops of antiseptic mouthwash, 2 drops of ammonia, and 1 drop of dishwashing liquid. Then I pour this energized "tea" into a handheld sprayer bottle, and spray my houseplants to clean them up and protect them from disease. ✉ **James L., MN**

THE OLD SWITCHEROO. Sometimes sensitive houseplants can be downright fickle about their water. If you have a plant that's lackluster and positively perk-less, try watering it with bottled water. Your plant may not care for the trace chlorine and fluoride that are in most tap water, so the filtered bottled water may be just what it needs. ✉ **Susanna S., CO**

BATHING BEAUTIES. When my local gardening store slashes prices on some houseplants that look like they've seen better days, I don't hesitate to take advantage of the bargains. I know that I can usually revive the plants by treating them to a shower once I get them home. I just mix 2 tablespoons of Epsom salts in a gallon of water, then fill

TAKE 5

Here are five not-so-common uses for tea in and around the yard and garden:

1. Use leftover tea to water your houseplants. It'll keep them happy and healthy.

2. Mist-spray indoor ferns with weak tea water three times a week to add humidity to the air.

3. Lay used tea bags in the bottom of your plant pots to cover the hole, yet still provide drainage.

4. Mulch outdoor plants with herbal tea leaves for a fragrant, protective layer against bugs.

5. Sprinkle the contents of used tea bags around your acid-loving shrubs to feed their habit.

a handheld sprayer bottle with the solution and spray the plants generously. Nine times out of ten, they perk right up. ✉ Pauline L., NY

TIMING IS EVERYTHING. Ever wonder when is the perfect time to water? Well, here's an easy indicator: Simply stick a pinecone into the houseplant's pot. The petals of the pinecone will open when the soil is dry, indicating that it's time to water, and close when the soil is wet. Wonder no more! ✉ Suzanne W., MI

BOTTOMS UP! Always water your African violets from the bottom. Simply fill a shallow container with warm water, and place the potted plant in it. It's an easy and rewarding way to treat your plants, and your violets will bloom almost continually. ✉ Melissa N., NE

SUPER WATER. The next time you water your African violets, don't use ordinary tap water. Instead, turn it into a healthier drink with the help of Epsom salts. Just add a pinch of Epsom salts to a pint of warm water, and use the mixture to water your plants. You'll be amazed by how big and lush they'll grow in just a short period of time. ✉ Marlene S., NE

Grandma Putt's Wisdom

When it came to watering houseplants, my Grandma Putt always said that there's good water and bad water. The best water, she said, is rain or melted snow. And the worst water? You guessed it—the stuff straight out of the tap.

The good news is that you can turn ordinary tap water into plant-friendly water by adding a layer of agricultural charcoal to the top of the soil in your plants' pots. It'll filter out additives like chlorine and fluoride, making the water perfect for your plants. And as a bonus, the charcoal will also keep your house smelling fresh.

Ask Jerry

Q: Jerry, I need help. My African violets look healthy, but they won't bloom. What can I do?

A: First, find a clean clay pot that's the same size as the pot your violets are currently in. Rub the inside of the clay pot down with apple juice, then transfer your African violets from their current pot into the clay pot, removing their lower layer of leaves. That should get 'em blooming like crazy!

RELY ON RUST. Here's a trick I learned that keeps my African violets blooming year-round: I simply push an old rusty nail into the soil. Presto—I get beautiful, bountiful blooms without fertilizing! ✉ Marybeth Q., NY

FANCY FOOTWORK. If you have a rabbit's foot fern that has so many "feet" that it's hard to water without making a mess, I've got the perfect solution. Just place a small funnel in between the branches and push it down into the soil. Then when it's time to give your plant a drink, pour the water directly into the funnel, and the moisture will be evenly distributed throughout the pot. And the fern's thick foliage will camouflage the funnel, so no one will ever know your secret. ✉ Larry P., MN

IT'S IN THE CARDS. I like to alternate the formulas I use for watering my houseplants so they're not always getting the same drink. To keep track of what formulas I use when, I print each recipe on an index card, and on the back of each card I keep a tally of the dates and the plants I used the tonic on. This simple tracking system put a permanent end to my formula mix-ups. ✉ Frankie L., TX

PUT MOLD ON HOLD. Sometimes houseplants can grow mold spores that continue to reproduce every time you water. To keep your plants well watered and keep the air you breathe clean and mold-free at the same time, stand a large hair curler in the pot, pushing it about an inch into the soil. Then cover the rest of the soil surface with aquarium gravel. Use the empty space inside the curler as your watering tube; meanwhile, the gravel will prevent the mold spores from becoming airborne. ✉ Bob E., UT

PAPER POT PLUG. Before repotting a houseplant, I always line the bottom of the new pot with a sheet of wax paper. This trick keeps the soil from falling out through the drainage hole as I settle my plant into its new home, saving me cleanup time. ✉ Lydia N., OR

FILTER FINESSE. Put a coffee filter over the drainage hole of a pot before you repot your houseplant. That way, the water will still drain properly, but the filter will keep the dirt from escaping through the hole. ✉ Priscilla W., SC

HOSIERY HELPER. When repotting a houseplant into a container that's got a drainage hole in the bottom, cover the bottom of the new pot with a piece of nylon from an old pair of panty hose. Then fill the pot with potting soil and your plant. The panty hose will keep the soil inside the container, but still allow for proper water drainage. ✉ Ed V., IA

A NEAT SHEET. Before repotting a houseplant, I place a used dryer sheet over the drainage hole, then add potting soil and the plant. When I water, the soil stays put in the pot. ✉ Doris B., WV

Jerry's Handy Hints

BREAK THE MOLD

→ You can prevent mold from making an appearance in the dirt around your houseplants by using activated charcoal. Just pour a layer of the charcoal (available at most pet-supply stores) on top of the soil. It's a practical filter that's attractive to boot!

ANOTHER GREAT IDEA!

NAIL YOUR PLANTS

Over time, watering your houseplants reduces the spaces between the soil particles in the pots, which drives the air out of the soil. Further waterings only increase soil compaction, which will gradually choke the plant to death. To keep this from happening to your houseplants, you need to aerate the soil. Take a long, large nail, and gently work it down into the soil. Repeat this process, making multiple holes throughout the pot, then water the plant. This "acupuncture" treatment is not intended to cure the situation, but it will give both you and the plant a breather until you find time to repot the plant in fresh soil.

DIAPERS DELIVER. To help keep potted flowers' thirst quenched, you can cut up the absorbent parts of unused disposable diapers and add them to the potting soil. The diaper pieces will retain enough water and keep your flowers satisfied—even when you're on vacation! ✉ Joannie S., IL

WHAT A GRIND. Save your coffee grounds and eggshells and use them as a soil additive when you're repotting houseplants. Just empty the used grounds into a pail each morning, and save the smashed, dry eggshells in a plastic bag. When you're ready to repot, mix the grounds and shells together and add them to your potting soil. In addition to making your houseplants happy, this mixture gives a great nutrient boost to roses. ✉ Allison L., NM

SUPER SOIL. To make fantastic houseplant soil, take about 10 pounds of dried compost and sift it through a screen until it is quite fine. Then moisten it with a bit of water and divvy it up into plastic bags. Microwave one *unsealed* bag at a time on "high" for five minutes. It'll be very hot, so give it plenty of time to cool. Then use the soil to pot your houseplants. ✉ Ray T., WI

Grandma Putt's Wisdom

Whenever I finished eating a banana at my Grandma Putt's house, I knew better than to throw away the peel. Why? Because using a banana peel was Grandma's favorite way to polish her big philodendron leaves. To use her secret method on any houseplant with large, smooth leaves, simply hold each leaf of the houseplant and wipe the surface with the inside of the peel. The natural oil in the banana skin gives the leaves a nice healthy shine.

MAYO MAGIC. To polish indoor plant leaves, put a little mayonnaise on a soft, clean cloth. Just rub it on with the cloth, and it'll disappear into a polished shine. ✉ Zanne G., GA

SCAT, CAT! If you're sick and tired of your cat chewing on your houseplants' leaves, do what I do and keep Fluffy away by sprinkling the leaves with a little cayenne pepper. After this spicy treatment, you can bet your pet won't be chewing on your houseplants anymore! ✉ Stella W., MI

OXY BOOST. To give your houseplants a boost of oxygen, mix 1 ounce of 3% hydrogen peroxide in 1 quart of water and pour the liquid into a handheld sprayer bottle. Mist the leaves with it, and then pour the remainder over the soil. Your plants will thank you for the supercharged soaking by growing faster and fuller, and producing lots more blooms! ✉ Yvonne T., CA

FEED BY THE FOOT. Here's my secret fertilizing trick: I cut the foot off an old pair of panty hose and fill it with timed-release fertilizer. Then I tie the end and set this small sack on top of the soil of my favorite potted houseplant. That way, my plant stays well fed all year long. ✉ Linda C., TX

BUG BLASTER. Here's how I keep nasty mealy-bugs off my houseplants: I mix 1 cup of black tea, 1 cup of warm water, 1 teaspoon of baking soda, and a few drops of dishwashing liquid in a hand-held sprayer bottle, and spray the solution all over my plants. I do this about once a month, and it keeps my houseplants pest-free. ✉ *Buella T., ON*

MITE WIPEOUT. If you've noticed that a web is growing in the branches of a potted plant, mites have probably invaded it. To get rid of the little buggers, give 'em a daily spray of Murphy® Oil Soap mixed into water. That should wipe 'em out in no time. ✉ *Thomas R., DE*

FOIL FUNGUS GNATS. If fungus gnats are pestering your houseplants, hit 'em hard with this lethal spray. Mix 1 part hydrogen peroxide and 3 parts water in a handheld sprayer bottle. Then allow the soil around the plant to dry after you've watered it, and saturate the plant with the mixture. Use the spray between waterings, but only when the soil is dry. After a few applications, there'll be no more gnats. ✉ *Jeff B., NY*

QUICK FIX

If you find a worm living in the root system of one of your houseplants, prepare a warm, soapy water bath in a large container, and soak your green pal in it until the worm cries uncle, and rises to the surface. Then pick him up and take him outside where he belongs.

SUPER-DUPER SOLUTIONS

HAIR SPRAY HELPER ● When aphids start plaguing your houseplants, reach for some hair spray and a plastic bag that's big enough to hold your plant and its pot. Spray the inside of the bag—not the plant—with the hair spray, and put your plant inside the bag. Fasten the bag tightly around the plant with a twist tie, and set it in an area that's away from direct sun (otherwise, your plant will cook to death). Wait 24 hours, then remove the bag. Those itty-bitty bugs will be history!

LOOKIN' GOOD. If you want to change the look of your faded houseplant containers, just grab a few stretchy tube tops from the girls' clothing department of your local discount store. You can choose from floral prints, solid colors, stripes, and so on. Stretch one top up the sides of each container, and you'll really perk up the look of your potted plants. ✉ Joan D., MI

ROOT, ROOT, ROOT FOR HOUSEPLANTS! If you've tried rooting houseplants in a glass of water with no luck, try my secret recipe: I add 2 drops of ammonia and ¼ teaspoon of 7UP® to fresh water in the glass each week to improve the process. It works for me every time! ✉ Bob L., CA

CONTAIN YOUR CUTTINGS. Here's a great way to give house-plant cuttings a good start. Take a 1-liter plastic soda bottle with a cap and remove about 3 inches from the bottom. Save the bottom for some other use, or put it in the recycling bin. Then plant your cutting in a pot and press the cut end of the bottle into the soil over the cutting. Leave the cap on for a few days so the moisture stays inside the bottle. This mini greenhouse will help your cutting quickly take root and grow into a sturdy young plant. ✉ Robin P., FL

QUICK FIX

Want to keep your potted impatiens growing and blooming all winter? In mid-September, cut them back, and leave them out-doors for 10 days in the shade. Then bring them indoors and place them in a southeast window for the duration.

POTTED PEPPERS. Try your hand at growing hot peppers on your windowsill in the winter. Simply surround the plants with rose geraniums, and your indoor garden will not only be full of room-brightening blooms, but will also produce a bumper crop of peppers. ✉ Linda B., IN

POINSETTIA POINTERS. Poinsettias require alternating periods of light and

ANOTHER GREAT IDEA!

CHRISTMAS ALL YEAR LONG

Take care of your Christmas cactus even after it's finished blooming. Start by placing it in a cool location, and water it just enough to keep the plant from wilting. Repot the cactus in April, and water it thoroughly whenever the soil begins to dry out. Around mid-September, cut back on watering (the soil should be on the dry side) and move the plant back to its cool location until flower buds form. Increase the water and temperature during blooming. If your Christmas cactus is only drooping—not blooming—give it a few days of cool weather (45° to 65°F) to trigger the blooming sequence. Then place it in a shady window until mid-October, and you'll have blooms by Christmas!

dark to keep them vibrant after their blooming season is over. So I put mine in a dark closet with a fluorescent light on a 12-hour-on/12-hour-off timer, and it helps them bloom again. If you give this a try, just be aware that it's easy to forget about the plants because they're out of sight, so write yourself a reminder to water them as needed. ✉ **Greg P., NY**

OIL YOUR CACTUS. To generate healthy blooms on my Christmas cactus, I put 2 tablespoons of castor oil around the roots in October. By December, it's full of fabulous flowers. ✉ **Cuba M., MI**

FEED YOUR ORCHIDS. Fertilize your orchids with one of Jerry's terrific tonics: Mix 1 can of beer, 1 cup of Epsom salts, ½ cup of ammonia, and 2 cups of water in a plastic bottle. Give each orchid ½ teaspoon of the solution every two weeks, and they'll reward you with loads of beautiful blooms. ✉ **Robert J., TX**

HOUSEPLANT HARMONY. If you want your houseplants to grow quickly, but you don't want to use chemicals, do what I do and play

Ask Jerry

Q: Do you know of any houseplants that'll help clean the air in my apartment? The neighbor below me is always cooking something smelly for dinner, and it's driving me crazy!

A: Spider plants and ferns both make terrific air filters. Get a few, and if that doesn't do the trick, get a few more. And if you can find them, gardenias will freshen your air beautifully.

classical music for your seedlings. And here's another tip: From time to time, add a little milk to their water. I guarantee you'll be happy with the results. ✉ Thelma F., FL

AIR OUT. When you recarpet your house, you'll love the new look, but your houseplants won't love the fumes that can linger long after installation. They may droop, lose leaves, and even die. So find your plants a temporary home away from newly carpeted areas until the air clears. ✉ Marina H., CA

MOIST AND MARVELOUS. If you bring a plant indoors for the winter, you must always keep some moisture in the soil—not a lot, but enough to keep it alive. Don't just stick it in the basement and forget about it, or when it's time to take it back outside, you'll be sadly disappointed. ✉ Shirley D., WI

WINTER WISDOM. Go ahead and bring your potted plants inside for the winter. But if they start losing their leaves, it means that your air is too dry. The solution? Add a humidifier to increase the humidity in your home. It'll help both you and your plants breathe a whole lot easier. ✉ Elliot Q., NJ

Outdoor Dwellers

RE-TIRE IN THE GARDEN. Recycle an old tire and make a lovely outdoor flower planter at the same time. Lay the tire flat on the ground, and cut around the top (what was the side of the tire when it was on a car) in a zigzag pattern. Then turn the tire inside out, set it on an old wheel, and paint both a bright color. Fill the wheel with gravel and the tire with soil, and then plant flowers to your heart's content. ✉ *Linda T., MI*

IT'S IN THE BAG. Here's my really lazy way of "container" garden-ing: I take a large bag of professional potting mixture, lay it flat on a board, make a few X slits in the bag, and plant a seedling in each X. I plant flowers and sometimes tomatoes. Then when frost rolls in, I extend my growing season by moving the bag and board into my nice warm garage. ✉ *Clair B., IA*

Grandma Putt's Wisdom

Grandma Putt would use her trowel or a knife to cut a circle around the plants she planned to put in pots for the winter. The circle was as big and deep as the pot each plant was even-tually going to go in. But instead of digging them out right away, she would leave them cut out like that in the ground. This gave her plants a chance to absorb the initial shock of being cut up before being moved. She watered them thoroughly, and then left them in the ground long enough for new rootlets to form within the ball.

After about three weeks, she lifted the new root-ball carefully out of the ground, and placed it in its new home (pot), where it was as happy and contented as if it had always lived there!

CLEAN THAT CLAY. Before planting your container garden, soak last year's lime-stained clay pots in a bucket filled with swimming pool pH-correcting solution, then rinse them well. They'll clean up and look as good as new. And they'll be ready for you to fill with beautiful flowers. ✉ Tori B., PA

IT'S THERE IN BLACK AND WHITE. Line your clay pots with a few layers of newspaper before filling them with soil and plants. The paper will keep the plants nice and moist, and as it breaks down over time, it'll add beneficial organic matter to the potting soil. ✉ Howard H., TX

TAKE 5

Here are five great uses for panty hose around the yard and garden:

1 When a cold snap strikes, block chilly winds by covering small plants with pieces of panty hose. Just slip a piece of hose over each plant, and pull the bottom closed.

2 Cover ripening fruits, vegetables, and sunflower heads with panty hose to protect them from nibbling insects, rodents, and birds.

3 Tie up vines and floppy plants with strips of panty hose to keep them on the up-and-up.

4 Scrunch panty hose into a ball and use the wad to polish the old jalopy without harming the finish.

5 Cut off a panty hose leg, tuck a bar of soap into the toe, and hang it near your outdoor faucet. Use it to clean off the dirt before you head inside.

LOVE THOSE LEAVES. Instead of spending big bucks on coconut husk pads to line my outdoor hanging flowerpots, I set aside a bagful of oak leaves when I'm raking them up in the fall. In the spring, I use these sturdy leaves to line the baskets, then fill the remainder with potting soil and plant my pretty flowers. ✉ Joanna M., NY

GO NUTS. Here's a great tip for making outdoor planters lighter and easier to manage: Fill the bottoms with foam packing peanuts before adding any potting soil. If your planters are exposed to a lot of wind, stuff the peanuts into old panty hose legs and tie the ends. Then place these "bags" in the bottoms of your planters. They'll still help lighten the load and improve drainage, but without the danger of being "gone-with-the-wind." ✉ Wanda K., IL

IN THE SWIM. When you know a rainstorm is headed your way, place a small plastic kiddie pool out on your deck or patio (or even your driveway) and set all of your potted plants in it. The rain will fill it up, and your plants will have a nice refreshing dip. ✉ Lori L., AL

SUPER-SOAK 'EM. I don't always have someone available to come by and water my outdoor potted plants when I go on vacation, so I came up with this solution: I soak my plants the night before I leave, then again early the next morning, and move them to a really shady spot. When I return a week later, my plants are still moist and cool. ✉ Donna G., MD

COLORFUL CONTAINERS. Save your children's old serving cups and bowls, superglue on another handle or two, then fill these colorful containers with potting soil and flowers and hang them from trees. They make a bright and attractive display, and you can move them around your yard for optimal light. ✉ Jim U., SD

AMARYLLIS AGAIN AND AGAIN. To get your amaryllis bulb to produce more blooms, remove it from the soil after the green foliage has died back. Cut the foliage off and let the bulb rest in a cool, dry place. When it's time for spring planting, place the bulb in the ground outside, leaving just a bit of the bulb showing. Keep it well watered and by July, you'll have glorious blooms once again. Dig up the bulb immediately after the first frost, and let it rest until the end of October. Replant it in an indoor pot, and voilà—another Christmas miracle! ✉ Martha C., ON

AMARYLLIS ACTION. Here's how I multiply my amaryllis. Once my plant is done blooming, I cut back on watering and place the bulb in a cool location. After a few weeks, I divide the bulblets and repot them. Come winter, I have several new plants to enjoy during the holidays. ✉ Camille B., PA

Ask Jerry

Q: I live in an apartment with a wonderful balcony that I can enjoy all year long because of my big glass doors. Are there any shrubs I can grow out there in containers that will also look good in the fall and winter?

A: You bet there are! Boxwood, juniper, cotoneaster, and many other shrubs come in compact varieties that will grow happy as clams in big pots. One of my very favorite shrubs for container growing is euonymus. It comes in both deciduous and evergreen versions, so make sure you look for one of the evergreen types to use on your balcony.

CHAPTER **15**

Bugs and Slugs

Flower Fiends

AWAY, APHIDS! To keep destructive aphids from ruining your beautiful roses, hang several long strands of banana peels over the branches of the bushes, skin side down. Replace them with fresh peels every two to three days, and your aphid trouble will soon be history. ✉ **Wilma R., CO**

FIT TO A TEA. Rid your roses of aphids with this garlic and parsley tea. Just put 2 tablespoons of minced garlic and ½ cup of parsley flakes in 3 cups of water, boil it down to 2 cups, strain out the solids, and cool. Put 1 cup of the liquid in a 20 gallon hose-end sprayer, and spray your rosebushes. If you don't want to make the tea, you can plant garlic and parsley between your bushes. That'll do the trick, too! ✉ **Christine E., CA**

Grandma Putt's Wisdom

As far as my Grandma Putt was concerned, the best program for fighting off bugs and disease in her flower garden was a good cultural preventive maintenance program. She made sure her plants got plenty of sunlight, and she watered, fed, and weeded them regularly. She also gave them a shower with the following tonic from time to time: ¼ cup of soap (she used lye-based), ¼ cup of antiseptic mouthwash, and ¼ cup of chewing tobacco juice in 5 gallons of rainwater (which she also collected). That took care of even the toughest problems.

CHEW ON THIS. I use a wad of well-chewed gum to remove aphids from my plants. I simply remove the gum from my mouth, and press it against the affected plant leaves. It grips the little pests tightly, and then I pitch the sticky mess into the trash. This also works to remove eggs left by tent caterpillars. ✉ Cynthia M., CA

MAKE MINE MARIGOLDS. Are aphids bugging your prized roses? Here's an easy—and attractive—way to protect your beautiful blooms: Plant marigolds in between the bushes. You'll never have aphids again! ✉ Brenda T., MO

A SOAPY SOLUTION. To protect your plants from aphids and leaf rollers, try this soapy solution: Mix 2 teaspoons of dishwashing liquid and 1 cup of vegetable oil in a handheld sprayer bottle. Shake it up, add a quart of water, and lightly mist the plants. ✉ Earlene K., TX

PUNGENT PROTECTION. I found an easy way to stop aphids and other pests from attacking my rosebushes. I put a peeled clove of garlic at the base of each of my rosebushes, and they haven't been pestered since. ✉ Carmen P., NM

LURE IN THE LADIES. Having a few ladybugs hanging around your roses will keep the aphids away all summer long. Lure the ladies to your garden by planting umbrella-shaped flowers and fragrant herbs and giving them plenty of water. ✉ **Linda L., CA**

SPRAY AWAY INSECTS. If insects are infesting your flower garden, fight back with this powerful spray: Mix ½ cup of orange cleaner and two squirts of flea-and-tick-control dog shampoo with enough water to fill a handheld sprayer bottle. Then spray your flowers liberally to stop insects in their tracks. ✉ **Linda A., OR**

WAGE WAR ON WHITEFLIES. Whiteflies can be a pain in the hibiscus to get rid of. Here's how I conquer these pests: I place plastic grocery bags over the infected branches, and leave them on overnight. By morning, the dew in the bags has already trapped and killed many of the adult flies. I remove all the bags, and wipe the nests off the undersides of the leaves with a paper towel that's been dipped in mayonnaise. Then I attach sticky traps to the branches to catch the rest of the invaders. ✉ **Catherine B., CA**

Ask Jerry

Q: How can I give proper "room and board" to those cute little ladybugs?

A: It's simple, but it's also fairly dangerous for your plants. Ladybugs need a steady diet of aphids, an insect that kills many plants. The problem is that ladybugs eat so many so fast that they soon eat themselves out of house and home! So you'll need to provide aphids if you want the ladybugs to stick around. Just keep in mind that you may be inviting a whole lot of trouble into your garden.

ANOTHER GREAT IDEA!

TOMATOES TO THE RESCUE

Protect your flowers from whiteflies with this time-tested tomato potion: Put 2 cups of chopped tomato leaves in a pan with 4 cups of water, and bring the water to a simmer (not a boil). Then turn off the heat and let the mixture cool. Strain out the leaves and add ½ teaspoon of dishwashing liquid to the water. Pour the solution into a handheld sprayer bottle and spritz the affected plants from top to bottom. Just remember that tomato leaves are poisonous, so don't use this spray on any plants that you intend to eat.

SWEET SURRENDER. Honey is a terrific helper when it comes to getting rid of whiteflies. Just heat some honey in a microwave, then brush it onto bright yellow 5-by-7 index cards with a pastry brush. Place one card in the middle of each plant that's infested with whiteflies. The pests will be attracted to the cards, get stuck in the honey, and die. Then you can just pitch the card and be done with it. ✉ Karen S., AZ

PLANT PARTNERS. Plant alyssum here, there, and everywhere, all around your garden. It smells great and needs very little attention. But most importantly, it'll keep whiteflies away from your other garden beauties. ✉ Mark K., CA

PUT A HALT TO HOPPERS. Is something eating your gardenia buds? It could be grasshoppers—they love to sneak in at night to snack on those irresistible blooms. But if you cover your gardenias at night with a garbage bag, the hoppers won't be able to get to them. In the morning, simply pull the bag off so you can enjoy your beautiful flowers. ✉ Jonelle A., TX

MEALYBUG BLASTER. Whenever I find mealybugs lurking on my flowers, I make a batch of this bug blaster: I mix ¼ teaspoon of ground cloves with ¼ cup of rubbing alcohol. I let it steep overnight, then use a cotton swab to dab the mixture right on the mealybugs the next day. It stops 'em dead in their tracks. ✉ Tom B., PA

STUCK ON YOU. Here's how I keep gnats away from my outdoor flowerpots—I hang a couple of sticky fly catchers near my container garden. As new gnats hatch, they get stuck on the paper, and soon enough, the gnats are gone. ✉ Annette S., WA

GO FOR GARLIC. Garlic oil makes a spot-on bug repellent and insecticide, and that's why I use this potent potion from Jerry: Mince 4 cloves of garlic, cover them with mineral oil, and let them soak for at least 24 hours. Then add 2 teaspoons of the oil and ¼ ounce of dishwashing liquid to 2 cups of water. Stir thoroughly, and strain the mixture into a glass container. When it's time to spray the bad bugs, mix 2 tablespoons of the oil with 2 cups of water in a handheld sprayer bottle, and go to town! ✉ Minnie W., FL

PERFECT POWDER PROTECTION. Give your plants even coverage when using a powdered bug killer by placing the insecticide in

---

SUPER-DUPER SOLUTIONS

MOVE ON, MEALYBUGS! ● The surest way to control a mealybug infestation is to remove the bugs. Wipe them off with a damp cloth, handpick them, or use a cotton swab dipped in alcohol to remove them. Check for egg sacks, and wipe those off as well. If the infested plants are in pots, keep them isolated from healthy plants. If they're out in the garden, check them every day until you get the infestation under control. Then wash your plants every week or two with a solution of 2 tablespoons of dishwashing liquid per half gallon of lukewarm water. Rinse them with water of the same temperature, then mist-spray them with a weak tea water solution.

a large flour sifter. Then crank the handle as you're walking through your garden. There's no muss, no fuss, and no pain in the back, either! ✉ Donna P., KS

A PENNY EARNED... Here's a great use for all those old pennies in your coin jar. Older pennies were made out of copper, so if you can find a few that were made before 1982, set them around your garden to prevent slugs from attacking and damaging plants. Slugs do not like copper, and they will steer clear! ✉ Moe L., ON

SLUGFEST. To keep slugs and snails away from my flower garden, I sprinkle dry yeast into a plastic lid filled with water, then place the lid on the ground near my plants. The slimy critters are attracted to the yeast smell, slither into the lid, drink their fill, and quickly die. ✉ Bonnie P., MO

TRUE GRIT. If slugs are destroying your garden, get some bird grit (intended for pet birds, it's available at pet-supply stores), and sprinkle it around your flowers. It will not only keep the slugs away,

Ask Jerry

Q: Last year, something ate the leaves off all of my marigolds. Could it have been slugs, and if so, what can I do to prevent a repeat this year?

A: It sure sounds like slugs to me. This year, apply a mixture of 25% aluminum sulfate and 75% pelletized lime with your handheld spreader once every three weeks to the areas you want to protect. Also, set out shallow pie tins filled with leftover beer for the tough guys—they'll fall in and drown themselves!

but it'll help your garden grow, too! Bird grit contains lots of calcium and charcoal, which are both great garden boosters. ✉ Susan J., OH

SPRAY 'EM AWAY. Protect your precious perennials from damaging slug attacks with this simple solution: Mix 2 cups of water with 1 tablespoon of ammonia in a handheld sprayer bottle. Then knock the slugs off your plants, and give 'em a big ol' squirt while they're squirming on the ground. ✉ Judy D., IN

A CORNY FIX. I've found that cornmeal helps keep slugs and snails away from my flower garden. I just sprinkle it on the ground around and among my flowering plants, and the slimy pests keep their distance. ✉ Luana E., CA

QUICK FIX

Using beer to lure slugs to their demise works great, but the cost, even if you're buying the cheap stuff, can really add up. So switch to store-brand grape juice and stock up when it's on sale. It works just as well, but costs considerably less than beer.

Fruit and Veggie Menaces

THE APPLE OF MY EYE. To make a codling moth trap for my apple trees, I cut an opening in one of the panels of a plastic milk jug opposite the handle. Then I mix equal parts of vinegar and water, and pour the solution into the jug until it's 1 inch deep. I add a few tablespoons of blackstrap molasses, and hang one trap in each apple tree. I check the traps every week, and remove the trapped moths. Try this, and you'll be eating worm-free apples in the fall, that's for sure! ✉ Reggie E., IL

PUT IT IN APPLE PIE ORDER

→ If you spray your apple trees but still have worms, you probably already had a problem before you started spraying. It generally takes more than a year or two for fruit trees to recover from an infestation. So you must follow a regular spraying program year-round. Start with dormant oil in the fall, follow it up with lime sulfur spray in early spring, and apply liquid fruit tree spray every 14 days throughout the growing season. Then get ready for a bushel full of prize-winning apples.

CONTROL CODLING MOTHS. For quick control of destructive codling moths, put a red cup in your apple tree's limbs, and fill it halfway with molasses. Once the cup is full of moths, empty it, refill it with molasses, and replace it in the limbs. Keep this up for the entire growing season, and you'll have the healthiest apples around! ✉ Meghan L., WA

WOO WOODPECKERS. I enlist woodpeckers in my battle against apple worms. They'll come calling if you hang suet in your apple trees. Woodpeckers will flock to the free meal and hang around to polish off the larvae for dessert. ✉ Denise Q., PA

THAT'S JUST PEACHY. Stop peach tree borer damage before it starts by circling your peach trees with nut-shells and hulls—black walnuts are best, but any type of nut will do. Bury some of the shells and hulls about 2 inches into the soil around the tree, and scatter several around on top of the ground about 6 inches from the trunk to just beyond the tips of the outermost branches. That'll do the trick. ✉ Stephen M., SC

PRISTINE PEACHES. I use this homemade trap to keep peach tree worms from attacking my fruit: I stir 1 cup of vinegar and 1 cup of sugar into 1 quart of water. Then I fill a jar with the mixture and hang it from the tree when it's in full bloom. The worms are more attracted to this trap than they are to my peaches. ✉ Anne G., GA

TREAT THE TRUNKS. Here's a super-simple way to keep borers out of your fruit trees. Just mix wood ashes with enough water to make a paste, and spread it on the tree trunks up to a height of 2 feet or so. If you do this, both female moths and newly hatched larvae will seek lodging someplace else. ✉ **Elise W., PA**

FLOUR POWER. If the leaves of your strawberry plants become rolled up tight, you can bet it's the dirty work of leaf rollers. Spring into action by dusting your plants with flour. The baby caterpillars will eat the stuff, swell up, and die. Clip off and throw away any rolled-up leaves—don't compost them!—and your plants should bounce back and give you a healthy crop of berries. ✉ **Brenda R., MO**

WEEVIL WIPEOUT. When strawberry root weevils attack your strawberry and raspberry plants, foil them with this old-time trick: Spread a sheet on the ground under your plants. Then two or three hours after the sun sets, when the weevils are enjoying their dinner, go out and jostle your plants' foliage. Weevils can't fly, so they'll come tumbling down onto the sheet. Carefully gather it up and dump the contents into a tub full of soapy water. ✉ **Herman L., KY**

Grandma Putt's Wisdom

Fruit tree borers are a nemesis to all who grow their own peaches, plums, apricots, and apples. My Grandma Putt's method literally painted out borers with a solution made up of 1 gallon of cheap-grade interior latex paint (exterior paint may damage some young trees) and 3 gallons of water. You'll need less water if you're going to apply the solution by brush rather than spray. Either way, apply the "paint" to the trunks of the trees in late July, and your borer troubles will be over.

BERRY BUG TRAP. To keep moths and black bugs off your raspberries, mix 2 cups of sugar, ½ cup of vinegar, and 1 banana peel in a 1-gallon plastic milk jug, then add enough water to the jug until the liquid reaches 2 inches below the top. Hang the open jug in a nearby tree or set it among your raspberry bushes, and leave it in place all summer long. You'll be amazed at how many insects your trap will catch! ✉ Jeannette H., WI

GET HOPPING. To get grasshoppers to hop on by, just mix 2 cups of flour with 1 cup of baking powder and sprinkle it on your vegetable plants. It won't kill the hoppers, but it'll stop them from eating your precious greens. ✉ Ellen F., MO

CALLING ALL BIRDS. Birds are our best line of defense when it comes to getting rid of pesky grasshoppers, so try this neat trick to attract fine-feathered friends to the hopper feast: Mix 1 part molasses with 9 parts water, and pour the mixture into shallow containers

Ask Jerry

Q: My raspberries get two rings around the tip where the berries should be forming. Then the tip bends over and dies. I have also noticed a worm between the two rings. What is this, and how can it be prevented?

A: It sounds like an infestation of raspberry cane borers. As soon as you see a tip wilt, cut it off below the rings. Remove all the old canes after you harvest the berries, and spray the plants with Murphy® Oil Soap at the rate of 1 tablespoon per gallon of water to prevent future infestations.

like cat food or tuna fish cans. Then set the cans out in your garden and sprinkle bread crumbs or sunflower seeds all around them. Grasshoppers will zero in on the sweet water, while birds will home in on the hoppers, crumbs, and seeds. ✉ Timothy L., IL

MIGHTY MOLASSES MIX. Every summer, grasshoppers descend on my garden. But I've figured out how to spoil their fun—with molasses. I just sink jars up to their rims in my garden beds, then fill each one with a mixture of equal parts molasses and water. The hoppers dive right into the drink and stay there! ✉ Ellen P., NJ

RADISH RESCUE. I keep root maggots away from my radish plants by crushing bran cereal and putting it in the holes along with my seedlings. My plants grow up healthy, strong, and maggot-free. ✉ Georgia D., KY

NET RESULTS. Need a pesticide-free way to keep moths off your cabbage plants? Try bird netting—it's reasonably priced, lets in light and air, and won't blow away like row covers do. And it sure beats picking pests off by hand. Make a frame out of wood, and attach the netting to it. You'll still be able to get to your veggies, but the moths will be thrown for a loop! ✉ Pat F., ID

GET GRILLING. And when you're done with the barbecue, take those leftover charcoal ashes and put them to good use in your garden. Sprinkle the ashes around your cabbage and broccoli plants to keep cabbage worms away. It's all-natural, and the worms absolutely hate it. ✉ Sonia M., IL

Jerry's Handy Hints

ONE GOOD TURN

→ Here's a great way to combat plant-eating grasshoppers. Since the destructive hoppers spend the winter as eggs in the soil, get on top of the problem by turning your garden soil under as early as you can in the spring. You'll destroy lots and lots of eggs.

ANOTHER GREAT IDEA!

BUTTER 'EM UP

If you love buttermilk as much as I do, here's a little secret you ought to know: Cabbage worms can't stand the stuff. So every time you empty a carton, rinse it out and pour the milky liquid on your plants. Even watered down, it'll send those predators packing, pronto!

FOIL THEM WITH FLOUR. Early in the morning, while the dew is still on the plants, sift flour over your cabbages using a flour sifter. Cabbage worms will crawl out on the cabbage plants and coat themselves in the flour. Then as the sun dries the dew—and the flour—the worms will be starched stiff, and you'll be rid of them once and for all. ✉ **Fae S., IA**

HOSIERY HELPER. I control cabbage worms with an old pair of panty hose. I just cut off a leg from the knee down, and pull the foot part over each cabbage. The nylon stretches as the cabbage grows, and the plant still gets plenty of air, light, and moisture that it needs. ✉ **Gary L., MI**

SUPER-DUPER SOLUTIONS

PLANT PURPLE ● Cabbage butterflies tend to zero in on green plants and leave purple and reddish types alone. So use that knowledge to your advantage. When you place your next seed order, look for winners like 'Red Rookie' cabbage, 'Purple Head' cauliflower, 'Violet Queen' broccoli, and 'Rubine' Brussels sprouts. There are plenty of varieties available, so peruse catalogs, Web sites, and heirloom-vegetable books for the latest and greatest, or the oldest and tastiest, types.

A SOUR SOLUTION. To keep caterpillars from feasting on my cabbage plants, I make a solution of sour milk and a little lemon juice or vinegar, and spoon it into the center of each plant. It does the trick every time! ✉ Patricia R., FL

Grandma Putt's Wisdom

Whenever my Grandma Putt's pine trees shed their needles, she'd scoop up the prickly things and put them in a big bucket. Then anytime she needed to fend off cutworms, slugs, or other soft-bodied crawlers, she'd scoop out some needles and scatter them around the base of each vulnerable plant. Just like that, problem solved!

GO POSTAL. Hang on to those advertisement postcards that literally fall from between the pages of your magazines. You can fold them in half lengthwise, and turn them into cutworm collars for your plants. Now that's what I call recycling! ✉ Ronald S., PA

COLLAR CUPS. I use empty yogurt cups to make cutworm barriers. I just cut off the bottoms and press the remaining cups, cut side down, into the soil. They make perfect weatherproof collars around my tender young seedlings. ✉ Greg T., NM

WEEP NO MORE. Make reusable cutworm collars for your seedlings by cutting 5-inch sections from plastic weeping tile (found at building-supply stores). Set the collars around each plant, pushing one end into the soil, and you're good to go. ✉ Gerald M., IL

NAILED AGAIN. I place a nail in the soil alongside each of my cabbage, tomato, and other seedlings to stop cutworms from eating them. I don't know why, but it sure does do the trick for me! ✉ Richard I., MN

Q: Earwigs invade everything in May, eating my carrots, beets, zinnias, beans, and cabbages as soon as they come through the ground. What can I do?

A: Earwigs feed by night. During the day, they hide in damp, shady places. To set a trap for these pests, loosely roll up several sheets of newspaper, dampen the tube, and set it in a shady spot. Hordes of earwigs will crawl inside while the sun shines. As evening approaches, before they mosey on out for dinner, grab the tube and unroll it over a tub of soapy water. Or you can simply toss the whole shebang on your compost pile and pour hot, soapy water on top.

TOTALLY TUBULAR. Need a cheap, easy, and effective cutworm collar? Then do what I do and save the cardboard tubes from your paper towel rolls and cut them into 3- to 4-inch lengths. Push an inch or so of each mini tube into the soil around young plants, leaving about 2 inches above soil level to protect your tender seedlings from hungry cutworms. ✉ Sandy S., MO

I'LL DRINK TO THAT! You can use plastic drinking straws to keep cutworms off your transplants. Cut the straws into 1½-inch pieces, and slit them lengthwise. Slip a section around each stem before transplanting, then press the bottom of the straw into the soil as you put the plant into the ground. ✉ Mark G., IL

IT'S IN THE CAN. When my garden is playing host to an infestation of earwigs, I fill a few empty tuna cans with molasses and set them out among my plants. The sweet, sticky goo is a big hit with the earwigs—they eagerly climb in, but aren't able to escape. Then I just toss out the cans and replace them with new ones until no more earwigs appear for the gravy train. ✉ *Phyllis S., AZ*

DOWN TO EARTH. If earwigs are wigging you out, sprinkle some diatomaceous earth (available at your local home-improvement or hardware store) around areas they favor—in other words, anyplace that's dark and moist. ✉ *Gregory P., CA*

ERADICATE EARWIGS. Say good riddance to bad bugs! Bathe your plants in soapy water to get rid of earwigs, and keep 'em away for good. Just add a few drops of dishwashing liquid to a handheld sprayer bottle, and fill the bottle with water. Mix well, then take aim and fire away at the pincered pests! ✉ *Evelyn P., NY*

Grandma Putt's Wisdom

My Grandma Putt taught me about four outstanding good-neighbor plants that can help your vegetables fight off insects. Believe it or not, they're neither herbs nor vegetables; they're flowers! The fabulous four I'm talking about are old-fashioned marigolds (the kind that smell so spicy), nasturtiums, geraniums (both red and white), and poppies. Grandma used all four as an outside border around her vegetable garden. For good measure, sometimes she even chopped, squeezed, and then mixed them up with an old eggbeater to make organic insect repellents. If you try this, be sure to dilute the beaten-up pulp with 10 parts water in your hose-end sprayer.

For those of you who live in the South, don't forget to put a few tobacco plants (*Nicotiana*) in with your vegetables. They smell wonderful and are among the very best bug killers you can buy.

SPUD SAVER. Bothered by potato bugs? Then try my recipe for relief: Mix 4 tablespoons of whole wheat flour, 1 teaspoon of dishwashing liquid, and 1 quart of warm water in a handheld sprayer bottle, and squirt the solution on your potato plants. The sticky spray will either trap the bugs and kill them, or it'll ruin their digestive tracts when they eat, and they'll die. Either way, you win—and the bugs lose their free lunch. ✉ Elaine E., ME

ANOTHER GREAT IDEA!

CLEAN SWEEP

If squash bugs are buggin' your cucurbits, reach for the wet/dry vac. Put an inch or two of soapy water in the reservoir, then go out into your garden early in the morning, hit the "on" switch, and sweep up those bad bugs. If you don't have a wet/dry vac, use a handheld vacuum, and empty the buggy contents into a bucket of hot, soapy water.

BEETLE BUSTER. To get rid of potato beetles, start with a clean glass jar that has a tight-fitting lid. Fill the jar with powdered lime, screw the lid on, and poke some holes in it. Then go out and sprinkle the lime on your potato and nightshade plants every two weeks, and anytime after it rains. It'll keep your potatoes safe from those nasty pests. ✉ Andrea E., VA

QUASH SQUASH BUGS. When squash bugs invade my garden, I fight back by putting a dab of white all-purpose glue on each egg cluster. It prevents the eggs from hatching, plus it's much easier to dab the eggs with glue than to scrape them off, and the glue won't damage the leaves. Check your plants frequently, and apply glue to any new egg clusters right away. ✉ David D., MI

WORTH THEIR WEIGHT IN GOLD. I've discovered that marigolds make the perfect squash bug repellent. Give this trick a try next planting season: Before you set out your squash plants, plant a crop of marigolds, spacing them so there's room to plant your squash in among the flowers. I guarantee that your vegetables will be untouched by squash bugs. ✉ **Yolanda S., NM**

NOT JUST FOR VAMPIRES . . .
Yep, I'm talking about garlic. If you're having problems with squash bugs or cucumber beetles in your garden, simply sprinkle the plants with garlic powder, step aside, and literally watch the little buggers drop and run for cover. ✉ **Kerry S., MI**

Rx FOR SQUASH.
I use disposable syringes to inject liquid Bt directly into the stems of my squash plants. This way, I'm able to kill borers without having to split open my plants' stems. I give the first injection as soon as I see flowers starting to bloom on the vine, then follow up with a shot every week throughout the growing season. ✉ **Rose T., IL**

BURIED TREASURE.
Don't let the bad bugs get to your squash before you do. As soon as you notice holes in the lower stems, bury the stems almost to the leaves. It'll take a little time for the plants to get reoriented, but at least you won't lose them altogether. ✉ **Charles G., VA**

TAKE 5

Here are five not-so-common uses for sugar in the yard and garden:

1 Nix nematodes by tilling in 3 pounds of sugar per acre of soil in late fall.

2 Trap insects by sprinkling equal parts of flour and powdered sugar on plants in the morning before the dew dries.

3 Feed future pie ingredients by making fertilizer for strawberries and rhubarb. Combine 5 pounds of dry garden food with ½ cup of sugar.

4 Attract hungry hummingbirds with a mixture of 1 part sugar to 8 parts hot water, replacing the mixture every four days.

5 Remove gasoline spots from the lawn by sprinkling 6 parts gypsum and 1 part sugar over the entire area and watering well.

CABBAGE WAKE-UP CALL. To perk up sickly cabbages that worms or bugs have been pestering, try this trick: Mix flour with a little sugar and cayenne pepper, and dust the mixture on your plants in the morning while they're still damp with dew. It'll repel the pests, and in no time at all your cabbage will be looking healthy again. ✉ Kelly Y., WI

PINE PROTECTION. Before planting your vegetable garden, do what I do and spread a 2-inch layer of pine sawdust over the bed and turn it into the soil. It'll keep nematodes under control for at least two growing seasons. ✉ Donald L., CA

RHUBARB REVENGE. To deal with garden pests, I make a rhubarb potion to keep the buggers under control. I simply boil 3 medium-sized rhubarb leaves in 1 gallon of water. After the mixture cools, I pour it through cheesecloth to filter out the solids, then mix in 10 drops of dishwashing liquid. I spray this solution on my plants using a handheld sprayer. In addition to repelling pests, this potion helps prevent blight on my tomatoes. ✉ Michael H., WA

SUPER-DUPER SOLUTIONS

DON'T LET 'EM SNATCH THE PATCH! ● If little slugs are hiding in your lettuce, and traps don't seem to be solving the problem, it's going to take an all-out effort to reclaim your lettuce patch. Here's a trick to get you started: In the evening, lay pieces of burlap over the ground around your lettuce, and dampen them just a bit. The next morning, you should find a bunch of those slimy little guys hiding under the cloths. Rinse the fabric out in a bucket of warm, soapy water, put it back in place, and repeat the process for five days. Try to keep the rest of your garden area as clean as possible, and add a scratchy barrier around your beds (such as diatomaceous earth or sandpaper collars) to keep the pests from coming back around.

LOVE YOUR LETTUCE. If you love to grow lettuce, but can't stand battling the slugs that want to eat it all before you can get your hands on it, try this clever trick: Break up several clean, dry eggshells and sprinkle them in the garden all around the plants. The slugs will slither elsewhere, and you'll have lots of yummy lettuce—all to yourself! ✉ Linda P., OH

GO FOR THE SHINE. To keep slugs away from your garden treasures, grab a roll of aluminum foil. For single-stemmed plants (like tomatoes), put a 1-inch strip of foil around the bottom of the stem. For many-stemmed plants (like dahlias), place a ring of crinkled foil around all of the stems. The slugs will definitely steer clear. ✉ Pat E., WA

SAVED BY SPICE. I sprinkle dried ginger around my plants to keep slugs away. Try it, it really does work! Just remember to apply more ginger after every rain and after watering your garden. ✉ Sarah S., ON

GREAT GRIT. To keep slugs away from your garden, surround each plant with a wide ring of sand. The gritty barrier will thwart any slugs that try to raid your produce. ✉ Shirley H., CA

PLUCK AND DUNK. This isn't for the squeamish, but I use this slug-busting technique to keep my garden clear of the slimy pests. I just pluck slugs off my plants with a snap-shut clothespin (like I'm using tweezers), and toss 'em into a can filled with soapy water. That shows 'em who's boss! ✉ Debra H., NH

SLUG BLASTER. Here's a simple way to send slugs to their graves: Fill a handheld sprayer bottle with 1 part ammonia and 2

QUICK FIX

Trap slugs by setting out citrus rinds, cabbage leaves, or potato chunks among your plants in the evening. Come morning, you'll be able to scoop up the traps, slugs and all, and drop 'em to their doom in a bucket of water laced with a cup or so of rubbing alcohol or ammonia.

parts water. Anytime you see a slug, blast it with a big ol' squirt. You'll be delighted at what this does to the slimy little creatures! ✉ Donna S., WA

HIT THE TRAIL. Slugs won't cross a wood ash trail. So instead of throwing them out, sprinkle the ashes from your fireplace around your tomato plants and other garden gems that are bothered by these destructive pests. ✉ Clettyce S., IN

Backyard Pests

LAY A TRAP. If bugs are a problem in your backyard, make your own great bug catcher from items you probably already have in your kitchen. First, grab an empty plastic milk carton out of the recycling bin. Rinse it out and fill it with 1 cup of white wine vinegar, 1 cup of sugar, and 1 banana peel. Add warm water until the carton is one-third full. Slosh it around to mix it, then add cool water until the carton is half full. Hang the carton from a rod or pole in the area of your yard where the bugs are causing the most problems, and you'll see a noticeable decline in their population. ✉ Alice S., IA

SHOO, FLIES. To keep flies from buzzing around your porches and doorways, half fill a ziplock plastic bag with water, and hang it over the entryways. I know it sounds crazy, but the water refracts the light and scares the flies away. ✉ Doreen D., WA

LET'S FLY AWAY. Keep annoying flies away from your picnic area (and you!) with this nontoxic repellent: Mix equal parts white vinegar and mouthwash in a handheld sprayer bottle. Then spray it around your picnic table or blanket, and even on yourself. I guarantee that flies won't bother you anymore. ✉ Denise B., OH

Ask Jerry

Q: My husband wants to get one of those electric bug zappers to kill the mosquitoes in our yard. I've heard that they don't really work very well, and I'm afraid that all it's going to zap is our peace and quiet. Am I right?

A: Yes and no. Those gadgets zap bugs all right—just about every kind, including the good guys. What they don't kill, however, are mosquitoes. Most zappers use light to attract their prey, and mosquitoes aren't attracted to light; they're out for blood, so they zero in on the smell of carbon dioxide, which mammals give off. If your hubby insists on using an electric gizmo, steer him toward a machine that uses CO_2 to quietly lure skeeters to their death.

SOAP FOR SKEETERS. Put a few drops of lemon-scented dishwashing liquid in a white plate filled with water, and set it out on your deck rail. It will attract mosquitoes and keep them away from you and your backyard guests. ✉ Barbara R., MI

EAU DE RELIEF. When you're working outside, the last thing you want is to be pestered by mosquitoes. So do what I do and head 'em off at the pass by putting a fresh dryer sheet under your hat. Skeeters can't stand the smell, so they stay far away! ✉ Ed R., WV

SKEETER SPRAY. Pretend you're the father in *My Big Fat Greek Wedding* and arm yourself with a spray bottle of Windex® whenever you spend time outside. As soon as mosquitoes start buzzin'

around, let 'em have it. A quick spray of the cleaner will make skeeters drop immediately. ✉ Rachel Z., AZ

B BITE-FREE. I've discovered that if I take vitamin B for a week, mosquitoes avoid me like the plague. I don't know what the science is behind this trick—I just know that it works! ✉ Leslie R., CA

Grandma Putt's Wisdom

My Grandma Putt had a dandy way to cut down on the mosquito population: She'd fill some old pans with water, add a few squirts of dishwashing liquid, and set them outside. When the skeeters set down to lay their eggs, they couldn't get up again!

ALL HANDS ON DECK. To keep your deck area free of hornets and wasps, try using balloons. Blow up a balloon so that it fits into a paper lunch bag, then tack the bag up in the area bothered by the flyers. As the breeze moves the paper bag, the vibrations from the balloon inside scare hornets and wasps away. ✉ Judy D., ON

KEEP 'EM MOVING ON. If you've got wasps or bees scouting out nesting areas near your house, put out the "No Trespassing" sign with some citronella. Place a citronella candle bucket (with the lid off) as close as possible to the area being considered—or already inhabited—by wasps or bees. They will quickly decide not to make their home there! ✉ Julie J., IN

BLAST AWAY. When you find wasps and their nests, give them a blast of ammonia from your hose-end sprayer. Really soak the insects and their homes; the wasps will drop like rocks, and the nests will eventually dry out and fall off eaves and other hard-to-reach locations. ✉ Marie L., NY

CLEAN HOUSE. To keep wasps from taking over your birdhouses, put a few mothballs in the houses in early spring. And hang a handful of mothballs in old knee-high nylons in your garage, on your porch, or anywhere else that wasps are likely to try to build new digs. ✉ Evelyn L., MO

FEEDER FIX. Wasps used to love hanging out at my hummingbird feeders until I found this deterrent: I dab a little vegetable oil on the ports surrounding the feeder holes. Wasps can't get to the sugar water, so they're no longer interested in my feeders. And that leaves them available for the hummers to enjoy. ✉ Sharon B., IN

Ask Jerry

Q: I have a problem with yellow jackets and wasps. Are there any plants that will repel them?

A: I don't know of any plants that deter yellow jackets—but a lot of people plant flowers to attract them! Wasps and yellow jackets prey on garden pests and pollinate plants, so they can be very helpful in your garden. If you still want to get rid of them and don't want to go near their nests, try to avoid attracting them in the first place. Put food away promptly, don't leave ripe fruit in your garden, and keep the garbage can lids on tight. To really send 'em off, fill several cans with equal parts ammonia and water, and then hang the cans in and around your yard. Ammonia is a definite wasp deterrent.

READY, AIM, FIRE. I use hand-to-hand combat on fire ants by mixing 1 part all-purpose orange oil cleaner with 10 parts water in a handheld sprayer bottle. Then I take aim and fire on the little devils' hills and they soon disappear. ✉ **Charlotte M., AL**

THEY HIDE, YOU SEEK. If you have fire ants in your yard, but you're having trouble finding all their hills, try this trick: Seal one end of a 2-foot-long plastic pipe (about 2 inches in diameter), and secure it on the handle of your lawn mower, sealed end down. Buy a dozen or so surveyor's flags from a hardware store (30-inch wires with small flags on top), and put them in the pipe on your mower. Then the next time you mow, every time the blade chops off the top of an ant nest, pull one of the flags out of the pipe and stick it into the center of the nest. When you're done mowing, walk around the yard, and as you pick up the flags, treat each nest with your favorite fire ant killer. After a few mowings, you'll have an ant-free lawn, and you'll be able to keep it that way all season long. ✉ **Noreen K., MS**

ANT BLAST. To get rid of outdoor ants, simply place household bleach in a handheld sprayer bottle, take aim, and fire directly on ants and their hills. It's a blast! ✉ **Zanne G., GA**

BORAX CHASER. Here's a simple way to stop an ant intrusion: Just sprinkle some good old borax around the foundation of your house to keep the pests outside—where they belong. ✉ **Kate E., MO**

SUPER-DUPER SOLUTIONS

ANTI-ANT A-PEEL ● You can get rid of fire ants without using pesticides, but first you've got to save a lot of orange peels. Mix them (the more, the merrier) with 5 gallons of water in a bucket, and let 'em steep for about a week. Strain, then pour the liquid over the fire ant mounds, or anywhere else you find these bad bugs lurking!

BRING IN THE BIRDS. To get rid of ants that are invading your garden, hang a bird feeder above their hills. The birds will flock to the feeder, and the ants will head to the hills to find new digs because they certainly won't want to live so close to their natural enemies! ✉ Todd L., PA

ANT ATTACK-TICS. I sprinkle dried coffee grounds around my plants and shrubs to keep ants away. Then when I want to get rid of ants for good, I mix equal parts of boric acid powder and apple mint jelly and put globs of it right on their anthills. *Caution:* Keep this mixture away from children and pets. ✉ Ellen L., MO

GET IN LINE. You can use cinnamon to prevent ants from invading your house, garage, and tool-shed. Simply pour a line of the ground spice across any entry points to keep the pests away. ✉ Lori L., WA

TURN UP THE HEAT. I've found a great ant deterrent in my spice rack: chili powder. I just sprinkle the powder around an army of ants and watch 'em run like crazy in the opposite direction. ✉ Nicholas E., CA

A STICKY SITUATION. Ants want that yummy sugar water in your hummingbird feeder as much as the little hummers do. Your job is to keep them away, so try sticking a few strips of double-faced carpet tape to your feeder's hanger. The ants will get stuck to it, leaving the sweet liquid for the birds. ✉ Jenna M., MI

GOOD GREASE. Keep ants from climbing into your hummingbird feeder by spraying the bottom of the support pole with cooking spray. The little buggers will slip and slide and never make it to the feeder. Just remember to spray it again after each rain. ✉ Jolene P., PA

TAKE 5

Here are five not-so-common uses for chalk in your yard and garden:

1 Keep ants out of your storage shed, garage, and other areas by drawing a heavy chalk outline near the entryways.

2 Stop slugs dead in their tracks with a thick chalk line.

3 To prevent a calcium deficiency from developing in your tomato and melon plants, grind up some chalk and sprinkle it on the soil around the plants.

4 Boost your newly planted seeds to new heights by sprinkling a little ground-up chalk over them in their planting beds. This works well on seedlings, too.

5 Throw a stick or two of chalk in your toolbox to protect your tools from rust. Replace it every year or so, and your tools should be rust-free for life!

HEAD FOR THE HILLS. I get rid of huge anthills in a snap by simply pouring boiling water over them. Then I poke into the hill with a stick, and pour more water inside, making sure I get the steaming liquid deep down into the nest. That usually does the trick. ✉ Robbie T., IL

A JARRING SOLUTION. I say "good riddance!" to pesky sugar ants by dissolving ½ cup of sugar in a cup of warm water, then combining it with 1 cup of borax. I lightly stuff four baby food jars with toilet paper, and pour the liquid mixture into the jars. I put the lids on, and shake the bottles to saturate the toilet paper. Then I poke about six holes in the top of each lid with a hammer and nail, and set the jars around the anthills, or wherever I see an ant infestation. The ants are attracted to the sugary sweetness and go right for the mixture through the holes in the lids—but once they get into the jars, they can't get out. ✉ Ronda P., OR

SIMPLE SYRUP. Here's an easy recipe for getting rid of ants: Mix equal parts of borax and confectioner's sugar with enough water until it's a syrupy consistency. Put the mixture in small, flat pans, and place them wherever you see ants. The ants that eat the syrup will die, and the ants that eat the dead ants will die, too. Eventually, you won't have any more ant problems! ✉ Karen F., MI

THE CUKE CURE. I've discovered that ants can't stand the smell of fresh cucumber. So whenever I peel a few cukes, I scatter the peels anywhere I've seen ants. Believe me, they clear outta there in no time. ✉ Tom R., IL

IT'S A WRAP. It's frustrating to see ants on the march up the trunks of your trees. So do what I do and wrap a band of carpet tape or double-sided masking tape around each trunk. The tape won't harm the tree, but it will trap the ants as they try to scamper

ANOTHER GREAT IDEA!

GOTCHA!

To trap ants before they wander far from their home, try this no-fail trick: Put a piece of tape over the drain hole in the bottom of a flowerpot and set the pot upside down over the anthill. When the ants come up out of the hill, they'll scamper up the inner sides of the pot. Within a day, your trap should be so full of ants that you'll hardly be able to see the sides. Then just pick up the pot and drop it into a bucket of boiling water. Problem solved!

up it. Be sure to inspect the tape every few days and replace it when it's covered with the pests. ✉ **Marcie R., DE**

PEE FOR TREES. Believe it or not, you should pour human urine around the trunks of trees that are being destroyed by carpenter ants and beetles. Treat the trees in early spring, out to an 18-inch perimeter, then again about three weeks later. It may seem crazy, but it really works! ✉ **Ron D., MI**

ERADICATE BOX ELDERS. Every few years, box elder bugs seem to be everywhere. I stop 'em in their tracks with this sudsy spray: I pump five squirts of liquid hand soap into a handheld sprayer bottle, and fill the remainder with water. I spray this mixture anywhere I see the bugs crawling. To cover a larger area, I fill

SUPER-DUPER SOLUTIONS

QUIT BUGGING ME ● If you've been overrun by box elder bugs in the past, take action now to keep them from entering your home as the weather cools and they hunt for warm living quarters. Here's what you need to do:

- Repair or replace damaged window and door screens.

- Repair or replace damaged screens in roof and soffit vents and in bathroom and kitchen fans.

- Seal areas where cable TV wires, phone lines, other utility wires, pipes, outdoor faucets, dryer vents, and similar objects enter your home.

- Seal small spaces with caulk. For larger spaces, use polyurethane expandable spray foam, copper mesh, or another appropriate sealant.

- Install door sweeps or thresholds on all exterior entry doors, and install rubber seals along the bottoms of garage doors.

a 20 gallon hose-end sprayer with liquid hand soap, and spray areas of infestation to the point of runoff. ✉ Anna M., MN

SUCK 'EM UP. When box elder bugs invade your home, the quickest way to get rid of them is to use your vacuum cleaner to suck them up. When you're done, simply dispose of the bag. These bugs can also be trapped rather easily under boards or folded paper; then all you'll have to do is check the trap every day. ✉ Mike R., CT

CREEPERS, JEEPERS. Here's a simple way to keep creepy crawlers like caterpillars and worms from crawling up your patio plants—use tape. Just wrap transparent tape sticky-side out around the plant stems. This invisible deterrent won't spoil the plants' appearance, but it will spoil the pests' fun! ✉ Tina W., ND

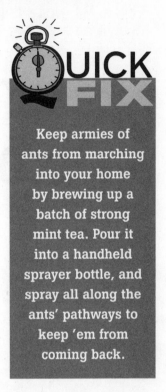

QUICK FIX

Keep armies of ants from marching into your home by brewing up a batch of strong mint tea. Pour it into a handheld sprayer bottle, and spray all along the ants' pathways to keep 'em from coming back.

WHAT A JARRING SURPRISE! If you've got earwigs crawling all over your deck, stop 'em in their tracks with this sweet treat. Pour about half an inch of molasses into some glass jars, then add enough water to reach about three-quarters of the way up. Stir until the water and molasses are thoroughly mixed, and set the "beverages" out on your deck and among any nearby plants. The earwigs, which have a real sweet tooth, will drop in for a drink, and they'll stay long after the bar closes! ✉ Tommy L., PA

America's Best
Practical Problem Solvers

CHAPTER 16

Critter Control

Birds

TIE A YELLOW RIBBON ... To discourage hungry birds from eating your yummy garden goodies, pound several 12-inch stakes into the ground. Wrap fishing line from one stake to the next, until all of the stakes are connected, and then tie brightly colored ribbon from the line. The ribbon will flutter in the breeze, and voilà! No more breakfasting birds in your garden. ✉ **Jessica H., NM**

CLEVER CUP COVERS. When your baby plants are just peeking through the soil and all the neighborhood birds seem to have their eyes on them, use this clever cover for your seedlings: Remove the bottoms from tall, clear plastic cups and, using one cup per plant, push the cut end of the cup into the ground so it surrounds your plant. Your seedlings will be safe, and you'll be entertained watching the birds try to peck through the clear plastic! ✉ **Jennifer H., WA**

SNAP, CRACKLE, PLASTIC. I scare birds away from my crops with black plastic. I simply cut 3-foot-long strips from black plastic garbage bags and tie them to nearby trees, shrubs, fences, and stakes. The wind takes care of the rest—the flapping, snapping plastic strips scare the dickens out of the birds, and my crops stay nice and safe. ✉ Nick L., NC

PANTY HOSE PROTECTION. If you have a grapevine, it can be tough to keep the birds away from the developing fruit. Here's a creative solution. Simply cut the legs off an old pair of hose, then cut them again at the knee. Tie one cut end of each piece with a brightly colored piece of yarn, and fit the panty hose "bags" over each bunch of grapes. Finish by tying the other end with more yarn. The birds won't be able to get at your grapes, and you can let everyone know that as long as the grapes are covered with the panty hose, they aren't ripe enough for nibbling. ✉ Nancy M., UT

Ask Jerry

Q: Here's a problem that's driving me bonkers! I have a small garden that's got sandy soil. The blasted birds have taken it over as a dusting haven. I've tried all sorts of remedies, and the only thing that works is to keep the ground soaked, or cover the whole area with plastic. Unfortunately, neither of these methods helps a garden grow! Do you have a solution?

A: My advice is that you either put netting up high enough so you can walk and garden under it, or use a landscape fabric that lets food and water through, but keeps birds (and weeds) out.

TAKE

Here are five not-so-common uses for aluminum foil around the yard and garden:

1 Hang strips of aluminum foil on wire just above your plants to electrically charge the air around them, and keep birds away.

2 Keep gnawing critters away from tender young tree trunks by loosely wrapping them with aluminum foil about 2 feet up from the ground.

3 Place aluminum foil around plants to keep cats from doing their duty, and to keep certain insects away.

4 Wrap aluminum foil over a container, then poke a hole through it to keep cuttings upright while you're rooting them.

5 Place a piece of foil behind outdoor lights to make them brighter.

MUSIC TO YOUR EARS. If birds are gathering in your fruit trees, pecking at the produce before you can get your hands on it (and sink your teeth into it!), put your old CDs to good use. Hang the disks in your trees and let them sway in the breeze. The reflections from the sun will scare the birds away. ⊠ Marlene G., CA

BYE-BYE, BIRDIES. I keep birds from harvesting my fruit crop with help from my Christmas tree decorations. I hang several silver and gold ball ornaments from the branches of each of my fruit trees. Then when sunlight reflects off the bright balls, the birds steer clear. ⊠ Sue R., TN

NET RESULTS. When birds are picking and squirrels are eating every apple on my trees before they ripen, I cover the trees with tree nets. They are cheap, light, easy to use, and best of all, they work! ✉ Douglas R., IA

BONUS BUTTONS. I've discovered this pretty slick trick to keep the birds from eating my blueberries: I plant some blue bachelor's buttons (cornflowers) among my berry bushes. The blue flowers bloom as the berries ripen, and for some reason, the birds stay far away. ✉ Mary H., WA

PLAYING CHICKEN. You can protect your strawberries from birds by laying a long strip of chicken wire across the plants. The feathered feasters won't like getting their feet tangled up, so they'll fly right on by. ✉ Aldyth H., KS

STOP PIGEON PROBLEMS. To keep pigeons from roosting on the ledges, nooks, and crannies of my house, I stretch out metal Slinky® toys and tack them down on both ends along the eaves. They wobble around in the breeze, and the pigeons don't like that at all. ✉ Diane L., MO

QUIT PECKIN' ON ME! Stop woodpeckers from pecking holes in your wooden siding with this scare tactic. Just hang aluminum pie plates and/or place pinwheels near the area. The reflections off the pie plates and the near-constant movement of the pinwheels will send the birds flying! ✉ Marshall K., RI

POND-ER THIS. If you have a pond or lake on your property, you know what a pain in the grass wandering ducks and geese can be when they start moseying around. Here's how I solved my fowl problem: I pounded several small stakes into the ground at the water's edge, then connected

QUICK FIX

Nothing against our fine-feathered friends, but having them build their nests in the potted flowers and hanging baskets that adorn your deck can be a bit, well, inconvenient. To encourage them to seek out more welcoming digs, cover your pots and baskets with pieces of chicken wire. Then as the plants grow, pull them up through the openings.

them with string wrapped around each stake about 6 inches off the ground. Ducks and geese won't cross the line, so they no longer mess up my property. ✉ **Richard W., MI**

LET'S TALK TURKEY. Are wild turkeys roaming your back 40, taking their fill of your flower seeds and seedlings? Then try one of these maneuvers: If your area is rather small, rope it off or put netting over it. If you're trying to protect a larger piece of real estate, scare the big birds away with strips of black plastic bags hung on wires spaced throughout your yard and garden. ✉ **Michelle R., MD**

Deer

DISCOURAGE DEER. You can protect your garden from hungry deer by making a clear fishing line "fence." Just stretch the line between two posts and wrap the ends securely around each post. Make two rows of line—one about 1½ feet up from the ground, and the other about 3 feet up. The deer will wander over for their bedtime snack, and as soon as they feel the invisible line touching them, they'll skedaddle on out of there. ✉ **Debbie A., MI**

MAKING SCENTS. I sprinkle cinnamon and ground black pepper all over the soil around my garden to keep deer away. For whatever reason, it works like a charm! ✉ **Barbara D., WA**

NOW HAIR THIS. If you want to keep deer, groundhogs, and other varmints out of your corn patch, scatter some human hair clippings around the stalks. Reapply fresh clippings after each rain, and your crops should stay critter-free for the duration. ✉ **Nick L., NC**

CALLING ALL CLIPPINGS. You already know that human hair clippings sprinkled around your garden will keep hungry deer away,

Ask Jerry

Q: I had a big problem with deer digging into my roses and lettuce, possums poaching my strawberries, and raccoons treating themselves to my tomatoes. So I scattered mothballs around my planting areas, and I didn't lose another thing all season long. But now I'm wondering, will the mothballs hurt the plants?

A: It all depends on how heavily you applied them—too much of a good thing can be trouble no matter how "safe" it may seem. So I'd rather you rake 'em up at the end of each growing season, and properly dispose of them.

but what if you're—well, let's just say it—bald? Then head on over to your local barbershop and ask for a couple bags of clippings. You can even offer to sweep them up yourself. When you get home, sprinkle the hair wherever deer are a problem. ✉ **Gina F., TX**

A STINKY DEER DETERRENT. Deer can't stand the scent of humans, so save your old shoe insoles, and drop one into each leg of an old pair of panty hose. Then cut off the legs and tie the nylons to a branch or fence post near any plants that are being munched on. The deer will take one whiff and move on to fresher-smelling fare. Just be sure to change the contents of the hose at least once a month to keep the scent fresh. ✉ **Barbara B., VA**

SAY IT WITH SOAP. Say good-bye to roaming deer by sticking bars of soap in old panty hose legs or onion bags and hanging the sacks from fences and tree branches near your gardens. Deer don't like the smell of the soap, so they'll steer clear. ✉ **Janine M., MI**

Cats and Dogs

IN THE BAG. If you put out trash bags instead of garbage cans, you know that roaming cats, raccoons, and other critters will quickly chew through the plastic and scatter the contents. Keep 'em away by spraying the bags with a window cleaner that contains ammonia. That'll do the trick. ✉ Dolly A., MN

A THORN IN THEIR SIDES. The next time you trim your rose-bushes, save the clippings and put them around your garden, covering them with a little soil or bark dust to hold them in place. The prickly terrain will discourage cats from hanging around and digging in your beds. Plus, you get to recycle your yard waste for free! ✉ Carole B., OR

SCAT, CATS! I don't like the neighborhood cats doing their business in my yard and garden. So to keep them away, I liquefy hot cayenne and jalapeño peppers in a blender. Then I put the peppers in a hand-held sprayer bottle and add some lemon-scented dishwashing liquid, castor oil, beer, and human urine. I spray this potent solution all over my lawn and gardens. When the kitties visit, they find less than purr-fect conditions, and head off in search of another lawn to litter! ✉ Maureen C., GA

Jerry's Handy Hints

A CITRUS SOLUTION

→ Keep frisky felines out of your flower beds by spraying the perimeters with a mixture of 2 tablespoons of orange or lemon extract per gallon of water, using a handheld sprayer. Cats hate the smell of citrus!

FORK IT OVER. I've found an easy way to keep the neighborhood cats out of my freshly prepared garden: I plant plastic forks, with their tines up, all around the bed and in between the rows. The kitties don't get comfy enough to find a potty spot, so they quickly move on. ✉ Jessica W., CA

GATHER YE PINECONES . . . And bring them inside to enjoy in seasonal baskets. Come spring, crumble the pinecones and sprinkle them in your garden. Cats will keep away because they don't like the prickly pinecones poking at their tender paws. ✉ Maureen W., ON

STICK 'EM UP. My cats used to attack my seed-starting trays, making a huge mess and ruining all my hard work before I could get a chance to plant. Then I figured out a way to keep them from setting foot near my work space: I lay strips of duct tape, sticky side up, along the edges of the table where I keep my trays. Now my cats stay away. ✉ Betsey B., NH

HOT STUFF. Add a crushed, dried chili pepper, seeds and all, to a gallon of water. Let it soak overnight, strain out the pods and seeds, and pour the remaining liquid into a handheld sprayer bottle. Then spray your garden plants with the peppery water, and cats will steer clear! By the way, this hot spray will also keep indoor cats away from your houseplants. ✉ Jennifer M., NM

GO-GO, DOGGIES. Who let the dogs out? Who cares, as long as they stay out of your yard! You can keep 'em out by sprinkling

Ask Jerry

Q: Is there anything I can do to help a lawn survive my two female dogs? I'm really desperate for a solution.

A: Overspray your turf with 1 cup of dishwashing liquid in your 20 gallon hose-end sprayer, and then apply gypsum over the area at the recommended rate. One week later, overspray the same area with my Lawn Saver Tonic: 1 can of beer, 1 cup of ammonia, and 1 can of regular (not diet) cola mixed in a bucket and poured into your 20 gallon hose-end sprayer. Apply to your lawn to the point of runoff. This treatment will combat all but the worst dog "spots." (You may have to reseed those.) Then, to prevent damage in the future, after your dogs use the yard for their "business," use a garden hose to soak the area. This'll dilute the dogs' urine to a nitrogen-rich fertilizer your lawn will love.

powdered tobacco around the edges of your property. It does the trick every time. ✉ **Donna S., NC**

CLEVER CONDIMENT. I put a tablespoon of ketchup on my dog's dinner every day, and now I no longer get brown patches on my lawn marking his favorite potty spots. And as a bonus, my pooch loves the ketchup's flavor, so he gobbles up his kibble. ✉ **Brian L., BC**

FRUIT VS. FIDO. Keep your pooch (and everyone else's) out of the garden by sprinkling a few fresh orange or lemon rinds around the plants. Since dogs can't stomach the smell or taste of citrus fruit, they'll stay away. Just be sure to replace the rinds once they've dried out and lost their scent. ✉ Teresa V., ID

OUCH! I had a big problem finding "gifts" from neighborhood dogs in my garden. Then I planted a prickly pear cactus in the area, and there was no more "doo" in the morning dew! As a special bonus, these plants spread quickly and produce gorgeous, paper-thin blooms. ✉ Diana K., TX

I LIKE LIME. Dead brown spots in your lawn that crop up wherever your dog does his business can be a real eyesore for any pet owner. So do what I do and pour 2 cups of lime into a rinsed-out gallon milk jug, and fill the remainder with water. Then every time your dog tinkles on the grass, pour about a cup of the limewater on the spot. Your dead spots will green up, just like that! ✉ Charles V., PA

SUPER SCOOPER. Cut the bottom off a half-gallon plastic milk jug, and use the remaining half (with the handle) as a "pooper scooper" to dispose of piles left in your yard by roaming neighborhood dogs. Simply rinse it off after each use and hang it by its handle in the garage or storage shed. That way, you'll always have it handy. ✉ Helen R., OR

ANOTHER GREAT IDEA!

DOGGY DO!

If you have a male dog, you may notice white rings developing around the base of your trees. The rings mean that Fido's simply left his calling card behind after doing his business. Don't be alarmed—the white rings just contain extra nitrogen. Leave them alone and water the trees well, and everyone will be happy.

Field Mice

GET 'EM PLASTERED. Here's an old-time method for killing pesky field mice organically. Simply mix flour, cornmeal, salt, and plaster of Paris in an old pie tin. Place the tin near the infested area alongside a bowl of water. Mice will feed on the salty mixture, and then drink the water. The next thing you know, the plaster will harden—inside the mouse! ✉ Robin K., CA

DO THE MASHED POTATO. To get rid of mice, set out shallow containers of instant mashed potatoes with a dish of water nearby. The mice will eat the powdered potatoes, drink the water, swell up, and die. ✉ Tom C., DE

TRIM THE TREES. I keep my trees and shrubs off hungry rodents' dinner menus, even during prolonged deep-winter freezes. What's my secret? Simply this: In late fall and then again in January, I prune my trees and spread the trimmings on the frozen ground. The hungry critters eat the pruned branches and leave the growing trees alone. ✉ Peter R., NY

BAIT THE BUCKETS. Here's a trick I learned from my grandpa: how to trap plant-munching mice with 5-gallon plastic buckets. Set each bucket upright near a shrub and put your bait in the bottom (I use chunky peanut butter). The mice will scramble up and over the edge, jump in to get the goodies, and stay put. Unless you release them, they'll quickly die of starvation or be eaten by hungry predators. ✉ Nick D., IL

QUICK FIX

To stop mice, rabbits, and other backyard pests from nibbling on your just-planted fruit trees, wrap the saplings from the top of their root-balls to about 1 foot up their trunks with aluminum foil. It's twice as nice at any price!

Gophers

GET GOPHERS GOING. I know that sunflower windmills (found at lawn and garden centers) do great work getting rid of gophers. You simply stick 'em in the ground wherever you see damage, and the vibrations will drive the gophers batty in no time. But those garden-center ornaments can get pricey. So I found a less expensive solution—I buy toy windmills. They do the same fantastic job of keeping gophers away, but at a fraction of the cost. ✉ Jodi H., WA

COUNT ON KITTY. You can get rid of gophers fast with old kitty litter. Just take the box full of well-used litter, and dump the whole shebang into an open gopher hole. Then using a garden hose, saturate the area with water. The gophers won't take long to get the hint, pack their bags, and hit the road. ✉ Nancy C., NM

DOWN THE HATCH. Frustrated with gophers that are determined to stay no matter what you bombard them with? Then show 'em you mean business. Pour a cup of ammonia into a 2-gallon watering can, filling the remainder with water. Shovel off the top of the gopher's hole, pour in the ammonia water, and put the dirt back over the opening. Then watch those gophers skedaddle. ✉ Mary N., OK

Grandma Putt's Wisdom

Gophers can eat their way through a garden in no time flat, but my Grandma Putt had a fragrant way to evict them from their cozy tunnels. She'd soak rags in ammonia and stuff one into each tunnel entrance. The hungry rascals took one whiff and beat a fast track to another dining establishment!

Moles

MOVE ON, MOLES. I send pesky moles packin' with this one-two punch: First, I puncture their tunnels with holes spaced about 2 feet apart. Then I sprinkle chili powder into each hole and cover it with dirt. The moles soon head for the hills. ✉ **Regina L., WA**

BLOWIN' IN THE WIND. If you've got some old glass milk bottles lying around, put them to good use in your garden. Fill each bottle halfway with water and place them throughout your garden where moles, gophers, and other unwelcome guests are a problem. When the wind blows across the tops of the bottles, the noise will scare the marauders, and send them on their way. ✉ **Denise C., OR**

BEAN THERE, DONE THAT. You can take care of problems with moles by planting castor beans near their runs. This bitter-rooted plant will drive the burrowing rodents away. Then keep 'em away by pushing the hulled seeds of the plants into their empty runs. *Caution:* Castor beans are toxic, so handle them with care, and keep them away from children and pets. ✉ **Ernestine D., OK**

Ask Jerry

Q: To keep moles from building runways under the deep snow next winter, would it help if I cut my grass extra short in the fall?

A: No, it would only put the grass under further stress. It sounds to me like voles are the real culprits, so pick up some traps at a local hardware store, and bait them with peanut butter.

HAIRY HELPER. I've found a great way to get moles to vacate my property. I fill their holes with a mixture of human hair and chopped fresh garlic. That makes 'em leave in a hurry! ✉ **Karen B., MI**

LEAVE IT TO LAXATIVES. If moles are making mincemeat of your backyard, then try this trick: Find the largest hole you can, and put two squares of ex-lax® chocolate tablets into it. The moles will eat the laxative and become extremely—er—uncomfortable. I'm not sure exactly what happens, but let's just say they won't be bothering you anymore. ✉ **Peggy G., MI**

CHEW ON THIS. Place half a stick of Juicy Fruit® chewing gum into several mole holes in your backyard. The odor will entice them and they'll gobble the pieces up. Too bad for them—because Juicy Fruit is lethal to moles! ✉ **Bill P., MI**

SUSHI FOR MOLES? This remedy will make moles move along: Dip a piece of raw fish in salt, and drop it into an active run. The moles will want nothing to do with it, or your backyard. ✉ **Victoria S., IL**

SCENTED SEEDS. To keep moles from eating pea seeds, put a small amount of kerosene on a paper towel, and place it in a paper

TAKE 5

Here are five not-so-common uses for cotton balls in the yard and garden:

1 Deter moles by dropping cotton balls soaked in castor oil along their runs.

2 Ward off garden moths by soaking cotton balls in lavender oil and hanging them from sticks between your plants.

3 Force forsythia by soaking a cotton ball in ammonia and placing it in a bucket of warm water with a forsythia branch. Cover the branch with a plastic bag, and it will burst into bloom.

4 Say adios to aphids by gently dabbing a weak mix of alcohol and water on your houseplants.

5 Polish houseplant leaves by rubbing them with a cotton ball moistened with milk.

bag along with the pea seeds. Shake the bag, let it sit for about 20 minutes, then plant the seeds as usual. The moles will be repelled by the kerosene smell, and they'll leave your pea seeds alone. ✉ Betty L., MI

Rabbits

SNAKE SURPRISE. Lay toy rubber snakes around areas in your garden where rabbits are taking advantage of your "all-you-can-eat buffet." Just be sure to change the snakes' positions from time to time to keep the bunnies on their toes and away from your garden bounty. ✉ Dabney C., OH

RAISE THE BAR... Of soap, that is. I wrap a strong-smelling bar of deodorant soap in netting, and tie it to the fence around my garden to discourage rabbits and other four-legged foragers. If you don't have netting, you can drop the bar of soap into the toe of an old nylon knee-high. Either way, the strong scent will send bunnies scurrying. ✉ Delia R., NY

ANOTHER GREAT IDEA!

RUN, RABBIT, RUN!

Here are a couple of tried-and-true methods for keeping rascally rabbits out of your garden: Start by sprinkling cayenne pepper and/or mothballs in any area where bunnies are nibbling. Then try interplanting tansy, rue, and rosemary—any one of those three herbs will make your garden undesirable to rabbits.

BUNNY BARRIER ● To keep rabbits (and other four-legged pests) out of your garden, whip up a batch of this All-Purpose Varmint Repellent: In a small bucket, mix 2 eggs, 2 cloves of garlic, 2 tablespoons of hot chili pepper, 2 tablespoons of ammonia, and 2 cups of water. Let the mixture sit for three or four days, then paint it on fences, trellises—anywhere unwelcome critters are carousing.

GET 'EM SNEEZING. Are rabbits getting to your peas? Then lightly sprinkle white pepper over the tops of the plants, and the bunnies will hop-hop-hop-*achoo!* right out of your precious garden patch. ✉ Carolyn S., MN

PEPPERY PROTECTION. Silly rabbits won't damage your tender tree seedlings if you spray the trunks with grafting spray, then follow up by dusting them with cayenne pepper. It's bye-bye bunnies! ✉ Richard G., NV

IF YOU CAN'T BEAT 'EM . . . I discovered a foolproof way to stop rabbits from devouring my garden goodies—I gave them their own garden! I buried a wire-mesh fence 10 inches deep around my own garden, then circled the outside of the fence with treats that rabbits like best. Now they stick to snacking on their own yummy greens and leave mine alone! ✉ Aldyth H., KS

HANDY HOLDERS. If you put out mothballs or other repellents to scare away bunnies, then you know how vigilant you must be to replace them after every rain. Well, here's this lazy woman's solution: I use clean, empty margarine tubs as holders for repellents in my garden. I simply punch ½-inch holes around the upper sides of the tubs, fill them with a repellent to just below the holes, put the lids on, and place them in suitable areas. Rain or water won't wash the repellents away, so they do their job a lot longer. ✉ Sandy M., MI

AN OCTOPUS'S GARDEN. You can frighten rabbits, birds, and other curious pests away from your garden with an octopus scarecrow. Simply cut a large green trash bag into eight long strips, and staple them to a paper cup. Attach the cup to the top of a 6-foot stake, and set it in the center of your garden. The sight and sound of the wind blowing through the plastic "arms" will scare the daylights out of the critters. ✉ Gerald M., IL

Raccoons

THIS MAKES SCENTS. If raccoons are digging up your plants and/or loitering on your lawn, do what I do and scatter Irish Spring® soap shavings around your property. The strong scent keeps 'em clean away. ✉ Stacy B., CA

BANISH THE BANDITS. The corn you planted was for you to enjoy, not those pesky raccoons. So outsmart the little bandits by planting a couple of pumpkins in the corn patch. As the pumpkins grow, train their vines to run through the cornstalks. The raccoons don't like stepping on the prickly vines, so they'll steer clear of your yummy corn. ✉ Jenna R., WI

HOW SWEET IT IS. Tired of chasing raccoons away from your sweet corn? Then sprinkle mothballs between the rows. They'll keep the raccoons from nibbling on your ears of corn. ✉ Melinda G., NY

QUICK FIX

If raccoons are chowing down on your corn, dust the ears with cayenne pepper or baby powder, or dab the silks with a nylon stocking that has just a touch of perfume on it. Also, you can interplant cukes, gourds, pumpkins, or squash to keep 'em away.

SHAKE THINGS UP. Just before my sweet corn is ready for harvest, I sprinkle a few shakes from a can of ground black pepper on the largest ear on each stalk. The pepper sticks to the silk, and it stops those rascally raccoons from wreaking havoc in my cornfield. ✉ Erma A., IA

TOWELS IN THE TRASH. I stop marauding raccoons from ripping my garbage apart with this neat trick: I dip a large wad of paper towels in sudsy ammonia, dribble six drops of hot sauce on the wet toweling, then drop it into my trash can. No more raccoon raids! ✉ Kathy D., NY

LEAVE IT TO LEMON. If raccoons are attacking your trash, leave a few lemon peels scattered about for the garbage-loving rascals to munch on. They'll get sick from the citrus and leave your trash alone. ✉ Guy M., IL

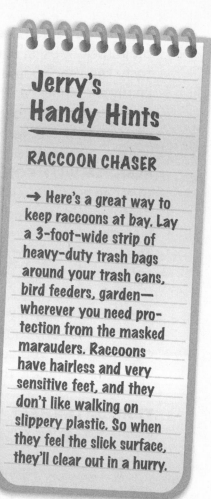

Jerry's Handy Hints

RACCOON CHASER

→ Here's a great way to keep raccoons at bay. Lay a 3-foot-wide strip of heavy-duty trash bags around your trash cans, bird feeders, garden—wherever you need protection from the masked marauders. Raccoons have hairless and very sensitive feet, and they don't like walking on slippery plastic. So when they feel the slick surface, they'll clear out in a hurry.

Squirrels and Chipmunks

DRINKS ARE ON THE HOUSE. If squirrels and chipmunks are getting to your plump, juicy tomatoes before you are, try this trick: Place a bowl of water in each corner of your garden. The little critters just might drink the water instead of sucking the juice from your mouthwatering tomatoes. ✉ Ellyn M., MN

SQUIRRELS FIND IT UN-A-PEELING. I stop squirrels from raiding my garden by using orange peels. I simply peel several oranges (I try to keep each peel in one long piece), and then hang the peels on my garden fence. The citrusy scent keeps squirrels away. If you try this, just remember to replace the peels as soon as they dry up and lose their aroma. ✉ John P., FL

FOOL 'EM WITH FOIL. Chipmunks are so darn cute and they think they can get away with anything. Unfortunately, they're also very destructive! I stopped them from digging in my potted plants by placing crumpled aluminum foil strips along the top of each pot. The little critters climb up, but once they reach the foil, they turn right around and never come back. ✉ Nancy D., MI

A WISE CHOICE. If you add a plastic owl or two to your yard, you'll frighten away any squirrels that are eating your nuts, strawberries, or other garden goodies. The squirrels will be unpleasantly surprised the next time they drop by for a snack. ✉ Cindy L., NY

TURN UP THE HEAT. To keep squirrels from eating what's growing in your garden, all you have to do is sprinkle your plants with

Ask Jerry

Q: Chipmunks are burrowing under our raised porch, near the garage, under the driveway, and in my sprinkler valve box. I've tried mothballs—and I think they actually like them! What can I do?

A: Get a couple of friendly cats, and the chipmunks will pack up and move out. If you're not a cat person, I'm afraid you're at the trap stage; use peanut butter as bait.

cayenne pepper. The pepper won't hurt the plants, but the squirrels will avoid it like the plague. ✉ Karl K., MI

SKIRT AROUND THE ISSUE. It used to be that as soon as green fruit appeared on my walnut tree, the squirrels got to work, and I could never enjoy my crop. Since the squirrels have to climb the tree trunk to get to the goodies, I came up with this deterrent: I shaped a long piece of wire fencing into a "skirt" for the tree. I attached the top of the skirt to the trunk a few feet off the ground and made the wire flare out at the bottom (make sure the bottom of the skirt is a foot or so off the ground). Now I get to harvest a huge crop, and the nut-hunting squirrels go away empty-handed! ✉ Isabell B., CA

POLISH YOUR PUMPKINS. I figured out a way to keep pesky squirrels from raiding my pumpkin patch: I use furniture polish. I just spray a little lemon-scented furniture polish on my future jack-o'-lanterns, and the snack-seeking squirrels leave 'em alone. ✉ Kathryn S., OH

SPICE UP THE SEED. If squirrels are ransacking your bird feeders, here's how to keep them away—just put a little cayenne pepper in with your birdseed in a ziplock plastic bag. Shake the bag well, and use the mixture in your feeders. The squirrels can't stand the heat, but the birds won't even notice! ✉ Patricia F., MA

GIVE 'EM THE SLIP. Squirrels were driving me nuts because they were raiding my bird feeder every time I refilled it. Then I figured out how to outsmart 'em by greasing up the feeder pole with petroleum jelly. The first time one of those furry-tailed critters made a leap for the goodies, it hit the pole and slid down like a fireman—all the way to the ground! ✉ Tonya S., NC

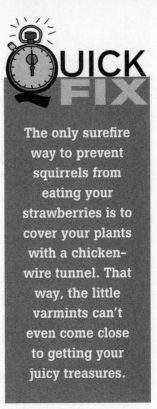

QUICK FIX

The only surefire way to prevent squirrels from eating your strawberries is to cover your plants with a chicken-wire tunnel. That way, the little varmints can't even come close to getting your juicy treasures.

Woodchucks, a.k.a. Groundhogs

GET 'EM WHERE IT HURTS. Woodchucks can be hard on your zucchini plants, for sure—they eat the leaves right off the stalk. But believe it or not, they can't stand the zucchini itself. So stick your extra zucchinis right in their holes, and when the veggies start to rot, the woodchucks will hightail it outta there! ✉ Tamara B., PA

IT'S A GAS. When woodchucks show up for dinner at your house, bring on the gas by setting a soup-size can of gasoline at each of the critters' tunnel openings. It won't take long before the woodchucks move on out. ✉ Angela K., MA

LET IT SINK IN. To keep woodchucks out of your flower beds, sink large, empty laundry detergent caps into the soil among your plants, and fill them with a mixture of 1 part bloodmeal to 2 parts water. The bloodmeal won't vanish into the soil when it rains, so it keeps on repelling those four-legged garden pests for a long time without giving your plants an overdose of nitrogen. ✉ Sam P., NJ

Grandma Putt's Wisdom

Grandma Putt foiled woodchucks by planting bitter-tasting, but great-looking, flowers around the perimeter of her garden. She knew that if the furry fellas took a nibble of marigolds, nasturtiums, wormwood, or yarrow, they'd give up and go elsewhere for dinner. And you know what? She was right!

PART 4

Odds and Ends

America's Best
Practical Problem Solvers

CHAPTER 17

Garage Gear

Tools of the Trade

STOP RUST IN ITS TRACKS. I tuck a few sticks of chalk in my toolbox to attract moisture that would otherwise cling to the metal. It's a simple way to keep your tools rust-free. ✉ Paul R., FL

SMOOTH TOOLS. Here's a way to keep the wooden handles of all your tools smooth and splinter-free—apply a fine coating of hair spray to them and let it dry thoroughly before you put the tools away for the day. ✉ Denise F., ME

WELL-DRESSED HANDLES. Use mayonnaise on your tool handles so they stay smooth, clean, and free of cracks. Just rub them down with a mix of 2 parts mayonnaise to 1 part lemon juice. Apply the mix with a soft, clean cloth and rub it in well. ✉ Sue N., NJ

PRE-WINTER PREP. The gardening season may be over, but before you put your yard tools away for the winter, protect them from destructive rust by rubbing the metal parts down with a bit of petroleum jelly. That way, they'll be ready and able to do their jobs come spring. ✉ **Mark B., OR**

KEEP 'EM ORGANIZED. Save your empty prescription bottles and use them to corral various sizes of nuts, bolts, screws, and nails in your toolbox. If you've got clear bottles, you'll be able to see what you need at a glance. ✉ **Richard C., IL**

AN EGG-CELLENT SUGGESTION. I put clean, empty egg cartons to work in my workshop and garage. They're perfect for organizing nuts and bolts and any other small items, keeping them right at my fingertips. ✉ **Don A., PA**

Grandma Putt's Wisdom

My Grandma Putt came up with this magical mix to keep her wooden tool handles in fine fettle, shielding them from cracking and splintering. Use it to wipe down all of your handles about once a month, or whenever you notice that the wood is starting to look a bit pale and dry.

In a glass jar with a tight-fitting lid, mix 1 part white vinegar, 1 part boiled linseed oil, and 1 part turpentine. To use, pour some of the mixture on a dry microfiber cloth or an old cotton sock, and rub it up and down the handle until the whole thing is covered. Wait about 10 minutes for the liquid to soak in, and then repeat the treatment. Wait another 10 minutes, and wipe any excess off with a clean, dry cloth. Screw the lid on and store the leftover potion in a cool, dark place—it'll keep indefinitely.

ANOTHER GREAT IDEA!

THUMB S.O.S.

Here's a real thumb saver—use an old comb to hold small nails in place when you're hammering them. That way, you'll hit the nail, not your finger.

LET LOOSE. If you're having a hard time getting a screw loose, apply a bit of cooking spray to it. It'll loosen right up so you can get on with the job at hand. ✉ Melanie W., ON

SOAP DOES THE TRICK. Before driving a screw into wood, rub it on a bar of soap, making sure you get the soap into the grooves. This'll help the screw sink into the wood more easily. ✉ Danny B., WI

QUICK FIX

Your pruning shears will work better and last a whole lot longer if you keep them lubricated. But there's no need to make a mess by oiling them. Instead, rub the moving parts down with an old tube of lip balm.

MATCH THIS. Got a screw hole that's a tad too big for the screw? Fix it with a wooden kitchen match. Just dip it in some glue, stick it into the hole, and break it off flush with the surface. The screw should go right in and stay put for a good long while. ✉ Louis S., AZ

MAKE THE CONNECTION. Nuts, bolts, and pipe connections will fit together easily—and not rust together later—when they're lubricated. But don't fuss with oil or goop; just coat them with some hair conditioner before you screw them in place. ✉ John P., CA

GET A GRIP. I always wrap the tips of my metal files with several layers of masking tape. The tape provides a comfortable grip for my fingers and makes it less likely the file will slip and slide when I'm using it. ✉ Pete C., NH

LET CLEANER HEADS PREVAIL. To help prevent a hammer from slipping, you need to clean the head every once in a while. To do so, work it over with a piece of sandpaper until it's shiny and clean and ready to do a bang-up job. ✉ **Craig V., NM**

KEEP CAULK FLOWING. Once you've opened up a tube of caulking, it'll quickly dry out. To prevent this from happening, place the tube upside down in a glass jar with just enough water to cover the nozzle. Then when it's time to use it, remove the tube, dry it off, and caulk away! ✉ **Ellen H., PA**

EXTEND FILTER LIFE. You can save a lot of money on wet/dry vacuum filters by keeping them clean with old panty hose. Cut a leg off one pair of hose, fit the stocking over the original filter, and fasten it securely. Then when the stocking is dirty, remove it and replace it with a clean one. Your original filter will last much longer, while your workshop and garage stay clean. ✉ **Susan S., WA**

CONTAIN YOUR TWINE. Keep a ball of twine from getting all tangled up by storing it in a clean yogurt container. Poke a hole in the cover and feed the end of the twine through. Drop the rest of the ball into the container and replace the lid. If you want to be able to just yank at the twine, put a stone in the bottom of the container before you insert the ball. The weight will prevent the container from tipping over as you pull out the twine. ✉ **Peggy K., IN**

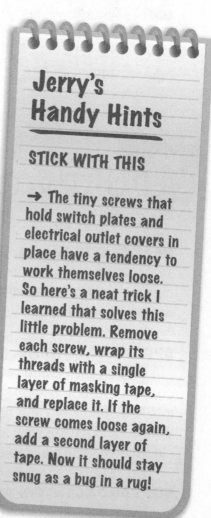

Jerry's Handy Hints

STICK WITH THIS

→ The tiny screws that hold switch plates and electrical outlet covers in place have a tendency to work themselves loose. So here's a neat trick I learned that solves this little problem. Remove each screw, wrap its threads with a single layer of masking tape, and replace it. If the screw comes loose again, add a second layer of tape. Now it should stay snug as a bug in a rug!

Ask Jerry

Q: How can I neatly store power tools and paint cans that are too heavy for pegboard hooks to support?

A: Get yourself some plastic milk crates and use sturdy hooks to attach them to a wall, with the openings facing out. The crates are strong enough to hold your tools and filled cans, and they'll take up a lot less space than ordinary shelves would.

The Old Jalopy

NEAT SEAT CLEANER. To clean up stains from your car's fabric seats and floor mats, scrub the spots with a brush that's been dipped in a solution of dishwashing liquid and vinegar. The stains will be gone, and there will be no lingering odor. ✉ Isaac T., TX

SPRAY AWAY STAINS. Windex® does wonders inside your car—not only on the obvious places like the windows, dashboard, and cup holders, but also on seats and floors, where stains have soaked into the upholstery and floor mats. All it takes is a simple spray of Windex and a wipe with a sturdy cloth, and the interior will be as clean as the day you drove your car off the lot! ✉ Debbie L., OH

SOFT AND SCENTED. Avon Skin So Soft Original Bath Oil doesn't just make your skin silky smooth—it will give a glossy new appearance

Want to fog-proof your car's windows? It's a snap: Just rub a bar of soap over the glass, and then polish it to a shine with a clean, soft cloth. This trick works just as well on diving masks and ski goggles, too.

to vinyl car seats, too! Just wipe it on with a soft cloth, and buff it off. Not only will your car seats be shiny, but the inside of your car will also smell nice. ✉ **Anna M., IL**

ONE, TWO WINDOW WASH. I clean my car windows lickety-split with just a bucket of hot water, two cloths, and a box of baking soda. After wetting one of the cloths, sprinkle it with baking soda, and rub it on the windows. Then wet the other cloth, and use it to wipe the glass clean. That's all there is to it. ✉ **Betty S., NY**

WIPE THOSE WIPERS. There's no point in cleaning your windshield if you don't take care of the wipers, too. To get at the grease and grime that accumulate on windshield wipers, use a little baking soda on a damp sponge. It'll take the gunk right off. ✉ **Holly B., TN**

EASY DOES IT. Here's a handy hint: Keep a clean chalkboard eraser in the glove compartment of your car. Then the next time your windows steam up, just erase the fog away! Your windows will end up clear and streak-free every time. ✉ **Lydia F., FL**

ANOTHER GREAT IDEA!

SOCK IT AWAY

Carry an orphaned clean sock (100 percent cotton is best because it's so absorbent) in your car. When you need to clear fog from your windows, simply slip the sock over your hand and give the glass a few well-placed swipes.

Grandma Putt's Wisdom

Even before I learned how to drive, my Grandma Putt taught me how to put out small gas, oil, or engine fires: Stand a safe distance away and throw baking soda at the flames. To this day, I keep a big old container of soda in my garage and in the trunk of my car just in case—and you should, too!

BAKING SODA FOR BATTERIES. When corrosion builds up on your car's battery, clean the posts and cable connectors with a baking soda paste. Mix 3 parts soda to 1 part water, dip an old toothbrush into the paste, and scrub away. ✉ Fern T., CT

CLEAN WITH COLA. I de-gunk my car battery with cola. Just pour a can of it over the cables and watch it bubble away the built-up corrosion. Then wipe any residue away. ✉ Jim T., TX

JELLY PROTECTION. If you coat the terminals on your car battery with petroleum jelly, it will prevent corrosion and crud from building up. Plus, your car will run more smoothly. ✉ Barry L., WA

GIVE BUGS THE BOOT. I've found that with a can of WD-40® you can do just about anything. My favorite use? I spray some on the front bumper of my car before a summer drive to keep bugs from sticking to it—even on long trips. ✉ Mark M., MT

DEBUG YOUR BUGGY. Remove extra-stubborn stuck-on bugs from your car with a fabric-softener sheet, which will not hurt the chrome or paint. Start by hosing down your car, and then use a wet fabric-softener sheet to scrub off the bugs. (The fabric softener in the sheets helps to loosen the "guts.") Then rinse your vehicle to get the remains off, and wash it as you normally would. ✉ Jody S., LA

A SAPPY SOLUTION. You found a nice shady parking spot, but now your car is covered in pine sap. To remove the sticky stuff, spray it with a little WD-40® and let it soak in for a minute. Gently wipe off the residue with a soft, clean cloth. ✉ John V., FL

HEAD OFF TROUBLE. The next time your car's headlights need cleaning, rub them down with white non-gel toothpaste on a soft, clean cloth. Then fold the cloth over to a clean section and polish the paste off. You'll have a much brighter view of the road ahead.
✉ Christopher L., MN

COLA AND CHROME. Don't let a little rust on your chrome bumper spoil the look of your hot rod. Just pour some cola into a bucket, dip a medium-abrasive scouring pad in it, and go to work. You'll restore the shine in no time flat. ✉ Jay V., BC

BRIGHTEST BUMPERS. You've just restored an old car, and now you want to show it off. So make sure the chrome bumpers are sporting the most amazing shine in town! To do so, mix a paste of baking soda and water. Gently rub it into the chrome, then buff it off with a soft, clean cloth. ✉ Sherrine H., AR

MAYO TO THE RESCUE. Having trouble removing an old bumper sticker? Pull off what you can, then rub some mayonnaise into the sticky residue. Work the mayo in with your fingers, and scrape off the rest of it with a plastic knife or an old credit card. ✉ Sherry H., KY

Jerry's Handy Hints

WINDSHIELD WIPE

→ When you're cruisin' down the highway at 55 miles an hour (or more), the bug bodies pile up fast and stick on hard. But a little club soda will take them off in a jiffy. Simply pour the bubbly stuff into a handheld sprayer bottle, apply it to the splatters, and wipe them off with paper towels, old panty hose, or a soft, clean cloth. No more bugs!

GOOD-BYE, GREASE. You can make grease, tar, or pine pitch practically slide right off your car. How? Simply by slathering on the mayo. Put a generous glob of mayonnaise over the offending gunk, let it sit for a few minutes, then wipe the mess off with an old, clean towel. ✉ Tim G., RI

TOUGH ON TAR. Got tar spots on your car? Here's an easy way to remove them without damaging your auto's finish. Pour some lubricating oil on a soft, clean cloth and rub it into the marks. Once they're gone, wipe the area with soapy water to remove any oily residue. ✉ Mel L., NJ

RIM RENEWAL. Use a handy dandy Mr. Clean® Magic Eraser® to rub away any dirt and dust that are gunking up your car's tire rims. Dampen the eraser, then rub the scum until the rims are shiny and clean. ✉ Daniella F., NJ

BRUSH UP YOUR RIMS. I use a bottle brush to clean those hard-to-reach areas on my car's rims. Just spray the brush with a little degreaser, and lightly scrub until the grime vanishes. ✉ Jennie G., OH

RAIN, RAIN, GO AWAY. Forget those fancy (and pricey) products that promise to repel rain from your windshield. Instead, clean the outside of your car's glass as usual, then wipe the surface with rubbing alcohol. The next time it starts raining, the water will slide right off—no wipers required! ✉ Terri H., NC

ANOTHER GREAT IDEA!

PB & TAR

To get tar off your car, reach into your pantry and pull out the peanut butter. Rub a generous spoonful onto the tarry marks, then wash the spots away with sudsy water.

WINTER WARNING ● If there's a winter snow or ice storm warning for your area and your car is going to be parked outside, cover the exterior door locks with masking tape. That way, you'll be able to peel the tape off the locks and get into your vehicle after the storm hits.

THIS SPUD'S FOR YOU. Try this thrifty trick to repel rain from your car's windshield. Cut a large baking potato in half and rub the cut surface all over the outside of your windshield. The rain will roll right off. ✉ **Steve R., OK**

MAKE SNOW GO. To keep snow from sticking to your car's windshield, rub the glass with an onion that's been cut in half crosswise. It works every time! ✉ **Ed B., VA**

NEWS YOU CAN USE. To keep your car's windows from frosting up this winter, wet a crumpled piece of newspaper with rubbing alcohol, and wipe it all over the exterior glass. Then rub the windows dry with a fresh piece of newspaper. Repeat this trick every week for frost-free glass no matter what Mother Nature dishes out. ✉ **Trudy E., MO**

I'VE GOT YOU COVERED. If you're tired of waking up to cold winter mornings and having to scrape snow and ice off your windshield, make it easy on yourself with this trick. Use an old rug runner to cover the windshield on frosty winter nights. Place it carpet side down, and secure it to the window by closing the ends in the front doors. In the morning, you can just roll up the rug and hit the road without lifting a scraper. ✉ **Karen W., OK**

ASHES FOR TRACTION. In icy weather, keep a sealed bag of wood ashes in your trunk. They'll come in mighty handy if you start to slip and slide all over the place—just throw some under your car tires when you need an instant grip. ✉ **Dottie C., ON**

GOOD TO GO. If you live in an area that gets icy or snowy weather, be sure to keep a bag of nonclumping cat litter in your trunk. Then if you get stuck, you can sprinkle some around the tires and be purring along in no time at all. ✉ **Cuba M., MI**

SCRAPPY DO. At the start of winter, stash some good-size carpet scraps in the trunk of your car. Then, if you get stuck on icy pavement, all you have to do is pull out the carpet and place the scraps under your tires for traction. ✉ **Lewis R., VT**

Ask Jerry

Q: Road salt really does a number on my car's finish every winter. Is there more I can do besides normal car washing to protect my vehicle?

A: You're right in wanting to keep that road salt off your car—it can shorten your vehicle's life span considerably. So keep this simple recipe handy and use it every time you come home from a drive on wet, salt-treated roads. Mix 1 cup of kerosene and 1 cup of dishwashing liquid in a bucket of water, and use a sponge to rub the salt deposits away. <u>Note:</u> Kerosene is flammable, so use this mix with caution and in a well-ventilated area.

America's Best
Practical Problem Solvers

CHAPTER 18

More Good Stuff

Kitchen Curiosities

SIP STAIN-FREE. To remove coffee stains from inside a thermos, fill it with hot water, and drop in a denture-cleaning tablet. Put the top back on and leave it sit overnight. The next morning, rinse the thermos with soapy water, and it'll be fresh, clean, and ready to use. ✉ *Debbie M., SC*

ONE LUMP OR TWO? I place two sugar cubes in my silver coffee-pot and store it with the lid off. This helps prevent a musty or stale odor from developing in it. ✉ *Monica R., OH*

DOUBLE DISHCLOTHS. Are you tired of tossing your disposable dishcloths after only a few uses? To make these handy helpers work harder and last longer, try this trick. Take two new, unused

QUICK FIX

To clean food out of graters, use a little dishwashing liquid on an old, sterile toothbrush, and scrub away!

cloths, stack one on top of the other, and sew them together. ✉ **Myrtle P., OR**

GIVE CONTAINERS NEW LIFE. As plastic food-storage containers get old, they tend to fade and get sticky. To bring your containers back to their original color and nonsticky texture, soak them in a solution of half heavy-duty cleaner and half water for approximately 15 minutes. Then rinse, dry, and put them back to good use. ✉ **Laura D., TX**

A DRY IDEA. When you wash resealable plastic bags, do you hang them over the faucet or in some other inconvenient place? Here's a simple drying rack you can make that keeps those wet bags out of the way. Cover a piece of Styrofoam™ with aluminum foil, and poke three holes in the surface. Stick a plastic straw into each of the holes, and place the bag over the straws to hold it open while it dries out. ✉ **Liz G., NJ**

ALUMINUM AGAIN. Don't throw away disposable aluminum foil cake or pie pans. I recycle and reuse mine after cleaning them with an old, sterile toothbrush. Just fill each pan with warm, soapy water

Grandma Putt's Wisdom

Here's how my Grandma Putt kept her cutting boards germ-free. First, she wiped down both sides of the board with a mix of 1 part white vinegar in 2 parts water. If you're cleaning a plastic board, you can wipe it dry right away. For a wooden board, let the solution sit for five minutes before drying it. And there's never a need to rinse; the vinegar smell will disappear as it dries.

and gently scrub the crevices with the brush. Rinse well and the pans can be put back to work. ✉ **Maryanne H., TX**

SIMPLE SPONGE SANITIZER. You'll keep your kitchen sponge free of bacteria if you spray it with a mix of water and bleach in a handheld sprayer bottle. Then zap it in the microwave for a few seconds, and your sponge will be germ-free! ✉ **Jackie G., OH**

LEMONY FRESH. Rub a fresh lemon into a sour-smelling sponge, then rinse it in lukewarm water. It'll smell as fresh as it did when it was new. ✉ **Terry A., NH**

OVERNIGHT ODOR CURE. I put powdered carpet freshener in my garbage disposal once a month to keep it smelling fresh. Just pour an entire container of the freshener into the disposal, and let it sit overnight. In the morning, turn on the cold water and run the disposal for a minute or so, and you'll be left with a nice clean scent. ✉ **Elaine B., MI**

Jerry's Handy Hints

RACK IT UP

→ Don't pitch that smelly old sponge! Instead, clip it to a dishwasher rack with a clothespin, and wash it along with your next load of dishes. When the cycle is done, your sponge will be as good as new! If you don't have a dishwasher, you can get the same results by soaking that stinky sponge in cold salt water every few weeks.

CITRUS CLEAN. Here's how to freshen up your kitchen and garbage disposal at the same time. Put a handful of citrus peels into the disposal (from whatever you have on hand), turn on the cold water, and run the disposal. The fruit rinds contain citrus oil that will cut grease in the disposal and give your kitchen a nice citrus smell at the same time. ✉ **Martha K., WV**

LEMON SODA. For a fast and easy drain deodorizer and degreaser, drop half of a fresh-cut lemon into your disposal followed by ½ cup of baking soda. Run the disposal, and your whole kitchen will smell lemony fresh. ✉ **Maggie R., NV**

ANOTHER GREAT IDEA!

UNDER COVER

The rubber cover that keeps food from splattering when you use your disposal can get real slimy. To keep it clean, scrub it regularly—inside and out—with an old toothbrush that's been dipped in hot, soapy water.

SIMPLY PRICELESS. Price tags and other adhesive labels never seem to peel cleanly away without leaving a sticky residue behind. One way to loosen up the gunk without making a bigger mess is to saturate the sticker with baby oil. Once the oil has soaked in, let it sit on the tacky area for about an hour, then you can simply wipe the residue away. ✉ Kathy B., IN

To remove a jar lid that just won't budge, put a piece of sandpaper, rough side down, over the lid and twist. It should come right off. And remember this: The larger the grit, the firmer your grip will be.

HELP FOR A STICKY SITUATION. Sticky residue from labels and tape can be removed quickly and easily with aerosol air freshener. Just spray the surface where it's sticky, then wipe the area with a paper towel. ✉ Daneen K., NY

SAY "NUTS" TO GUNK. I've found that peanut butter can get rid of sticky gunk on almost any hard surface. Just coat the mess with peanut butter, and leave it on for an hour or so. Then wash the peanut butter—and the sticky residue—off with a wet cloth. Wipe the item dry with a second clean, dry cloth. ✉ Lois P., FL

HANDY BANDS. If you're having trouble taking the lid off a jar, wrap a couple of rubber bands around the side of the jar. That way, you'll have something to grip, and the lid will come off a heck of a lot easier. ✉ Lourdes G., CA

Grandma Putt's Wisdom

My Grandma Putt was a big believer in recycling, and glass jars were one of her favorite things to reuse. But getting the labels off the jars . . . well, that was quite a chore. So instead of soaking and scrubbing, she used this clever trick: She'd saturate the label with cooking oil, wait 5 to 10 minutes for the oil to soak into the glue, and peel the label off. Then all it took was a little soap and water to remove the oil and leave the jar sparkling clean.

GET A GRIP WITH GLOVES. Don't struggle with tight jar lids. Instead, put on a pair of rubber gloves, grip the lid with one hand and the bottom of the jar with the other, and twist. ✉ Jacqueline D., ON

LID LIFTOFF. When I need to remove a tight jar lid, I slip the front end of a spoon under the lip of the lid and press down on the spoon handle. This releases the pressure and makes it easier (even for people with arthritic hands) to get the lid off. ✉ Kimberly P., OH

Grime Stoppers

CLEVER COIN CLEANER. Taco sauce is a dandy thing to have on hand when it comes to polishing your coin collection. Just dip your coins in the sauce, rinse 'em off, and finish by wiping them with a soft, clean cloth. ✉ Darla B., MI

CORRAL YOUR COINS. Don't waste time searching for loose change in the house or in your car. Instead, keep coins in empty plastic film canisters (the kind 35-millimeter film comes in). At home, you'll be able to easily grab the change you need for tipping delivery persons; when traveling, you'll have exact change right at your fingertips for toll booths and vending machines. ✉ Pete C., PA

TICKLE THE IVORIES. If you have an old piano that's got ivory keys, they're probably yellowed with age. You can restore their long-lost luster by rubbing them with a lemon. Simply cut a lemon in half, dip the cut side in table salt, and rub it over the piano keys. Let the keys dry, then wipe them with a soft, clean cloth. Use the same cloth to buff the ivory to a bright finish. ✉ Lois K., UT

CLEAN KEYS FOR A SONG. I clean my piano's plastic keys with vinegar. Start by making a solution of 1 tablespoon of white vinegar in 1 quart of water. Dip a chamois or soft, clean cloth into the solution and wring it out so that it's just damp. Then wipe down the keys. The vinegar smell goes away quickly, so you won't have to rinse. ✉ Donna L., MI

KEYS THAT PLEASE. Whether your piano keys are made of ivory or plastic, you can clean them with a couple of common household products. First, put some white non-gel toothpaste on a soft, clean cloth and gently rub it onto the keys. Then take a second clean cloth, dip it into some milk, and use that to rinse the paste off the keys. Finish up by buffing with another soft, clean cloth. Now that's music to your ears! ✉ Abbie G., NY

Jerry's Handy Hints

COUNT YOUR PENNIES

➜ If you're like most folks, you end up with a pile of loose change on your dresser top after emptying your pockets or purse. Keep it neat by dropping your change into a clear glass jar or bowl. This way, you'll have the satisfaction of watching how quickly those coins add up. Then when the container is full, deposit the contents into your investment account, or use the cash to buy yourself a special treat.

ANOTHER GREAT IDEA!

FACE THE MUSIC

If you have an old piano with ivory keys, you know they can turn yellow faster than you can play "The Yellow Rose of Texas." So keep them clean and bright with this neat trick: Put just a dab of plain yogurt on a soft, clean cloth and wipe down the keys with it. Then use a clean, damp cloth to buff the keys to a brilliant white shine.

SEND SOOT PACKING. Soot can build up fast on the exterior of a wood-burning stove. So here's how I make the job of cleaning it up a whole lot easier: Sprinkle baking soda on the surface, and scrub it down with a wet cloth. When you're done, dry it off with a soft towel. That's all it takes. ✉ Maureen H., MI

KEEP IT CLEAN. Clean dirty grout in a brick or stone fireplace by spraying whitewall tire cleaner directly onto the grout. Rub it in with newspaper, then wipe it off with a clean cloth that's been dipped in a solution of 1 tablespoon of vinegar in 2 cups of water. And there's no need to rinse; once it's dry, your grout will look like new. ✉ Ed B., PA

FOIL THE FIRE. You know what a mess it can be to clean out your fireplace. I solved that problem by lining mine with heavy-duty aluminum foil. Now whenever it's time to clean out my fireplace, I simply roll up the foil, take it outside, and dump the ashes into my garden. ✉ Mina A., NJ

ASHTRAY ANSWER. Can't stand the smell of ashtrays even after you've washed them? Me neither. So try this refreshing technique: Rub a clean ashtray with a used fabric-softener sheet. I've found that it removes cigarette residue and leaves the ashtray smelling nice and fresh. ✉ Lynnette J., MS

Grandma Putt's Wisdom

Ashes can go flying everywhere when you sweep out your fireplace, so try my Grandma Putt's quick fix to make the chore less of a hassle. Simply sprinkle damp coffee grounds over the ashes. The flyaway ash will clump up around the moist grounds, making it a cinch to sweep them up with your fireplace brush and dustpan. And play it safe like Grandma did—put the ashes into a metal container for extra insurance against an accidental fire.

NEW LIFE FOR OLD ASHTRAYS. Do you still have old ashtrays stashed away? Bring 'em out and use 'em as pet-food dishes. Gather the largest glass or ceramic ashtrays you have, wash them well, and fill 'em up with your pet's food. Fill the deepest one with water for a small pet like a guinea pig or rabbit. ✉ Michelle M., PA

FAN-TASTIC IDEA. If you haven't checked your attic fan vent lately, you may be surprised to find it coated with a greasy, dusty buildup. Don't panic—you can clean up the mess easily with a paste made from baking soda and water. Gently scrub it on with a soft brush, then wipe it off with a clean, wet cloth. ✉ Theresa K., OK

DEFY THE DUST. It's always a chore to dust off ceiling fans, but here's a way to cut down on the number of times you'll have to drag out a stepladder to get the job done. The next time you clean your ceiling fan, finish up with a light coating of ArmorAll®. Simply put some on a soft, clean cloth, and rub it right on the blades. Dust won't stick as easily, which means you won't have to clean those hard-to-reach fan blades nearly as often. ✉ Pamela M., WV

KEEP PLANTS PRETTY. I quickly clean my silk plants by spraying them with a fabric-refresher spray. They end up looking clean and smelling fresh. Best of all, the spray won't fade their bright and beautiful colors. ✉ Carrie T., WA

SEE WHAT I MEAN? When I need to cut grime on TV screens, mirrors, or windshields, I use a half-and-half mix of rubbing alcohol and warm water. It won't leave any streaks or smears, and it's much cheaper than store-bought window cleaners. *Note:* Not all television sets are alike, so check your owner's manual before using any product to clean your TV screen. ✉ Julia H., MI

HOSIERY HELPER. Computer screens are fragile and should only be cleaned with something gentle; in fact, most manufacturers recommend using products that are specifically made for this purpose. Others say that using rubbing alcohol, or distilled water with vinegar, is just fine. Regardless of what cleaner you use, you'll need a soft cloth to apply the liquid, and what's softer than panty hose? Wet the panty hose with the cleaner, and gently wipe it onto the screen. Make sure you turn the monitor off first; that way, you'll be sure to leave the screen streak-free. ✉ Denise R., NJ

WIPE OFF WOES. You've already started writing on your white-board when you realize you grabbed the wrong pen. Now your board is marked up with permanent ink, not the dry-erase kind you intended. Not to worry! Just saturate a cotton ball with nail polish remover, and dab at the spots until they wash away. Then rinse the whole thing off with soapy water, and just like that, your board will be clean as a whistle! ✉ Carol M., OH

Jerry's Handy Hints

EX-SMOKER'S STORAGE SOLUTION

→ A friend of mine who kicked the habit years ago gave me this clever idea: When you're searching for containers to organize supplies in your home office or hobby room, reach for your retired ashtrays. They're just the right size for holding small necessities like paper clips, pushpins, rolls of tape, and the like.

Sewing Secrets

FIX IT WITH FLOSS. The next time you need to sew a button on a shirt, use unwaxed dental floss instead of thread. It's so strong and holds so firmly that you will probably never lose that button again. ✉ Sharon O., LA

TWIST AND GO. What do you do when you're in a rush and a button on your shirt falls to the floor? Grab a twist tie and strip the paper coating off it. Then "thread" the wire through the buttonholes and the cloth, and twist it closed on the inside of your shirt. Now get going! ✉ Regina S., ID

HASTY HEMMING. In a hurry and your hem is hangin'? Do what I do: Simply put it back in place with duct tape. It's only a temporary fix, but it does the trick. By the way, this works great on pant cuffs as well as dress and skirt hems. ✉ Barbara L., RI

SEW SMOOTH. Before you start a hand-sewing project, run your needle and thread through an unused fabric-

TAKE 5

Here are five not-so-common uses for fishing line:

1 Use it to reattach buttons to clothing—it's a lot stronger than thread!

2 Hang a picture by attaching the line securely to the screw eyes on the back of the frame, and hang it high.

3 String popcorn on it in the winter to make a great treat for the birds.

4 Wrap it between two or more poles to make a trellis for cucumbers.

5 Attach it to the tops of poles around your garden for an "invisible" fence to keep deer out.

QUICK FIX

To take the hassle out of needle threading, coat the end of the thread with clear nail polish. Let it dry, and then thread it right through the needle. You'll be amazed at how easy it is to hit that eye on the very first try.

softener sheet. This trick will keep the thread from clinging to the fabric and prevent it from getting tangled. ✉ Kate R., CA

NO MORE CLING. I always attach a small safety pin to the hem of my skirt or slacks to get rid of annoying static cling. There's no messy (and pricey) spray required! ✉ Eleanor Y., NC

KEEP 'EM COVERED. Fusible interfacing is easy to use, and it gives your sewing project a crisp look. To keep from accidentally "fusing" the interfacing to your iron or ironing board, put a paper towel between the fabric and the iron, and another one between the fabric and the board. That way, you won't get any sticky residue on your iron or cover. ✉ Lenora B., CA

SALT FOR SMOOTH IRONING. If your iron's not pressing as smoothly as it used to, a buildup of starch and other residue could be the culprit. To remove it, I sprinkle a layer of salt on a sheet of wax paper. Then I warm the iron up and rub it over the salt. The salt granules scrub any residue off and the wax from the paper helps the iron glide more smoothly. ✉ Deborah W., NM

ANOTHER GREAT IDEA!

RUB OUT STATIC

To remove static electricity from clothing, rub a damp sponge over the garments. The sponge should be only slightly damp so you can do this even while you're dressed.

Grandma Putt's Wisdom

I sometimes wonder if my Grandma Putt didn't invent the first nonstick iron. Whenever hers got a little balky, she'd wax the bottom to make it glide. Her trick took just a few seconds: She'd simply run the hot iron over a block of paraffin she kept wrapped in a cotton cloth within easy reach at the end of her ironing board. At the touch of the hot iron, the paraffin melted through the cloth, leaving a thin, smooth coat of wax on her iron. After a while, the cloth became stiff with wax, which made the job go even faster.

GOOD FOR THE SOLE. The base of your iron, also known as the soleplate, is easy to keep clean if you use a little toothpaste. Just apply a dab of white non-gel toothpaste to a cold, nonstick iron with a soft cloth and polish away. Then wipe up the residue with a clean, damp cloth. ✉ Gerri M., WI

ALL DOLLED UP. If a cherished doll has become marked up with ink, don't trash it. Instead, try rubbing some peanut butter into the spot, then wiping it away with a damp cloth. The mark should come right off. ✉ Kristin K., MI

SMOOTH DRESSER. As difficult as it may be for you to help your child put clothing on her dolls, imagine how hard it is for her to do it herself! So make it easier on both of you by sprinkling the dolls with cornstarch first. You'll be happy at how easily the clothes slide right on. ✉ Martha T., NY

SECOND LIFE FOR LINT. Here's how I put my dryer lint to good use: I gather enough of it to replace the stuffing in any of my daughter's stuffed animals that have lost some of their innards. It saves money and gives the toys a pleasant scent. ✉ Shirlene R., TX

How Sweet It Is

OUT WITH ODORS. I put fabric-softener sheets in my clothes hampers, suitcases, and stored picnic baskets. They do a terrific job of keeping musty smells away, and they leave a fresh clean scent behind. ✉ Monica R., FL

FOIL FOUL SMELLS. Musty basement? Pour cat litter into clean aluminum foil pie plates, and set them around the room to rid it of odors. Just replace the litter every six months or so to keep your basement smelling nice. ✉ Eileen G., NY

CLEAR THE AIR. To get rid of musty smells in your house, pour a little vanilla extract into small bowls and place them in several rooms on tables or shelves. You can also mix a few drops of vanilla with water in a handheld sprayer bottle and lightly spray it on your carpets and drapes to freshen things up. ✉ Linda L., GA

NOW YOU'RE COOKIN'. If you love to cook, but hate the odors that linger long after the meal has ended, keep a small bowl of vinegar on top of your stove. It'll absorb heavy cooking odors—even from the strongest-smelling foods like fish and onions. ✉ Donna W., NY

TAKE 5

Five not-so-common uses for fabric-softener sheets include:

1 Freshen things up by keeping sheets in your drawers and garbage cans. It'll clear the air in a hurry.

2 Collect pet hair by rubbing a sheet over your clothes or furniture to attract the loose hairs like a magnet.

3 Rub a sheet on panty hose to eliminate static cling.

4 Hang them in your garden shed to keep the flies away.

5 Thread a sheet through your belt loop to repel hungry mosquitoes.

SUPER-DUPER SOLUTIONS

LIKE A WALK IN THE WOODS ● What do you do with a fresh Christmas tree after the holidays are gone? One of my favorite reuses is to put the tree to work freshening the air. Here's how: I pile small cuttings in a basket and place it on the floor of my bathroom to keep the air from turning foul. I use dried sprigs as kindling for a cozy fire; they give off that terrific piney scent. And I place evergreen needles in dishes and set them throughout my house. Whenever the air needs some freshening up, I just stir the needles to release their outdoorsy aroma.

A SPICY SOLUTION. To remove cooking odors from the kitchen, put cinnamon and cloves in a saucepan with water and bring it to a boil. Let it simmer on the stove until the air is fresh. ✉ Kim L., DE

ROOM DEODORIZER. To eliminate lingering odors from a room, I cut an onion in half and place it cut side down on a small, water-filled dish. I know it sounds stinky, but it works! ✉ Martha D., ON

ORANGE A-PEEL. Instead of roasting chestnuts on an open fire, try tossing some orange rinds into your fireplace. They'll pop, sparkle, and give off an oh-so-pleasant aroma. ✉ Tom T., NJ

THE AROMATIC ANSWER. For a terrific-smelling room, dab a little vanilla extract on the top of a lightbulb. Once the lamp is turned on, the bulb's heat will release the soothing scent into the air. ✉ Claire K., PA

AIR SCENTS. Here's a neat way to freshen up the air in any room. Take the cover off each heating vent, spread an unused fabric-softener sheet over the back of the cover, then replace it in the floor or wall. The sheet will scent the room and also help filter out dust. When the sheet gets dirty, replace it with a new one. ✉ Tina G., RI

APPENDIX

Fixers, Mixers, and Elixirs

Home

ADIOS, ANTS!

Say "so long" to invading ants with this surefire solution.

1 cup of sugar
3 tbsp. of borax
4 cups of water

Mix all of the ingredients in a large saucepan and bring to a boil. Remove the pan from the heat and let the mixture cool. Then pour it into several small containers, such as empty tuna cans, and set them out wherever you see lots of ants, but not where children and pets can get to them.

CLOG CLEARER

Try this quick mix to clear a clogged drain, quick as a wink.

½ cup of table salt
½ cup of baking soda
1½ tbsp. of cream of tartar

Mix all of the ingredients together, then slowly pour the powdery mixture down the drain. Follow with 2 cups of cold water. If the clog hasn't completely cleared, repeat this procedure up to twice more. And if you're still stuck with a sluggish drain, you'll have to bite the bullet and call in the plumber!

DIY DETERGENT

Make your own inexpensive, suds-free laundry detergent.

⅓ bar of Fels-Naptha® soap
6 cups of very hot water
½ cup of washing soda
½ cup of borax
6½ qt. of hot water, divided

Grate the soap and add it to a pan with the 6 cups of very hot water. Heat the pan until the soap is dissolved, then stir in the washing soda and borax. Continue to stir until all of the ingredients are dissolved and the mixture has thickened and looks like honey. Remove the pan from the heat, then mix the melted soap blend with 1 quart of hot water in a 6-gallon bucket. Add another 5½ quarts of water, and stir until completely blended. Set the mixture aside for 24 hours, then pour it into clean, plastic milk jugs for storage. For a regular load of laundry, add ½ cup of detergent per load.

EMBER Rx

If an ember or candle drops on your carpet and singes it a bit, you may be able to clean up the damage with this mixture.

1 cup of white vinegar
½ cup of talcum powder
2 onions, coarsely chopped

Mix all of the ingredients in a saucepan and bring to a boil. Remove the pan from the heat and let the mixture cool. Spread it over the stain and wait for it to dry thoroughly. Then brush away the residue and vacuum the area.

GRASS STAIN REMOVER

Wipe out grass stains on clothing in a snap with this wash day fixer.

1 cup of laundry detergent
1 cup of ammonia
2 cups of water

Mix all of the ingredients in a handheld sprayer bottle. Apply the stain remover directly on the soiled area just before tossing the clothes into the wash.

KITCHEN CABINET CLEANER

Grimy cupboards can make your whole kitchen seem dingy. This solution will wash away buildup and give them a fresh, clean smell, too!

1 cup of ammonia
1 cup of vinegar
⅓ cup of baking soda
1 gal. of hot water

Mix the ammonia, vinegar, and baking soda in a bucket, then stir in the water. Use this solution with a sponge or soft-bristled brush to spruce up your cabinets—inside and out!

MIRROR MAGIC

Take gunk and smears off your mirrors with a few swipes of this cleaner.

1 cup of rubbing alcohol
1 cup of water
1 tbsp. of white vinegar

Pour all of the ingredients into a handheld sprayer bottle. Spray the formula onto a microfiber cloth, and wipe the dirt away. That's all there is to it. Shine on!

PESKY PEST LURE

Here's a sure cure to keep pesky gnats and fruit flies from hovering around potted plants and fruit bowls.

2 tsp. of wine
5 drops of dishwashing liquid
2 tsp. of hot water

Mix all of the ingredients in a small glass bowl and set it out where the gnats congregate. They'll be drawn to it, and take the deadly plunge.

ROACHES ON A ROLL

Run roaches out of town with these killer "marbles."

16 oz. of boric acid
1 cup of flour
¼ cup of shortening
1 small onion, chopped
Water

Mix the ingredients together with enough water to form a stiff dough and shape into marble-sized balls. Roll them into all the dark, damp areas where roaches hide. They'll eat the marbles, drink water, and die.

SKUNK ODOR-OUT TONIC

When a skunk comes a-callin', reach for this easy remedy.

1 cup of bleach or vinegar
1 tbsp. of dishwashing liquid
2½ gal. of warm water

Mix all of the ingredients in a bucket and thoroughly saturate anything Pepe Le Pew has left his mark on. *Caution:* Use this tonic only on nonliving things.

SUPER LAUNDRY WHITENER

Here's a great recipe for keeping your white clothes, sheets, and towels bright white.

4 aspirin tablets
1 cup of hot water
1 load of dirty whites

Dissolve the aspirin in the hot water, then add the mixture to a warm-water load in the washing machine. For white clothes that are already yellowed, let the load soak for 30 minutes before you put it through the wash cycle.

SWEATY STAIN SOLUTION

Here's a laundry challenge that's been around as long as laundry itself: getting grungy perspiration stains out of shirt underarms. To treat white shirts, there's nothing better than this recipe.

½ cup of lemon juice, or 2 lemons
Hot water
1 additional lemon
Sunshine

Pour the lemon juice or squeeze the lemons into a half-full laundry tub of hot water. (If you're doing a full load, add twice as much lemon.) Soak your clothes for an hour or overnight, then put them through the wash cycle. Add the juice of one more lemon to the rinse cycle, and hang your clothes in the sun to dry. Lemon and sunshine combine to make nature's best bleach, and so far, nothing the detergent industry has come up with can top it!

Health and Beauty

ACHING MUSCLE MAGIC

Muscles are very temperamental, and every so often, you'll wake up in the morning or end your day with a muscle that certainly wasn't bothering you a few hours earlier. Ease your aches with a little of this minty mixer.

1 tbsp. of petroleum jelly
6 drops of peppermint oil
Warm water

Mix the petroleum jelly and peppermint oil in a small bowl, and put it in a larger bowl of warm water. Soak a towel in warm (not hot!) tap water, wring it out, and drape it over the troubled area. Leave it in place for three to four minutes. Remove the towel and then massage the warm jelly/oil mixture into your skin for soothing relief.

ANTI-ALLERGY JUICE

Besides helping to relieve your runny nose, weepy eyes, and other allergy symptoms, this jewel-toned elixir is chock-full of vitamins that will fine-tune your whole internal system.

3 parts carrot juice
1 part beet juice
1 part cucumber juice

Mix all of the juices together in a pitcher, and drink two to three 8-ounce glasses of it each day. Keep refrigerated.

BAD BACK EASER

Back pain is no laughing matter because it can be so crippling that it'll spoil your entire day. Relieve the pain with this herbal tea that's tailor-made for those moments when you need your schedule to keep running smoothly.

Dried chamomile flowers
Dried gingerroot slices
Dried peppermint leaves

Mix these herbs together, and add 1 teaspoon of the mixture to 1 cup of boiling water. Steep, covered, for 10 minutes. Strain out the solids and drink 1 cup three or four times a day to ease your back pain and keep your daily plans on track.

HANDY HYDRATOR

If you're suffering through a bout of diarrhea, it's important to stay hydrated. If you don't have a sports drink on hand, simply whip up a batch of your own.

4 cups of boiling water
½ tsp. of table salt
1 to 2 cups of infant rice cereal

Pour the water into a large pitcher and add the salt. Then gradually stir in the cereal. Drink up to 6 cups every four hours to keep yourself in the pink— er—the drink. Cover and refrigerate between uses.

HEAVENLY HAIR TONIC

When your hair looks good, you look good. And your hair will be gorgeous with this homemade elixir that adds body and style.

½ cup of commercial shampoo
1 beaten egg
1 tsp. of canola oil
½ tsp. of orange juice
1 cup of water

Mix all of the ingredients together and pour the blend into a plastic bottle. Use it once a week in place of ordinary shampoo. Your locks will love it—and you'll love your luscious locks! Refrigerate between uses.

HERBAL SOAK

If you're feeling achy all over (whether it's from your daily workout or just a tense day at the office), then you're going to need some serious pain-busting relief to get back to feeling 100 percent. For general pain, try this marvelous mixture in a soothing soak.

⅓ cup of dried chamomile flowers
⅓ cup of dried lavender
⅓ cup of dried lemon balm
2 cups of Epsom salts

Mix the chamomile, lavender, and lemon balm together in a large bowl. Scoop out ⅓ of the mixture, wrap it up in a muslin bag, and place the bag in your tub while you run the hot water. Then pour in the Epsom salts and swirl the water to dissolve the salts. Soak in the tub for 10 to 15 minutes, or until you break into a nice healthy sweat.

HOMEMADE ICE PACK

A nice cold pack can ease sore muscles, and the best part is that the effects of cold last longer than those of heat because it takes longer for your body to warm up than to cool off. To make an ice pack that molds to your contours, follow these easy instructions. You can make them anytime, so you'll always have one on hand.

4 parts water
1 part rubbing alcohol
2 ziplock freezer bags

Pour the water and rubbing alcohol into one ziplock bag, filling it, and zip it shut. Put the filled bag into the second ziplock bag to prevent leaks, and put the pack in the freezer. The next time you're in pain, pull the pack out and apply it to the injured area for 15 to 20 minutes. Since the alcohol won't freeze, the pack will have just enough give to it to easily mold to your particular curves.

A HONEY OF A CURE

When you can't stop coughing, don't worry if you don't have a bottle of cough syrup on hand. As long as you have a few staples in your cupboard, you can mix up a batch of homemade syrup right in your own kitchen!

1 cup of honey
1 tbsp. of apple cider vinegar
Juice of half a lemon

Combine all of the ingredients in a bowl or large measuring cup. Use 1 to 2 teaspoons per dose; cover and refrigerate between uses.

MILK-AND-HONEY ACNE AXER

Clear up zits and keep the acne away with this daily skin cleanser.

1 tbsp. of plain yogurt
2 tsp. of honey
½ tsp. of milk

Mix all of the ingredients in a small bowl, and apply the mixture to your skin. Leave it on for a few minutes, then rinse it off, and watch your face glow.

MINTY TEA

Ease nasty cold symptoms or simply calm down before bedtime by drinking this soothing tea.

2 tsp. of sugar
2 drops of peppermint extract
½ cup of hot to boiling water

Place the sugar in a mug, stir in the peppermint drops, and then add the water. Stir well, and drink it to calm a cough, loosen congestion, or relieve a nagging headache.

STRESS-BUSTING SOAK

Take the edge off with this great-smelling bath.

1 cup of powdered milk
1 cup of baking soda
1 cup of table salt
10 drops of vanilla or lemon extract
Empty, clean milk carton

Place all of the ingredients in the milk carton and stir well. Add about ¼ cup of the mixture to your bathwater, and soak away your stress-filled day.

SUN-SORE FACE SOOTHER

Spring has sprung, and you were so eager to start planting that you rushed out to the garden without applying any sunscreen—and you stayed outdoors way too long. Now your face is feeling the results. Instead of chewing yourself out, treat your face to this intensive treatment.

5 capsules of vitamin E oil
2 tsp. of plain yogurt
½ tsp. of honey
½ tsp. of lemon juice

Drain the contents of the vitamin E capsules into a bowl, and add the yogurt, honey, and lemon juice. Mix well, and gently apply the lotion to your face with a cotton ball. Wait about 10 minutes, and rinse with warm water. Your skin will feel like new!

TOES-TY GARLIC TEA

Tired of itchy, burning toes caused by athlete's foot or some other irritating fungal infection? Well, put your foot down—in a tub of garlic water! Garlic has been scientifically proven to stop fungal infections dead in their tracks.

5 to 6 garlic cloves
Rubbing alcohol
Warm water

Crush the garlic cloves, and drop them in a tub filled with warm water and a little rubbing alcohol. Gently place both feet in the tub, and let them soak for about 10 minutes a day.

Note: If you have diabetes, you should check with your doctor before trying this garlicky cure.

Lawn and Garden

A HOT TIP

When squirrels are invading your bird feeders, give the feeder poles and surrounding lawn areas a blast of this spicy brew.

Hot sauce
Castor oil
Murphy® Oil Soap

Combine equal parts of each ingredient in a handheld sprayer bottle, then spray the mixture all around your bird feeders. It'll keep those pesky squirrels away, but the heat won't bother the birds at all.

BUG-OFF BULB BATH

This spa treatment will help your spring- or summer-blooming bulbs fend off disease germs, as well as bulb mites and other cunning creatures.

2 tsp. of baby shampoo
1 tsp. of antiseptic mouthwash
¼ tsp. of instant tea granules
2 gal. of hot water

Mix all of the ingredients in a bucket. Then drop in your bulbs, and let them soak for two to three hours (longer for larger bulbs). And don't peel off the papery skins! The bulbs use them as a defense against pests. Then either plant the bulbs immediately or let them air-dry for several days before you store them—otherwise, rot could set in.

BULB BREAKFAST OF CHAMPIONS

Give newly planted bulbs a big boost with a taste of this terrific tonic. It's packed with nutrients and organic matter to provide a small but steady supply of food—just what's needed for balanced bulb growth.

10 lb. of compost
5 lb. of bonemeal
2 lb. of bloodmeal
1 lb. of Epsom salts

Mix all of the ingredients in a wheelbarrow. Before setting out your bulbs, work this hearty meal into every 100 square feet of soil in your bulb-planting beds. Or, if you're planting bulbs among other plants, work a handful of this mixture into the soil in each hole before setting in the bulb.

DISEASE DETERRENT

Whenever you prune a diseased tree or shrub, keep plant diseases from spreading with this potion.

¼ cup of antiseptic mouthwash
¼ cup of ammonia
¼ cup of dishwashing liquid
1 gal. of warm water

Mix all of the ingredients in a bucket, then pour the solution into a handheld sprayer bottle. Use it to drench all the pruning cuts on your plants, as well as your pruning tools.

FABULOUS FOUNDATION FOOD

Are you planning on setting out some new shrubs around your home's foundation? Then take the opportunity to build up the soil's fertility and organic matter at the same time with this foundation feast.

10 parts compost
2 parts bonemeal
2 parts bloodmeal
1 part kelp meal

Mix all of the ingredients in a wheelbarrow, spread a 2- to 3-inch-thick layer over the soil, and dig or till it in before planting. Each year, add a new ½-inch-thick layer around established shrubs, and scratch it lightly into the soil. Top it with shredded bark or other mulch, and your foundation shrubs will stay happy and healthy for many years to come.

FALL LAWN FOOD MIX

Come fall, your flower and vegetable gardens are slowing down, but your grass is gearing up for another burst of growth. So give it a taste of this fortified lawn food, and be prepared for a great-looking lawn that'll sail right through the worst weather winter can throw at it.

3 lb. of Epsom salts
1 cup of powdered laundry detergent
1 bag of dry lawn food (enough for 2,500 sq. ft.)

Mix all of the ingredients together, and apply at half of the recommended rate with a broadcast spreader.

FIT TO A TEA

Rid your roses of aphids with this parsley and garlic tea.

½ cup of parsley flakes
2 tbsp. of minced garlic
3 cups of water

Mix the parsley and garlic in the water and bring to a boil. Boil the liquid down to 2 cups, strain, and cool. Put 1 cup of the mixture in a 20 gallon hose-end sprayer, and spray all around and on your rosebushes. If you don't want to make the tea, plant garlic and parsley between all your roses. That'll do the trick, too!

FUNGUS-FIGHTER SOIL DRENCH

When foul fungi are fussin' around your soil, they can cause your veggies to produce poorly, wilt, or worse! Polish 'em off with this potent potion.

4 garlic bulbs, coarsely chopped
½ cup of baking soda
1 gal. of water

Mix all of the ingredients in a big pot and bring to a boil. Then turn off the heat, and let the mixture cool to room temperature. Strain the liquid into a watering can, reserving the garlic. Soak the ground around fungus-prone plants, taking care to pour very slowly, so the elixir penetrates deep into the soil. Then dump the strained-out garlic bits onto the soil, and work them in gently, so as not to disturb any plant roots.

GO FOR GARLIC

Garlic oil makes a spot-on bug repellent and insecticide, so give this potent potion a try.

4 garlic cloves, minced
Mineral oil
¼ oz. of dishwashing liquid
Water

Put the minced garlic in a medium bowl and add enough mineral oil to cover. Let soak for at least 24 hours. Then add 2 teaspoons of the garlic oil and the dishwashing liquid to 2 cups of water. Stir thoroughly, and strain the mixture into a glass container. When it's time to spray the bad bugs, mix 2 tablespoons of the soapy oil mix with 2 cups of water in a handheld sprayer bottle and go to town.

HOT BUG BREW

This sizzling beverage will deal a death blow to mole crickets, maggots, flies, and any other bug that's buggin' your plants.

3 hot green peppers (canned or fresh)
3 medium garlic cloves
1 small onion
1 tbsp. of dishwashing liquid
3 cups of water

Puree the peppers, garlic, and onion in a blender. Then pour the mixture into a jar, and add the dishwashing liquid and water. Let stand for 24 hours. Strain out the solids, pour the liquid into a handheld sprayer bottle, and blast the bugs to kingdom come. Repeat as needed.

MULCH MOISTURIZER TONIC

Mulching your flower garden in spring will go a long way toward minimizing weeding chores for the rest of the growing season. To really kick things into action, overspray your mulch with this fantastic formula.

1 can of regular soda (not diet)
½ cup of ammonia
½ cup of antiseptic mouthwash
½ cup of baby shampoo

Mix all of the ingredients in a 20 gallon hose-end sprayer, and give your mulch a nice cool drink. Add more mulch as needed through the season to keep it at the same depth. Treat it with this spray each time you re-mulch, then get ready to have the most bloom-filled beds on the block!

PET-FRIENDLY WEED KILLER

I hate seeing weeds sprout up in my lawn, but I also hate to use any type of weed killer that may harm my beloved dogs. If you, too, have been searching for a pet-friendly solution to your weed problem, here's the perfect recipe.

1 capful of vinegar
1 capful of baby shampoo
1 capful of gin
1 qt. of warm water

Mix all of the ingredients together and pour into a handheld sprayer bottle. Then get out there and shoot those weeds down. Repeat this tangy treatment weekly as more wicked weeds appear, and rest easy knowing that your yard is a safe haven for your pets.

SCAT, CATS!

Don't let the neighborhood cats do their business in your yard and garden. Keep them away with this hot potion.

Handful of cayenne and jalapeño peppers
Lemon-scented dishwashing liquid
Castor oil
Beer
Human urine

Puree the peppers in a blender. Then put the peppers in a handheld sprayer bottle and add equal amounts of the remaining ingredients. Shake well and spray this potent solution all over your lawn and gardens. When the kitties visit, they'll find less than purr-fect conditions, and go off in search of another lawn to litter!

SHRUB REVIVAL

If you have an old shrub that's starting to look its age, give it a new lease on life with this elixir.

1 can of beer
1 cup of ammonia
½ cup of dishwashing liquid
½ cup of molasses

Mix all of the ingredients in a 20 gallon hose-end sprayer. Drench the shrub thoroughly, including the undersides of the leaves. If you have any leftover mixture, use it on young shrubs, too.

SPUD SAVER

Bothered by potato bugs? Then try this recipe for relief.

4 tbsp. of whole wheat flour
1 tsp. of dishwashing liquid
1 qt. of warm water

Mix all of the ingredients in a hand-held sprayer bottle and squirt the solution on your potato plants. The bugs will either trap themselves in the sticky spray and die, or ruin their digestive tracts when they eat it, and then die. Either way, you come out the winner—and your potatoes come out bug-free.

VEGGIE TONIC

Vegetable plants really work up an appetite churning out all that good food for us, and even the most well-balanced diet needs a little kick now and then. So treat 'em to this tonic to keep things growing.

1 can of beer
1 cup of ammonia
4 tbsp. of instant tea granules
2 tbsp. of baby shampoo

Mix all of the ingredients in a 20 gallon hose-end sprayer, and spray all of your vegetable plants thoroughly, to the point of runoff. This super-nutritious tonic will turn them into lean, mean growing machines!

Index